Five Comedies

SUNY series, Women Writers in Translation
Marilyn Gaddis Rose, editor

Five Comedies

by

George Sand

Translated by

E. H. *and* A. M. Blackmore
and
Francine Giguère

STATE UNIVERSITY OF NEW YORK PRESS

Published by
State University of New York Press, Albany

For information, address State University of New York Press,
90 State Street, Suite 700, Albany, NY 12207

Production by Marilyn P. Semerad
Marketing by Fran Keneston

Library of Congress Cataloging-in-Publication Data

Sand, George, 1804–1876.
    [Plays. English. Selections]
    Five comedies / by George Sand ; translated by E. H. and A. M.
Blackmore and Francine Giguère.
        p. cm. — (SUNY series, women writers in translation)
    Includes bibliographical references.
    Contents: The Marquis de Villemer — Françoise — The paving
stone — The Japanese lily — A good deed is never wasted.
    ISBN 0-7914-5711-7 (alk. paper) — ISBN 0-7914-5712-5 (pbk. :
alk. paper)
    1. Sand, George, 1804–1876 — Translations into English. I. Title:
5 comedies. II. Blackmore, E. H. III. Blackmore, A. M.
IV. Giguère, Francine. V. Title. VI. Series.

PQ2397.B55 2003
842'.7—dc21
                                              2002030448

10 9 8 7 6 5 4 3 2 1

Contents

Introduction

Many famous novelists have written plays. Without going beyond the bounds of the English language, a list could include George Eliot's *The Spanish Gypsy,* Trollope's *The Noble Jilt,* Hardy's *The Dynasts,* Joyce's *Exiles,* Hemingway's *The Fifth Column,* Saul Bellow's *The Last Analysis,* the various dramatic works of Dickens, Henry James, Joseph Conrad, D. H. Lawrence, and Graham Greene; even, perhaps, the adaptation of *Sir Charles Grandison* attributed to Jane Austen. Similar lists could be compiled for other languages. Balzac and Zola, Gide and Mauriac, Manzoni and Verga all wrote plays.

Nobody, then, will be surprised to discover that George Sand wrote plays; and many readers, being familiar with the dramaturgic strengths and weaknesses of other celebrated novelists, will already know what to expect. Her plays will be the idle amusements of an active and talented writer—doodles scrawled during the hours when she wearied of her true vocation. They will interest us in the way that the secondary activities of distinguished minds always interest us—in the way that Michelangelo's sonnets and Tolstoy's chess games and Mendelssohn's paintings interest us. They will not display any profound dramatic gift, any true feel for the stage—how could they? But the author's talent, however misguided and misapplied, will still be there, and the works will still be worth an occasional visit for that reason.

The truth is different.

George Sand was a rare phenomenon among playwriting novelists—perhaps a unique one. She did not dash off two or three semiplayable dramas in her spare time. She wrote dozens of dramatic works, twenty-one of which (twenty-six, if we count adaptations written by other hands but more or less supervised by her) were produced in the major Parisian theaters. Many were commercial successes, and one, *Le Marquis de Villemer,* was among the

1

greatest stage hits of its era. Moreover, she worked hard, not only at writing scripts, but at every other aspect of theatrical life. She acted in her own plays and other people's. She directed actors at every possible level of the profession, from Sarah Bernhardt to the enthusiastic but utterly incompetent amateur. She designed sets and made costumes. She was familiar with the practicalities of stage lighting and scene changes. She collaborated. She adapted. She improvised and experimented. Surely no other novelist in history was so thoroughly steeped in the theatrical profession, or made such a success of it.

This becomes all the more notable when we reflect how few women, at any time and in any country, have succeeded as dramatists. Playwriting has always been a far more male-dominated occupation than poem writing or novel writing. Has any other female dramatist ever had twenty-one plays staged in the major public theaters of her country? Lady Gregory perhaps comes closest—but of course her plays were staged by her own theatrical company in an environment specially created by herself and her friends, which was hardly a major public theater in the same sense as the Comédie Française, Gymnase, and Odéon for which Sand wrote.

George Sand, then, had a theatrical career without parallel either among playwriting novelists or among playwriting women. In this respect, as in so many others, her activities stand apart: there is no one to compare with her.

Amandine-Aurore-Lucie Dupin was born in Paris on 1 July 1804. On her father's side she was descended from royalty, on her mother's side from peasantry—as she loved to point out. Her father died when she was four years old, and the dominant figure in her upbringing became her paternal grandmother, who eventually bequeathed to her the family estate of Nohant, in Berry. Between 1817 and 1820 she was educated at a Parisian convent, where, she tells us,[1] she wrote and acted in plays based on her recollections of the Molière comedies she had read. At the age of eighteen she married Casimir Dudevant, the superficially appealing son of a recently created baron; her two children, Maurice (who was to exert a major influence on his mother's theatrical career) and Solange, were born in 1823 and 1828 respectively. But Casimir proved to be a heavy-drinking womanizer with no interest in any pursuit more profound than hunting, and in 1831 she left for Paris, planning to earn her living as a writer. Initially her

energies went into drama as much as fiction: her first independent play, *Une Conspiration en 1537 (A Conspiracy in 1537)*, ante-
dated her first independent novel, *Indiana*, by almost a year. But
the play was neither performed nor (till 1921) published, whereas
the novel, published under the pseudonym "George Sand" in May
1832, became an immediate popular success. For the next few
years, therefore, she concentrated on prose fiction, writing the
series of novels that made her reputation. All the same, *Une
Conspiration en 1537* did exert an immediate, and highly significant,
influence on nineteenth-century French drama: Alfred de Musset
borrowed most of its situations, and even substantial chunks of its
dialogue, for his 1834 *Lorenzaccio*, which is now widely regarded as
the finest play of the French Romantic era.

Although the novel dominated her literary activities for the
next decade, Sand continued to write plays, or at least works in
dramatic form. The first of these to appear in print was *Aldo le
rimeur*, published in the *Revue des deux mondes* in September 1833;
the first to be staged was *Cosima*, acted at the Comédie Française
in April 1840 and highly praised by no less a critic than Théophile
Gautier despite hisses from the audience (at least on the opening
night). But the real turning point came during the second half of
1846, at Nohant, when the Sand family and friends began dab-
bling with amateur theatricals. This activity, at first so lightly un-
dertaken, became more and more intense as the years went by.
On the ground floor of the château a little theater was constructed,
and in it dozens of plays—some of them more or less improvised,
others fully scripted—were rehearsed, polished, and staged before
local audiences. There was also a puppet theater run principally
by Maurice. The live theater at Nohant remained active till 1863;
the puppet theater was still operating less than a month before
George Sand's death in 1876.

In parallel with this semi-private activity, the little theater's
leading spirit began writing more actively for the Parisian stage.
Some of the plays were adaptations of works already performed at
Nohant, but many were specially designed for the public theaters.
First came a dramatization of her 1847 novel *François le champi*,
staged with immense success at the Odéon in November 1849: it
ran for a hundred and forty performances. *Claudie* and *Le Mariage
de Victorine* followed in 1851; both, again, were highly successful.
From this time onward, George Sand was accepted not as a

playwriting novelist but as a leading dramatist in her own right, and fifteen further Parisian premières followed during the next twenty years, the last being *Un Bienfait n'est jamais perdu* in November 1872.

The theater had a relatively low status in that predominantly novel-oriented literary world. Even so, during much of the nineteenth century the Parisian stage was perhaps the most richly diverse, and therefore the most tolerant of dramatic inventiveness, in Europe. Where else, for instance, could Alfred Jarry's anarchic *Ubu Roi* (1895) have gained a hearing? There were highly literary, imaginative plays written by poets (Hugo, Vigny, Musset, Maeterlinck, Claudel), some of which, notably Hugo's *Hernani* (1830) and *Ruy Blas* (1838), were immediate stage successes, while others, such as the early plays of Musset and Claudel, were discovered to be eminently stageworthy long after they were written. There were the immaculately crafted "well-made plays" of Eugène Scribe (*Adrienne Lecouvreur,* 1849) and Victorien Sardou (*Tosca,* 1887), with their emphasis on plot and suspense. There was what S. B. John has described as "the drama of money and class," "the play about social life . . . that reflects the prosaic concerns of the age,"[2] epitomized by the work of Alexandre Dumas *fils* (though his best-known work, *La Dame aux camélias,* 1852, is hardly typical of his output) and Émile Augier (*Le Gendre de Monsieur Poirier,* 1854). There were thriving traditions of melodrama (especially after Frédérick Lemaître's success in *L'Auberge des Adrets,* 1823, and *Robert Macaire,* 1834) and farce (the works of Eugène Labiche and Georges Feydeau are perhaps the most familiar examples). Music-drama also flourished, and George Sand, with her various musical connections, was an attentive observer of it; Paris was widely regarded as Europe's leading purveyor of both grand opera (Gounod's *Faust,* 1859; Berlioz's *Les Troyens,* 1863; Meyerbeer's *L'Africaine,* 1865) and operetta (Offenbach's *Orphée aux enfers,* 1858, and *La Belle Hélène,* 1864; Lecocq's *La Fille de Madame Angot,* 1872). Finally, there was a rich subsoil of amateur theatricals in private homes, which generated, for instance, the much-loved family-and-friends operettas by Viardot and Turgenev. Sand's dramatic work drew, to a greater or lesser extent, on all of these traditions; and if it had its own individual touch, a theatrical world tolerant of so many different styles could easily find room for one more.

How naturally the dramatic form came to her may be seen from the fact that, even when she wrote novels, she tended to drift into passages of dialogue with speech prefixes, stage directions, and all the external trappings of drama: the conversation between the *fossoyeur* and the *chanvreur* near the end of *La Mare au diable* is a familiar example.[3] Indeed, some of her works, although designed to be read as novels rather than staged, are cast from beginning to end in dramatic shape, even to the point of being divided into acts rather than chapters. In a few of these cases the sense of theater is so strong that it is scarcely possible to tell whether the work was written solely for the reader (like Byron's "mental theater" and Musset's *spectacle dans un fauteuil*) or whether Sand might have had some thought of staging it. Take the 1869 *Lupo Liverani*, for instance. It is subtitled *A Play in Three Acts*, and it is adapted from the classic Spanish stage play *El condendado por desconfiado* (usually attributed to Tirso de Molina), to which it stands in approximately the relation that Sand's 1856 comedy *Comme il vous plaira* bears to Shakespeare's *As You Like It*. Yet *Comme il vous plaira* was offered on the Parisian stage, whereas *Lupo Liverani* was presented only to the reading public. The distinction between stage play and storybook, in Sand's work, is sometimes an extremely tenuous one.

It is now possible to understand, at least partly, why her theatrical career was so much more substantial than, say, Henry James's or Zola's. In the first place, she was inherently, and temperamentally, as much a dramatist as a novelist. She wrote more novels than plays simply because she lived in a culture that preferred prose fiction to drama; had the society around her been different, so would the main thrust of her literary activities. And in the second place, her experience at Nohant gave her an all-round practical grasp of the theater which no other novelist in history has had. She knew intimately what could and couldn't be done on the stage, not only in the major theaters of Paris, but also, and even more importantly, in amateur situations where severe constraints were imposed by the limited sets, costumes, and acting abilities available.

Her plays suffered, in miniature, the fate of her novels. The first generation of reviewers thought highly of them. Critics as various—and as hard to please—as Saint-Beuve, Gustave Planche, and Hippolyte Taine all praised them (Taine, indeed, compared her to the ancient Greek dramatists). Gautier, as we have seen, was a still earlier admirer. Even Jules Janin, whose political antipathy to Sand might have been expected to disqualify him altogether from appreciating her work, recognized that she had exceptional dramatic talents. In the English-speaking world they attracted no significant attention, but that was to be expected. No theatrical management in either Britain or America would have attempted to produce a play written by anyone so scandalous; indeed, in Britain the Lord Chamberlain would certainly not have given the necessary licence for public performance.[4] (Even so, her plays were repeatedly quarried for source material—usually without acknowledgement—by the English dramatists of the day.[5])

The second generation, while still respectful, was less enthusiastic. Literary fashions were changing; in a world increasingly intent on what it called "realism," Sand's plays, like her novels, were losing their attraction. Jules Lemaître, in his 1887 review of *Le Marquis de Villemer*,[6] shows the beginnings of the change. He admires the play, but he finds it "a very beautiful lie, almost entirely a fantasy—one of the most perfect examples of its type." What bothers him is the "goodness" of nearly all the characters. "To be sure," he concedes, "there is the Baroness d'Arglade. She is the wolf in this sheepfold; but she is such a tiny wolf, so far from being dangerous, and even her little touches of malice work out so naturally to the flock's advantage. Ah, what a big-hearted group they are! What a band of fine souls!" He prefers Musset's *On ne badine pas avec l'amour* because it contains "two or three truths which may not be new, but which have rarely been expressed with such poignancy: 'All men are liars, unfaithful, unreliable, chatterers, hypocrites, stuck-up and cowardly, despicable and sensual; all women are fickle, crafty, vain, inquisitive and depraved; the whole world is nothing but a bottomless sewer where shapeless monsters crawl and wriggle on piles of slime; but in that world there is one thing sublime and sacred, and that's the union of two of these so imperfect, so horrible creatures. People are often deceived in love, often wounded, often unhappy; but they do love, and when they're on the brink of the grave, they turn and look back and say: "I've often suffered, I've sometimes made mistakes, but I've loved. I am the one who has lived—I, and not some artificial being created by my own pride and frustration." ' "[7]

To someone of Lemaître's generation, a play that depicted "all men" and "all women" as evil seemed self-evidently more truthful than one that depicted "fine souls." The name that was repeatedly invoked by writers of his generation, to show how Sand *ought* to have portrayed the human race, was the name of Zola; and Zola himself, though he found "an immense charm" in George Sand's plays, complained that they were "not based on exact observation."[8] No real-life peasants ever did, or ever could, talk and think like the peasants in *François le champi*. Zola did not dismiss the plays entirely; while he found the stage version of *Mauprat* "altogether mediocre," he had high praise for the dramatized *Le Marquis de Villemer* and one or two other works; but he was already on the path that would lead to the dismissal of Sand's artistry by the next generation.

The twentieth century, with its predilection for waste lands and endgames, was of course generally out of sympathy with George Sand's literary work in any medium. The plays were not staged, as the novels were not read, and none of the leading critics of the century showed any sign of firsthand acquaintance with them.

Recently, hand in hand with the revival of interest in her other writings, there has naturally been a revival of interest in the plays. English-language readers have already been given an excellent full-length survey, Gay Manifold's *George Sand's Theatre Career* (Ann Arbor, Michigan: UMI Research Press, 1985), and a valuable translation of the drama-for-reading *Les Sept Cordes de la lyre*.[9] To some extent this is part of a broader reawakening of interest in the pre-Ibsenite theater throughout Europe. Pinero's early comedies have more appeal to present-day audiences than his Ibsenite dramas; Boucicault's Irish plays are being revived with success; we no longer make fun of Verdi's middle-period operas. In Sand's case the new interest is all the more noteworthy, since—for reasons which we have already discussed—her plays had never established themselves on the English stage even in the nineteenth century, as they had on the French.

The future vicissitudes of those plays, of course, cannot be predicted. No theatrical reputation, not even Shakespeare's, remains static from generation to generation; and even within a single generation, no two people will have identical tastes and preferences. All we can do here, therefore, is to report how Sand's work appears to a few readers at the beginning of the twenty-first century.

Perhaps the most striking feature, to our eyes, is the Scott-like (indeed Shakespeare-like) empathy with which Sand's characters—*all* her characters—are presented. Almost uniquely among

mid-nineteenth-century stage works, her plays contain no double-
dyed villains. The very worst troublemakers in them, such as the
gossipy Baroness in *Le Marquis de Villemer* or the excruciating
Dubuissons in *Françoise*, are viewed with affection and warmth—
even with relish. Moreover, the author seems no more at ease with
any one social group than with any other. The Marquise de Villemer
is a *grande dame* who could not even extend her friendship to you
without chilling your blood; the Louise of *Le Pavé* is an illegitimate peasant girl who has been a social outcast from her earliest
childhood; yet the former is depicted without the slightest hint of
insecurity, and the latter without the slightest hint of patronization;
George Sand looks them both straight in the eye. Here we reflect
what strength she drew from her peculiar ancestry—in contrast to
the majority of nineteenth-century writers, nearly all of whom
came from the middle classes. Dickens, for instance, has to look
up to study the Tite Barnacles, and down to study Little Emily; he
seems less comfortable with them than with characters of his own
social standing; he does not seem to view them from within. But
George Sand knows that she has in her veins both the peasant
blood of Louise, and the aristocratic blood of the Marquise; and
she instinctively feels them both to be her social equals.

   She draws another, similar, strength from her peculiar position as (roughly speaking) a woman leading a man's life. The entrenched sexual segregation of nineteenth-century civilization in-
terfered with most male writers' capacity to depict female characters, and most female writers' capacity to depict male ones. Look at
the heroines of Dickens, or the heroes of Charlotte Brontë. George
Sand, almost uniquely, is at home on both sides of this social barrier. Her Caroline de Saint-Geneix is no Agnes Wickfield, and her
Marquis de Villemer is no Mr. Rochester; the former is seen as
much from within as Jane Eyre, the latter as Arthur Clennam.

   Like all authors, Sand writes mainly about characters who
are temperamentally similar to herself. They tend to be exceptionally generous minded, with an exceptionally broad range of
interests and sympathies, because that is the kind of person she
herself is. This, of course, is what caused Lemaître to deplore the
predominant goodness of her characters, and the complaint is
still sometimes heard: even Gay Manifold, with *Le Marquis de Villemer*
particularly in view, objects to Sand's "overly idealized and virtuous heroines."[10] But the awkwardness of the phrasing here is re-

vealing. "Idealized" and "virtuous" can scarcely be treated as coordinate terms; and the addition of "overly" looks like an attempt to bolster a criticism which the critic herself senses to be in need of support. Idealized, as Gautier pointed out in his pioneering review, is precisely what Sand's heroines (and other characters) are not. The adverse reception of *Cosima* was due in part, he said, to the fact that its characters were *not* the purely good or purely bad creatures with whom audiences then (as now) felt most comfortable: "The public, which has been wrong before and is wrong now, can accept only demons and angels on the stage"; Sand's characters are drawn with "subtleties of nuance" which theater audiences are unaccustomed to see.[11] As we have observed, the heroine of *Le Marquis de Villemer* (Caroline de Saint-Geneix) seems as real as Jane Eyre—and for the same reason: most of her inner fiber comes directly from her creator's own temperament and life experience. George Sand has no need to draw generosity, tenacity of purpose, self-abnegation, and other such qualities from the realm of the ideal, because they lie so readily to hand in her own personal character (as her correspondence and other private documents show). Here again the temperamental similarity to Scott becomes relevant. Virtuous a figure like Jeanie Deans (in *The Heart of Mid-Lothian*) may be, but there is nothing of the ideal about her: what heroine in fiction seems more real? The reason becomes evident when we look across at Scott's *Journal* and see his own private responses to bereavement, bankruptcy, and public humiliation. The heroine's virtues are deeply rooted in her creator's own personality.

But questions of theatrical characterization must really be considered not in isolation, but in relation to the practicalities of performance. As every actor knows, almost any role can be made to seem either realistic or unrealistic, depending on how it is played. It is astonishing to see, on the page, the bareness and mediocrity of the *film noir* scripts which Humphrey Bogart invested with such specificity and reality in performance; on the other hand, Hamlet himself was made to seem an idealized nonentity in at least one twentieth-century movie. We may readily grant that a few of Sand's theatrical roles demand very special acting skills if they are to be brought to life. The Marquis de Villemer—surely one of the most complex and ambiguous heroes to stand on the mid-nineteenth-century stage—is perhaps the most

striking example; and we might say of him what T. S. Eliot said of
Harry in his own *Family Reunion:* "If he isn't haunted then he is
insufferable."[12] Nineteen players in twenty would make nothing of
the part; the twentieth would give it the inwardness—the
hauntedness—it demands, and the character would instantly spring
to life.

Looking back from the vantage point of the twenty-first century, it is not evident that the nineteenth-century "realists" whom
Lemaître admired were any more realistic than the so-called idealists who had preceded them. Who nowadays would maintain
that Zola's *La Terre*, with its two rapes in the same field in the
same afternoon, is grounded in more "exact observation" of rural
life (to use its author's own term) than Sand's *François le champi?*
Both writers are stylizing the world around them for the purposes
of their art; they are simply doing so in different ways. Sand chooses
mainly noble-minded characters, Zola mainly mean-spirited ones;
and why should either choice be judged inherently more legitimate, or likely to generate better artistic results, than the other?
The truth is that drama never was and never will be a matter of
"exact observation." Stylizations are to be found in the stagecraft
of all ages. The audiences who first flocked to the plays of
Shakespeare did not utter blank verse soliloquies when they were
alone; few of George Bernard Shaw's early spectators delivered
five-minute monologues in daily conversation with their friends
and family. To critics of Lemaître's generation and the next half
century, it may indeed have seemed that the best plays of their
own day were more truthful than those of any previous era; in
English, this position was most forcibly defended by William Archer.[13] But to us, looking back, it seems that Lemaître and Archer
were simply preferring one set of conventions ("lies" or "fantasies," in Lemaître's own terminology) to another.

"To judge of *Shakespear* by *Aristotle's* rules," wrote Pope in a
famous passage, "is like trying a man by the Laws of one Country,
who acted under those of another."[14] Most of the late-nineteenth
and twentieth-century critics had learned this lesson where
Shakespeare was concerned, but they failed to apply it to their own
immediate predecessors: they berated Sand and Ostrovsky and Verdi
for failing to write like Ibsen and Chekhov and Richard Strauss.

Lemaître's contrast between the "lies" of George Sand and
the "truths" of Alfred de Musset makes a neat piece of critical

writing. But the reality is more complex, as the critic unwittingly revealed when he quoted a passage of Musset to show what was missing from Sand's dramatic universe. More than half of the alleged Musset speech was actually written by Sand herself. Not, to be sure, its opening sentences. The statements that "all men are liars, unfaithful, unreliable," and so forth; that "all women are fickle, crafty, vain, inquisitive and depraved"; and that "the whole world is nothing but a bottomless sewer"—those are indeed Musset's own work, and if they express perennial "truths" (which we today may be less quick to concede than the contemporaries of Zola were), the credit lies with Musset and no one else. But all of the richer and more complex material that follows—from "people are often deceived in love" to the end of the scene—is taken verbatim from one of George Sand's letters to Musset.[15] Thus most of the contrast that Lemaître devised was not between Sand and Musset, but between Sand and herself: her writings were more multiform, and contained a greater diversity of viewpoints, than the famous critic consciously realized. He was willing enough to praise the profundity of her work, and to find truth in it—but only when it had some other writer's signature attached to it.

If we keep our eye on the content of George Sand's plays, and not on the author's name assigned to them (with all its attendant mythology), we may find that their world, though artistically stylized, is not as simplistic as Lemaître thought. Are the characters of *Le Marquis de Villemer* really models of unmitigated goodness? The Marquis himself is a liar, an adulterer, and, on his own testimony, a killer—in the sense of someone who has been specifically responsible for the death of someone else. (To say this is not to reread his character in an unhistorically modern light; the so-called idealists of Sand's century, or even earlier, were capable of summing up their noble-minded heroes with equal bluntness. Compare Gluck's celebrated evaluation of his *Iphigénie en Tauride* Oreste: "He's lying; he has killed his mother."[16]) The Marquise is a snob whose prejudices wreak most of the havoc that occurs during the play. The Duke is in every respect a broken reed; Diane is a well-meaning fool. It is true that George Sand lavishes on them the empathic generosity that she extends toward every character in her plays, and therefore judgments phrased in so unmitigatedly negative a way seem too harsh; but the same criticisms are made unevasively, though lightly, in the fabric of the play itself.[17] Only Caroline is free from major faults; yet if she has done little to deserve her sufferings, they are nevertheless (like, say, Cordelia's) largely of her own making. (Had Diane, with all her follies, been placed in the same situation, she would have cut instantly the Gordian knots that hold Caroline helpless for three and a half acts.) To us, then, looking at these dramas from a distance of well over a century, Gautier's account of them seems more accurate than Lemaître's. The characters of *Le Marquis de Villemer* are, as he said, neither "angels" nor "demons" (though the "subtleties of nuance" in their presentation can easily be missed, and therefore it is hardly surprising that Lemaître oversimplified them); and the most nearly faultless of them is dramatized at least as convincingly as the faultiest.

The mid-nineteenth century sorted most of its plays into three categories, which it labeled "tragedies," "comedies," and "dramas" (or "domestic dramas").[18] Recent theatrical experience would suggest that of these, the comedies generally have the greatest appeal to present-day audiences. Boucicault's *London Assurance* and Pinero's *Trelawney of the "Wells"* continue to charm and delight playgoers whenever given the chance to do so; the same authors' *The Octoroon* and *The Second Mrs. Tanqueray* are now rarely resuscitated (despite their popularity in their own day) and tend to be seen mainly as museum pieces. Justly or unjustly, Feydeau is revived more often than Becque, and Offenbach than Meyerbeer. Therefore, all the plays chosen for inclusion in the present volume are *comédies*, at least in the broad sense of the term. It must be stressed, however, that some of George Sand's *drames* (such as the 1851 *Claudie*) are impressive examples of their particular genre and deserve more attention than they have yet received.

It must be stressed, too, that Sand's plays cannot be contained within the standard nineteenth-century stereotypes in genre, any more than they can in characterization. Her *comédies* contain what the nineteenth-century theorists would have called "dramatic" situations (the celebrated third-act curtain of *Le Marquis de Villemer*, for instance), her *drames* contain "comic" ones. Looking further afield, her plays grade off insensibly in one direction into unscripted improvisations, and in another direction, as we have seen, into novels. Being less exclusively bound to the theater than the other major playwrights of her day, she was able to see it in a broader perspective, and to be less exclusively constrained by its conventions.

Le Marquis de Villemer (1864) was adapted from the 1860 novel of the same name. The novel is itself an impressive work—generally considered the finest of Sand's final period—but its author was far too experienced a hand to attempt to reproduce it unaltered on stage: the plot is drastically reworked with an eye to theatrical effectiveness, and the last two acts, in particular, are almost totally new. Alexandre Dumas *fils* is said to have added a few small touches to it, but these can no longer be identified—the manuscript is entirely in Sand's handwriting,[19] and the two authors so strongly admired, and were influenced by, each other's work that verbal or stylistic similarities are no proof of authorship. (There are many Dumas-like lines in the novel, to which he certainly did not contribute.) As with the majority of effective stage works by experienced playwrights (think of *Othello* or *King Lear*), the published script has a few inconsequential loose ends and inconsistencies—it is written for the theater, not the printed page. In the theater its power was immediately apparent. Sand's comments after the opening night are worthy of one of her own heroines: "Every scene was received with constant shouts and stampings of feet, even though the whole imperial family was present. In fact the emperor applauded just like everyone else.... Now, at night, quiet has been restored, the traffic has resumed, and I'm going to bed."[20]

Yet, as every writer on the subject remarks, there are other plays by the same author that might easily have had a similar reception. In Gay Manifold's words, "The characters [in *Le Marquis de Villemer*] are well drawn, the story line charming, the romantic intrigue engaging; but then these qualities apply equally to many others of Sand's pieces."[21] Among these, the one with the primary claim to the English-speaking world's attention would probably be *Françoise* (1856). This deft and original comedy has always been particularly admired by Sand's critics; indeed, her biographer Wladimir Karénine thought it the most interesting of all her plays.[22] Those who believe that Sand idealizes all her major characters should certainly contemplate Henri, the nonhero of *Françoise;* as Gautier observed, this is a central role without precedent in French (or perhaps any) dramatic literature. An even more striking disruption of theatrical convention occurs in the last act, when the worm turns and the downtrodden heroine finally stands up for herself—a situation reworked, in a very different context but just as effectively, at the end of *Le Marquis de Villemer.*

We have also included three one-act plays that illustrate Sand's ability to write for limited theatrical resources. Naturally these works are less substantial than the four-act plays—as the author herself was well aware: she described *Le Lis du Japon*, for instance, as a "little curtain-raiser," "a trifle" (*une bluette*)[23]—yet they are no less characteristic of their creator.

Le Pavé (The Paving Stone), a "story in dialogue," was published in the *Revue des deux mondes* on 15 August 1861 and staged at Nohant three weeks later. Sand herself stressed that the play was designed for a rural home and "would be less suitable for Parisian drawing rooms, which insist on wit—as well as the somewhat factitious artifices and superficial relationships that exist in polite society—rather than naïvety, and which rarely plumb emotions to any significant extent. In the country, sooner or later everyone becomes more serious and more simple. That isn't such a bad thing, as the good folk themselves say."[24] However, much to its author's surprise, two Parisian theaters promptly expressed an interest in the play, and it was staged professionally at the Gymnase in 1862. For commercial rather than artistic reasons, changes were made for the Paris production, glamorizing and melodramatizing the little piece (the male neighbor, for instance, became a female one); these are generally felt to weaken it, and our translation therefore follows the pre-Parisian recension published in the 1865 *Théâtre de Nohant*.

The other two one-act plays were designed specifically for Paris, and contrast strikingly in tone and style with *Le Pavé*. *Le Lis du Japon (The Japanese Lily)*, like *Le Marquis de Villemer*, is taken from one of George Sand's novels, *Antonia*, published in 1861. Again the adaptation is beautifully crafted and entirely self-sufficient: from beginning to end, not a syllable would suggest that the work had been written for any other medium.

Un Bienfait n'est jamais perdu (A Good Deed Is Never Wasted), the last of Sand's Parisian plays, has a special interest. It is her main work in a genre which Musset had made very much his own: the *proverbe*, the brief comedy designed to illustrate some proverbial saying (usually embodied in the work's title).[25] For a present-day amateur or university dramatic company with limited resources, it might make an excellent companion piece for some of Musset's works in the same genre—or, perhaps, for the other Sand one-act plays in the present volume.

Except for the correction of obvious errors, our translations follow the published texts issued with Sand's approval, which sometimes differ significantly from the manuscript drafts. Where plays were issued in her collected editions, we have used those: for *Françoise* and *Le Marquis de Villemer*, George Sand, *Théâtre complet: quatrième série* (Paris: Michel Lévy, 1866), and for *Le Pavé*, as already explained, George Sand, *Théâtre de Nohant* (Paris: Michel Lévy, 1865). For the other two plays, which came too late to be included in the collected editions, we have used the first editions: George Sand, *Le Lis du Japon* (Paris: Michel Lévy, 1866), and George Sand, *Francia, Un Bienfait n'est jamais perdu* (Paris: Michel Lévy, 1872).[26]

Sand, like most French dramatists, employed the so-called Continental method of scene-division: a new scene begins whenever a character enters or exits, and its opening stage direction lists all the characters currently on stage (including those who have remained on stage since the previous scene). Anglophone readers and performers will probably be most familiar with this custom from the plays of Ben Jonson.

In the lists of characters, we have occasionally added some information to clarify relationships; all such additions have been enclosed in square brackets to distinguish them from the author's own work. Elsewhere in the plays, square brackets have been used in the normal way to mark stage directions—all of which are Sand's own work.

Chronology

1804	1 July: birth of Amandine-Aurore-Lucie Dupin (George Sand).
1822	17 September: marriage to Casimir Dudevant.
1823	30 June: birth of her son Maurice.
1828	13 September: birth of her daughter Solange.
1831	4 January: Sand leaves for Paris to earn her living as a writer.
	June: Sand writes her first play (not intended for the stage), *Une Conspiration en 1537* (*A Conspiracy in 1537*), published in 1921.
1832	19 May: publication of Sand's first complete novel, *Indiana.*
1833	August–December: Alfred de Musset uses Sand's *Une Conspiration en 1537* as a major source in writing his play *Lorenzaccio* (first performed 1896; recent productions of it have sometimes included further material from *Une Conspiration en 1537*).
	1 September: publication of Sand's play for reading *Aldo le rimeur* (*Aldo the Rhymester*).
1837	1 January: publication of Sand's short dialogue *Le Contrebandier* (*The Smuggler*).
1839	15 April: Sand's play for reading *Les Sept Cordes de la lyre* (*The Seven Strings of the Lyre*) begins serial publication.
1840	29 April: première of Sand's first stage play, the five-act drama *Cosima* (at the Comédie Française).
	1 July: Sand's play for reading *Gabriel* begins serial publication.
1842	January and September: publication of Sand's short dialogues *Dialogues familiers* (*Private Conversations*).
1844	December: publication of Sand's short dialogue *Le Père va-tout-seul* (*Old Go-It-Alone*).

1846   8 December: the private theater at Nohant opens with *Le Druide peu délicat* (*The Indelicate Druid*), improvised from a scenario by Sand.

1848   6 April: première of Sand's one-act play *Le Roi attend* (*The King Is Waiting*, Comédie Française).

1849   23 November: première of Sand's three-act comedy *François le champi* (*François the Foundling*, Odéon), adapted from her novel of the same name.

1850   10 February: première of Sand's three-act comedy *Lélio* (Nohant), later published as *Marielle*.

        8 August: première of Sand's three-act drama *Claudie* (Nohant, with the author in the title role); first professional performance follows on 11 January 1851 (Porte-Saint-Martin).

1851   10 May: première of Sand's five-act drama *Molière* (Gaîté).

        17 July: première of Sand's three-act comedy *La Famille de Vanderke* (Nohant); first professional performance follows on 26 November, as *Le Mariage de Victorine* (*Victorine's Wedding*, Gymnase).

        4 October: première of Sand's three-act drama *Nello* (Nohant); first professional performance follows on 15 September 1855, as *Maître Favilla* (Odéon).

1852   3 March: première of Sand's three-act comedy *Les Vacances de Pandolphe* (*Pandolfo Takes a Vacation*, Gymnase).

        15 July: première of Sand's two-act comedy *Le Démon du foyer* (*The Devil at Home*, Nohant); first professional performance follows on 1 September (Gymnase).

        August: publication of Sand's play for reading *Les Mississipiens* (*The Mississippians*).

1853   29 July: première of Sand's three-act drama *Le Pressoir* (*The Winepress*, Nohant); first professional performance follows on 13 September (Gymnase).

        28 November: première of Sand's five-act drama *Mauprat* (Odéon), adapted from her novel of the same name.

1854   31 October: première of Sand's three-act comedy *Flaminio* (Gymnase).

1855   15 September: first professional performance of *Maître Favilla* (Odéon).

1856   15 February: première of Sand's one-act comedy *Lucie* (Gymnase).

3 April: première of Sand's four-act comedy *Françoise* (Gymnase).

12 April: première of Sand's three-act drama *Comme il vous plaira* (*As You Like It*, Comédie Française), adapted from Shakespeare.

1857 August: publication of Sand's play for reading *Le Diable aux champs* (*The Devil in the Country*).

1859 23 April: première of Sand's three-act comedy *Marguerite de Sainte-Gemme* (Gymnase).

1861 15 August: publication of Sand's one-act "story in dialogue" *Le Pavé* (*The Paving Stone*); première follows on 7 September (Nohant), and first professional performance on 18 March 1862 (Gymnase).

25 October: première of Sand's three-act "fantasy" *Le Drac* (*The Sprite*, Nohant).

1862 26 April: première of Paul Meurice's play *Les Beaux Messieurs de Bois-Doré* (Ambigue-Comique), adapted (with Sand's assistance) from her novel of the same name.

31 August: première of Sand's three-act fantasy *La Nuit de Noël* (*Christmas Eve*, Nohant).

1863 1 January: publication of Sand's five-act play *Plutus*.

1864 29 February: première of Sand's four-act comedy *Le Marquis de Villemer* (*The Marquis de Villemer*, Odéon), adapted from her novel of the same name.

28 September: première of Paul Meurice's play *Le Drac* (Vaudeville), adapted from Sand's 1861 Nohant play.

1866 12 August: première of Maurice Sand's play *Les Don Juan de Village* (Vaudeville), adapted (with George Sand's assistance) from her novel of the same name.

14 August: première of Sand's one-act comedy *Le Lis du Japon* (*The Japanese Lily*, Vaudeville), adapted from her novel *Antonia*.

1867 1 September: Sand's play for reading *Cadio* begins serial publication.

1868 3 October: première of Paul Meurice's stage play *Cadio* (Porte-Saint-Martin), adapted (with Sand's assistance) from her 1867 play for reading.

1869 15 September: première of the comic opera *La Petite Fadette* (Opéra-Comique), words by Carré, music by Semet, adapted (with Sand's assistance) from her novel of the same name.

1 December: publication of Sand's play for reading *Lupo Liverani*, adapted from Tirso de Molina's *El condendado por desconfiado*.

1870   25 February: première of Sand's five-act drama *L'Autre* (*The Other Man*, Odéon).

1872   7 November: première of Sand's one-act dramatic proverb *Un Bienfait n'est jamais perdu* (*A Good Deed Is Never Wasted*, Théâtre de Cluny).

1875   10 November: publication of Sand's one-act comedy *La Laitière et le pot au lait* (*The Milkmaid and the Milk Jug*).

1876   8 June: death of George Sand.

The Marquis de Villemer

(Le Marquis de Villemer)

A Comedy in Four Acts

Characters

Urbain, Marquis de Villemer [*son of the Marquise*]
Gaétan, Duke d'Aléria, *his brother*
Comte de Dunières
Pierre, *the Duke's valet*
Benoît, *servant of the Marquise*
Marquise de Villemer
Caroline de Saint-Geneix
Diane de Saintrailles
Léonie, Baroness d'Arglade

Scene: Acts 1 and 2, the Marquise's home in Paris; acts 3 and 4, the Château de Séval in the country.

Act I

A large drawing room in the Faubourg Saint-Germain,[1] *opulent and austere, with an antechamber at rear. Large double doors upstage. Large side door downstage left, leading to the Marquise's apartment. Fireplace downstage right. Side door midstage right, leading to Mademoiselle de Saint-Geneix's apartment. Piano midstage left. Pedestal table near the fireplace. Chairs, armchairs, etc.*

Scene 1

[*Monsieur de Dunières and the Marquise, both seated.*]

MARQUISE: So, my dear Dunières, shall we put it in a nutshell?

DUNIÈRES: Well, Marquise, you wish to find a wife for your son Urbain—even though he's the younger, and his brother is still a bachelor.

MARQUISE: My son Urbain. His brother is not marriageable.

DUNIÈRES: Why not? A charming man, witty, elegant. . . .

MARQUISE: Already forty.

DUNIÈRES: It's still a suitable age.

MARQUISE: That all depends. We don't broadcast our children's defects to the whole world; neither, therefore, do we hide anything from old friends, do we? My older son—attractive as he may seem to you, and as he sometimes still seems even to me— is a prodigal . . . an idler . . . and, on top of it all, a libertine and a bankrupt. Wouldn't that be a fine husband to offer a girl who deserves to enter life through a golden door, with all illusions about marriage intact? The Duke d'Aléria, then, is out of the question; and the person in question must be the Marquis de Villemer—my son Urbain. He's sensible and decent; everything I have belongs to him, since his brother has ruined me; and he can offer a good name, thirty-three years usefully employed, and a fortune that you know to be very satisfactory.

DUNIÈRES: Very good. And he's finally ready to think of marriage?

MARQUISE: Not in the least! That's what worries me, Dunières.

DUNIÈRES: Could he have some entanglement?

MARQUISE: I don't believe so. Judging from his lifestyle, he's free enough—he lives here with me, under my very eyes, caring for my every whim, working on a historical book of some kind. . . . You know he's writing?

DUNIÈRES: About the Villemer family, I presume?

MARQUISE [*rising*]: No, thank heavens; that's well enough known as it is. Our family tree has all its roots in solid ground and all its branches in broad daylight. We don't need to rid it of insects; we only need to graft it well, just as our ancestors did. Mademoiselle de Saintrailles is perfectly suitable. I admit that there were two alliances of doubtful virtue in her maternal ancestry, in the time of Henri IV. . . .[2]

DUNIÈRES: Ah yes, there was likewise a certain Hermine de Villemer in the time of Louis XV. . . . But, of course, that time it was the King himself.

MARQUISE: You say that your ward . . . She is indeed your ward, and dependent only on you?

DUNIÈRES: Diane de Saintrailles is an orphan; she is dependent only on her godmother—my wife—and her guardian—myself.

MARQUISE: And she is leaving the convent school . . . ?

DUNIÈRES: In a month's time; immediately after Pentecost.

MARQUISE: How old is she now?

DUNIÈRES: Just seventeen.

MARQUISE: Pretty?

DUNIÈRES: As a picture.

MARQUISE: Her character?

DUNIÈRES: Very cheerful, very childlike, a little fanciful; she's clever and imaginative; she knows her own worth; she dreams of paladins and chatelaines; she feels rich and free; she will marry only someone of her own choosing. She has often heard us talk about you—and your two sons. I must confess that I have a great liking for the Duke—he's entertaining, he makes me feel young again; but Madame de Dunières, being a serious-minded person, prefers the Marquis; and because we've sung their praises to one another so much, we've made Diane very eager to meet them.

MARQUISE: It will be extremely difficult to persuade Urbain to put in an appearance at your home. You people see everybody on earth, and he doesn't like to venture out of private life.

DUNIÈRES [*going upstage*]: We'll catch him by surprise! We'll bring Diane here, and, when your son has seen her once, he won't avoid opportunities to see her again.

MARQUISE: In the country for instance, where we're neighbors. You *are* going there this summer?

DUNIÈRES: Yes indeed! When are you leaving for Séval?

MARQUISE: Whenever you leave for Dunières.

DUNIÈRES: The end of June?

MARQUISE: The end of June let it be, then! And you have hopes? . . .

DUNIÈRES: Why not? They're delightful, these young people of ours! As soon as they see each other, they'll like each other; they'll get to know each other in the country, they'll fall in love, we'll give them our blessing, and they'll get married.

MARQUISE [*going to the fireplace*]: That sounds like a fairytale![3]

DUNIÈRES: Sometimes there's good sense in fairytales. . . . Come now, I'd be delighted to place my ward in the hands of a woman like you. [*He goes up to the Marquise.*] After all, between you and me, Marquise, feminine virtue is a rare thing nowadays.

MARQUISE: True; but one mustn't say so. [*Urbain enters at rear.*]

Scene 2

[*Dunières, Urbain, and the Marquise.*]

URBAIN [*carrying several opened letters*]: Here are the letters, mother. . . . [*To Dunières.*] Ah, is that you, Count? I didn't see you. How are you?

DUNIÈRES: Very well, thank you. I was just going to come up and shake your hand.

URBAIN: And the Countess?

DUNIÈRES: Rather poorly—bronchitis still.

URBAIN: What are the doctors saying?

DUNIÈRES: Oh, they're saying as much as they know; they're not saying anything.

URBAIN: You will present my apologies to her?

DUNIÈRES: Yes, you ungrateful lad! We know you're working. And you've recently been on a trip, too?

URBAIN: Yes.

DUNIÈRES: To study agricultural techniques?

URBAIN [*evasively*]: That's right.

DUNIÈRES: Did your brother go with you?

URBAIN: No; my brother claims that the only breathable air in the world is in Paris.

DUNIÈRES: Give him my compliments on his lungs, then.

MARQUISE [*rising*]: Yes—when we see him next! Not one visit for a whole month! [*To Urbain.*] Darling, these letters are perfect; I do thank you for them. [*She turns to Dunières.*] Just think, Dunières, for the past few days my boy has been reduced to acting as secretary for me; I've had to part with my old friend Artémise.

DUNIÈRES: Mademoiselle Dumoulin, your lady companion?

MARQUISE: She was becoming deaf, gluttonous, slanderous, and cantankerous. I found her another position, and I'm expecting a gem that Madame d'Arglade has found me, an old school friend of hers—from a very good family, I'm told—a Mademoiselle de Saint-Geneix. Do you know that name?—you seem to know by heart the entire French peerage, great and small.

DUNIÈRES: Saint-Geneix? Just a moment! Yes, very well indeed: lower Brittany. There was a judge, a gentleman of the legal profession. . . . On the other hand, there was also a Saint-Geneix who distinguished himself at Fontenoy.[4]

MARQUISE: Well, that won't alter the house too much. [*She goes to sit down at right.*]

DUNIÈRES: But now that I think about it, if she's a childhood friend of Madame d'Arglade's, surely she must still be a little young.

MARQUISE: No harm in that. All the same, she is older than the Baroness.

DUNIÈRES: I never heard of a woman who wasn't older than the Baroness. [*He sits down.*]

URBAIN [*near the fireplace*]: You're wondering that they allow her out on her own?

MARQUISE [*laughing*]: She is a widow!

DUNIÈRES: And she's still pining for her husband?

MARQUISE: Very necessary, in public!

DUNIÈRES: That's true. The public wouldn't know, otherwise.

URBAIN [*to Dunières*]: You're not very fond of the Baroness?

DUNIÈRES: Oh, I hardly know her. The Countess has always refused to receive her.

URBAIN: Nobody says anything against her, though?

DUNIÈRES: No, but she isn't really one of our circle; she just worms her way into it.

MARQUISE: Personally, I do receive her; she's a good woman, she entertains me, she knows all the news, she brings me gossip, she's a bit—how can I put it?—a bit of a case. Well, don't we all have our vices? She's mine. I'm told she has come up from sugar or cotton. . . . But her husband was a baron.

DUNIÈRES: Who isn't, nowadays?

MARQUISE: Anyway, the good widow is making herself extremely useful to me, and if she sends me the jewel she's promised, I'll forgive her everything.

DUNIÈRES: And you're expecting this jewel? . . .

MARQUISE [*looking at the clock*]: Right now, if she's punctual.

BENOÎT [*entering at rear*]: Mademoiselle de Saint-Geneix wishes to know if Madame is at home to her.

MARQUISE: Well, that's a good start. Show Mademoiselle de Saint-Geneix in. [*Benoît leaves.*]

DUNIÈRES [*rising*]: Good-bye, Marquise.

MARQUISE: We'll be in touch. [*Lowering her voice.*] Not a word of our plan to Urbain!

DUNIÈRES: Don't worry about that. [*He goes to take his hat from a hatstand behind the Marquise's armchair. Caroline enters.*]

MARQUISE: Come in, Mademoiselle [*Caroline curtseys*], and sit down. I'll be with you immediately.

DUNIÈRES [*in a low voice to the Marquise*]: Very presentable.

MARQUISE [*likewise*]: Oh? . . . I can't see from here, myself.

URBAIN [*to his mother*]: I can send off your letters, then?

MARQUISE: Yes, darling, and thanks again. [*Urbain kisses the Marquise's hand, and withdraws with a bow to Caroline.*]

DUNIÈRES [*to Urbain*]: Will you accompany me part of the way?

URBAIN: I'm afraid I can't; I have to work.

DUNIÈRES: Always the same, eh? [*They go out at rear.*]

Scene 3

[*Caroline and the Marquise.*]

MARQUISE [*seated at right*]: I must beg your pardon, Mademoiselle; now I am entirely at your disposal.

CAROLINE: Madame d'Arglade did promise to introduce me to you, Marquise; but when I arrived in Paris this morning and went to meet her, I found a letter from her saying that she had an urgent errand—a favor for one of her friends. . . .

MARQUISE: She is so obliging!

CAROLINE: She still hopes to have the honor of seeing Madame today; instead of accompanying me, she's to follow me.

MARQUISE: We can manage without Madame d'Arglade. [*She waves Caroline to a chair next to her.*] She can't speak any more good of you in your presence than she has spoken already. Well then, how old are you?

CAROLINE: Twenty-four.

MARQUISE: And you were at school with Madame d'Arglade?

CAROLINE: Yes, Madame.

MARQUISE: And you were friends?

CAROLINE: That is, Mademoiselle Léonie Lecomte was one of the "big girls," as we used to say, when I was one of the "little girls"; and she took me under her wing. She left school well before I did, and we lost touch with each other. But when some mutual friends told her about my sister's situation and my own, she remembered us; she knew that I was looking for a position as a companion, and she had the happy idea of recommending me to Madame.

MARQUISE: I'm much obliged to her. The only thing is, Madame d'Arglade told me you were older than she is.

CAROLINE: Thinking of what was best for me, no doubt, and fearing that my age wouldn't be sufficient assurance. But I do think I should be credited with two years for each year of misfortune.

MARQUISE: All the same . . . She also told me you weren't pretty, and I find you are.

CAROLINE: That's a matter of taste, Madame, and each person is entitled to their own opinion on the subject.

MARQUISE: You have some brains, I see.

CAROLINE: I try to have the kind that are suitable for my position.

MARQUISE: They're the rarest sort. Let's talk about your position then. First of all, the financial question. I've offered you eighteen hundred francs.

CAROLINE: Yes, Madame, and I've accepted.

MARQUISE: It isn't very much. But still, if you're not well off, my dear, I'm not rich myself. The comforts that you see around me don't belong to me. You could earn more somewhere else. . . .

CAROLINE: Your house would suit me better, Madame.

MARQUISE: Why? Let's be frank. What made you decide to accept such scanty remuneration to come and keep company with an old woman who is half blind and perhaps extremely tiresome?

CAROLINE: First of all, Madame, I was told you were intelligent and kindhearted; so I didn't think I would be bored in your company. Secondly, you are a true lady, so I shouldn't have to fear the humiliating aspects of being more or less a dependent. Finally, even if I should be unhappy, it's my duty not to remain idle.

MARQUISE: Still . . . judging from your breeding, you must have had some wealth?

CAROLINE: My father had a reasonable amount of money.

MARQUISE: How did he lose it?

CAROLINE: Because of his love for us. He wanted us to be rich; he risked his capital in the hope of doubling it.

MARQUISE: And ruined himself! What happened to your mother?

CAROLINE: I was so young when I lost her that I don't even remember her. I was nursed and brought up by an excellent woman whose husband was a trusted friend of my father's. Those good people were like family to us. When we lost our money, I had to part from them, much to my sorrow.

MARQUISE: And your sister?

CAROLINE: My sister married for love; her husband's only asset was his job. While she could give me hospitality, she did. Her husband died young, leaving her with four children. So now it's my turn to help her out.

MARQUISE: On eighteen hundred francs? It can't be done. Eighteen hundred francs for six people! Madame d'Arglade didn't tell me that.

CAROLINE: In the country, we can live on very little.

MARQUISE: In the country, in the country! Well, we'll try to arrange something about that.

CAROLINE [*kissing her hand*]: Oh, Madame—whether or not I have the good fortune to suit you, let me thank you for your kindness!

MARQUISE: Well, all I've seen in you so far has been good qualities—virtues, in fact. Let's move ahead to the weaknesses; I have to detect some, or it will be the ruin of me. Are you frivolous? Are you flirtatious?

CAROLINE: I am neither frivolous nor flirtatious, Madame.

MARQUISE: I have very serious reasons for asking that. If I take a young and pretty person under my roof, I'm taking on a heavy responsibility. Come now, haven't you had some little romance or other?

CAROLINE: No, Madame, I haven't had even the littlest romance.

MARQUISE: You've managed not to fall in love? How?

CAROLINE: Simply because I've never had the time to think of my own concerns. When I was seventeen I saw my father die from sorrow. And then the days of poverty came—after there had been a lot of work to pay off our debts. After that, there was my brother-in-law, whom we tried to keep from death's door as long as possible; my sister in despair, at her wits' end; her children to look after and bring up . . . goodness knows what else! When you hardly have time to sleep, you don't have time to dream.

MARQUISE: All the same—given how attractive you are—you must have been noticed, sought after?

CAROLINE: No, Madame; if you don't encourage minor persecutions, you don't have to deal with any major ones.

MARQUISE: I quite agree; those are sensible and impressive answers. So then, you're not afraid of what the future may bring?

CAROLINE: I'm not afraid of anything at all.

MARQUISE: And won't this personal solitude make you sad . . . moody?

CAROLINE: I am cheerful by nature, in good health, active and studious; that's my view of myself. I've never yet been too far out of my depth, so I think I can promise to be a good and honest girl.

MARQUISE: I'm sure you're speaking the truth there. Finally, we need to know if you really do have the little talents I require. Take off your gloves.

CAROLINE: What do I have to do?

MARQUISE: Chat, most importantly; and on that point I'm already satisfied. Then you have to read and play a bit of music. Do something with that piano for me. [*Caroline goes to the piano, and plays.*] Weber!⁵ As it happens, I'm very fond of his music, and you interpret him very well. That's excellent. [*She rises.*] I've just been thinking it over, my dear: I find I can give you two thousand four hundred francs.

CAROLINE [*having risen from the piano, goes up to her*]: Oh—Madame!

MARQUISE: Don't thank me so much for so little, you'll upset me. [*She crosses left.*] I know how you write—Madame d'Arglade has shown me your letters; you'll make an excellent secretary. So, my dear, I've come to know you, and I like you; now it's your turn to get to know me and see if you like me. [*Caroline reacts.*] Oh! I do want you to be fond of me. You're not just going to be one of the household, you're going to be one of the family. So, without further ado, let me reveal to you my habits, my obsessions, my weaknesses. My mind is very active and my body very lazy. I've been forbidden by my doctor to go out on visits.

I'm used to that; whether I'm in Paris or in the country, I never go out. . . . Then, too, I don't have any carriages any more, and I don't want my son to give me any. But you can run errands for me, and you have no objection to going in a cab?

CAROLINE: No, of course not—nor on foot, either.

MARQUISE: Next, I stay up very late, and I'm very talkative.

CAROLINE: All the better for me.

MARQUISE: You're charming. You do embroidery no doubt, and tapestry?

CAROLINE: Yes, Madame.

MARQUISE: I can't stand that; people count stitches, they get preoccupied. . . . Will you sacrifice your needle for me?

CAROLINE: Gladly.

MARQUISE: Oh—by the way—one handicap. I fall asleep sometimes, right in the middle of talking to you. It isn't boredom; my brain is in constant activity, and sometimes it just stops like a watch; you must leave me to my sleep, then, until it passes of its own accord; don't worry, I don't snore. Finally, I'm living here with my son the Marquis; he is melancholy by temperament; living alone with me, he thinks out loud sometimes; he's a good boy, but it saddens me. When there is a third person present, especially a person of note, he does take the trouble to be charming, simply out of politeness in the first place, and then gradually he becomes distracted from his own concerns. So, my dear, you'll do us both a great service if you don't leave us alone together too much. [*She moves to the left a little.*]

CAROLINE: But, Madame, if you did wish to talk of something private, how should I know?

MARQUISE [*sitting down at left*]: I'd let you know by asking if the clock is slow. That's all; will you have me just as I am?

CAROLINE: Yes, Madame.

MARQUISE: In that case, come here so that I can give you your deposit. [*She kisses her.*] Done: now you're mine.

CAROLINE: When does Madame wish me to take up residence here?

MARQUISE: When? Right away.

CAROLINE: Today?

MARQUISE: This moment.

CAROLINE: Then I'll go to the hotel and get . . .

MARQUISE: Your luggage? Not at all; we'll have it brought here. [*She rises, goes over to the fireplace, and rings the bell.*] You're no longer to leave me; that's final. Your apartment is ready; it's over there ... [*she points to the door at right*], mine is here [*she points to the door at left*]; there's only this drawing room between us. Take off your cloak and your hat. Here you are, right at home again.

CAROLINE: Oh, Madame, I thank God that he brought me to you! May I write to my sister and tell her how happy I am?

MARQUISE: That's very proper. [*She rings.*] I'll send old Benoît to take your orders. Off you go now, hurry along. [*Caroline goes out right. Benoît enters at rear.*]

Scene 4

[*Benoît and the Marquise.*]

MARQUISE: Benoît, please go and put yourself at the disposal of Mademoiselle de Saint-Geneix, who is coming to live with us; I am giving her that apartment. See that she doesn't lack anything, and notify Marguerite that I expect the young lady to be treated with the utmost respect and attention.

BENOÎT: Very good, Madame.

MARQUISE [*going upstage left*]: Baroness d'Arglade will be coming; you may let her in. [*Benoît goes to leave.*] Just a moment, Benoît. [*She sits at left.*] Have you found your successor for me?

BENOÎT: Not yet, Madame.

MARQUISE: We're not parting; you're entitled to retire here with us, that's understood; but I want you to live a long time, so you must have some rest.

BENOÎT: There's no urgency, Madame. I have a very good candidate in mind; I'm simply waiting on his decision.

MARQUISE: Very good, Benoît; we shall wait for him. Off you go now, Benoît. [*Benoît goes out right. Urbain enters at rear.*]

Scene 5

[*The Marquise and Urbain.*]

URBAIN: Well, mother, have you engaged Mademoiselle de Saint-Geneix?

MARQUISE: Don't talk to me about her! I'm in ecstasy; I think she must have put a spell on me.

URBAIN: Really? Tell me about it.

MARQUISE: I don't really know that I should. . . . I'm afraid of turning your head too!

URBAIN: Even assuming me to be capable of so sudden a passion, I hardly think you need fear that, under your own roof. . . .

MARQUISE: I'm well aware of your principles, darling! Just a little joke, and not, it seems, a successful one. What's wrong with you, Urbain? Are you bored here? Are you in love with someone who doesn't love you?

URBAIN: Not at all, seeing that you're the one I love.

MARQUISE: Yes—you do love me; you prove it, too; and just now I've added to the long list of sacrifices that you've had to make for me. I've promised Mademoiselle de Saint-Geneix . . .

URBAIN: Has she been driving a hard bargain, then?

MARQUISE: She took the utmost care not to do that, poor little thing! She's sacrificing herself for her family. I was touched . . . and now I'm almost sorry for it. We're not always in a position to do good.

URBAIN: Ah, but the very fact that you feel free to do it shows how much you trust me, mother.

MARQUISE: You're the best son in the world, and the most generous man. You're a good seventy-five per cent of what I live for.

URBAIN [*with a smile*]: You mustn't say that, mother; my brother has the right to half of your affection—possibly the more tender half.

MARQUISE: Your brother . . .

URBAIN: Neglects you; but once he's here, you'll forgive him everything.

MARQUISE: No, I'm putting him out of my mind; I have hardly any affection for him left.

URBAIN [*looking at the clock*]: Hardly any left! So, if he came here this very moment and surprised you, he'd be unwelcome?

MARQUISE [*with a start*]: Is he finally going to come, then?

URBAIN [*smiling*]: Aha! See what I mean?

MARQUISE: If he is coming, it's only because you've been out looking for him.

URBAIN: He was getting ready. . . .

MARQUISE: I don't care if he does expect complaints! Ruining me is one thing—but deserting me!

BENOÎT [*announcing with pleasure*]: The Duke d'Aléria.

Scene 6

[*Urbain, the Duke, and the Marquise.*]

MARQUISE: You're having yourself announced in my home nowadays, are you, my boy? Have I become a total stranger to you?

DUKE [*kissing her hand*]: The fact is, I was a bit embarrassed about presenting myself, mother dear; it'd serve me right if you'd forgotten my name.

MARQUISE: There are too many things that remind me of it.

DUKE [*going to put his hat on the piano*]: Bad things, eh?—Hello, Urbain.

URBAIN: Hello, Gaétan.

DUKE: You've been round to see me?

URBAIN [*sotto voce*]: Yes; there's something I have to discuss. [*Aloud.*] You'll be dining with us?

DUKE: If mother will allow me.

MARQUISE: You're hoping for a refusal? You won't get it. I'm going to dress; it's time. If need be, the two of you can do the honors for Madame d'Arglade. She's the only one I'm expecting. Urbain, please remind her that she's to dine with us, and thank her for her charming little friend.

DUKE: Madame d'Arglade has a charming little friend?

URBAIN: A new companion that she's found for mother.

DUKE: Mademoiselle Artémise isn't with us any more, then? Oh, so much the better! Believe it or not, mother, it was the thought of Artémise that kept me from showing my face here.

MARQUISE: So, you'll be coming more often from now on?

DUKE: Are you trying to make me say something foolish, mother? Well, I must warn you, my conversation has become quite sensible these days.

MARQUISE: Since when?

DUKE: Since some time ago!

MARQUISE: What's happened to you, then?

DUKE: Well, you know the sort of nonsense—dinners at fifty francs a head, horses at eight hundred louis, women at I don't know how much. . . .

MARQUISE: My boy!

DUKE: But mother, I've got over it! The dinners were too hot, the horses were too slow, the women were too fast. . . . All which frustrations led me, via boredom, to morality; so, at the moment . . . You'll see: I'll deliver a sermon.

MARQUISE: To whom?

DUKE: To Urbain.

MARQUISE: Good heavens, on what subject?

DUKE: On his idolatry of books, and his aversion to marriage.

URBAIN: You want me to get married?

DUKE: Yes, sir; that's what we all want; after all, our dear mother does have to be provided with some grandchildren. One of us is going to have to commit matrimony, and since it can't possibly be me—I'd never find a woman sufficiently abandoned by heaven and humanity alike—apart from Madame d'Arglade, and I don't wish to hear a word about her. . . .

MARQUISE: You could do worse.

DUKE: Oh, surely not! Think it over—a man who is just starting to behave himself!

MARQUISE: And how long is it going to last, this starting to behave yourself?

DUKE: Oh, it won't last, of course; but it will come back, and by dint of coming back, maybe some day . . .

URBAIN: What's wrong with the present?

DUKE: Just think of the past. . . .

MARQUISE: Come now, you're trying to spare me the pain of recalling it.

DUKE: Recalling it? That's a punishment I'd prefer to shirk.

MARQUISE: You're rather blasé about it.

DUKE [*touched, kissing her hand*]: Never!

MARQUISE [*likewise touched, kissing him*]: I am such an old softie!

DUKE: Aha! Again, please.

MARQUISE: No; it's more than you deserve.

DUKE: If I deserved it, I shouldn't be asking for it.

MARQUISE: All right—this evening!

DUKE: Once only? Even when I'm going away?

MARQUISE [*lowering her voice*]: No; once for each hour you stay here.

DUKE: Then I shan't go away any more!

MARQUISE: Liar! [*She leaves; the Duke sees her out.*]

Scene 7

[*The Duke and Urbain.*]

DUKE: Well now, brother, congratulate me on my happiness. I am forgiven—it doesn't seem to surprise you any more, and yet

there's every reason to be surprised. So, what did you want to
tell me?

URBAIN: When our mother is cross with you, she's miserable; and
when she forgives you, she's resuscitated. You ought to get yourself forgiven more often.

DUKE: Oh, this time, Urbain, there was a very serious impediment
to my coming here; but I can't say that to my mother.

URBAIN: And to me you can? . . .

DUKE: Do you want to know what it is?

URBAIN: Yes; what is it?

DUKE: Well, all right, it's rather embarrassing to say so, but the
bailiffs were camped in front of my premises because of a
business matter.[6]

URBAIN: You've come to that point?

DUKE: I'm afraid so!

URBAIN: How did you manage to get here today?

DUKE: Because I didn't come from home. My valet brought your
letter to . . . where I was. [*He laughs.*]

URBAIN: And where were you?

DUKE: I was under the eleventh tree on the left as you go into the
forest of Fontainebleau by the Melun road. That's where I re-
side, sometimes.

URBAIN: You?

DUKE: Well, it's still better than prison . . . and there really are
some entertaining aspects to the life of a nomad. People like
you go on a long journey when you want the experience of
travel; I, on the other hand, get it from everything around me.
I have, for instance, the most amazing valet—constantly full of
surprises. No matter where I sleep—whether it's in the city, at
the Golden Lion inn on some road or other, underneath a tree
like I did yesterday—there I find him when I wake up, with
everything laid out just as if we were back home: my kit open
alongside me, my cocoa piping hot on his portable spirit stove.
So, this morning, he had me shaved, combed, and dressed
under the aforementioned eleventh tree, and brought me the
morning papers to skim through while he was doing it. I've
read Monsieur de Clusey's speech;[7] it's very good—all the gov-
ernment has to do is sit tight.

URBAIN: You treat everything as a joke, Gaétan!

DUKE: I treat everything as a joke if it deserves to be.

URBAIN: Still, this isn't; if mother found out about it, she'd die of shame. We'll have to put a stop to it.

DUKE: Easily said.

URBAIN: Easily done, too. Here's the receipt for what you were owing. A man with your brains really shouldn't be reduced to marveling at his valet quite so much. You haven't any more debts, and you have a remaining income of twelve thousand pounds. [*He gives him the receipt.*]

DUKE: Urbain!

URBAIN: Well?

DUKE: You paid my debts?

URBAIN: Seeing you couldn't pay them yourself—yes.

DUKE: But mother had already paid them once!

URBAIN: She couldn't have paid them again—she hasn't got anything left.

DUKE: So now I've ruined you too?

URBAIN: Not entirely. What I have left belongs strictly to the Marquise. With any luck we can hold onto it for a long time, and she needn't know about what will happen after her.

DUKE: And you thought I'd just swallow the humiliation of owing the money to you?. . .

URBAIN: Remember, your heart is older than your pride; it ought to have the first say.

DUKE:[8] I don't care! I won't have it! We don't have the same father, we don't have the same name, you don't have any obligations towards me.

URBAIN: We do have the same mother, and that's quite enough. It's too late to refuse, anyway. Your creditors would hardly be inclined to give back what they've just taken. Now you have only one creditor left, namely me, and that one can afford to wait.

DUKE: What a wretched creature I am! Why. . . ?

URBAIN: Why didn't you yield to temptation and blow your brains out?

DUKE: That's right! That's what I should have done.

URBAIN: And add an irreversible injury to reversible ones? Even if you yourself don't care about anyone, there are still people who care about you.

DUKE: My poor mother; true.

URBAIN: Plus . . .

DUKE: Plus who?

URBAIN: Well, your valet . . . and me.

DUKE [*throwing himself into his arms*]: Oh, Urbain! . . .

URBAIN: Come now, Gaétan, let's have no more of that. I've simply done for you what you would have done for me.

DUKE: No, I couldn't have done it, I wouldn't have been able to bring it off; it's my destiny in life, I spoil everything. Urbain . . . Urbain, you know I never really felt close to you?

URBAIN: Oh, I know that. In my view, it's simply a matter of constitutional differences; but perhaps it's time we learned to like each other better.

DUKE: Oh—definitely! Forgive me: I do respect and admire and venerate you; you're so straight and good and exemplary, and I'm just an ungrateful brute and idiot! You're the best friend I have, and I've never appreciated it, and I've given over my time and my heart and my money—along with my father's and my mother's and yours—to rascals and, and . . . What can I do for you? Are you in love with someone? Does she need to be abducted? Does her husband need to be murdered? Do you want me to go to China—Siberia—hell? Tell me!

URBAIN: If you could manage to feel closer to me, that would even up the score.

DUKE: But I do—heart and soul! I wish I could find some immediate way of showing it.

URBAIN: There's one way that you possibly haven't thought of.

DUKE: No, I've thought of that—turn over a new leaf! All right, I will turn over a new leaf. Why not? I'm still young, goodness knows—you're not finished when you're forty, you're only a bit shopworn, that's all. I'll put myself in order—that's settled. It has to be done anyway. I'm not really in such a bad way, after all. I'll work at getting my health and youth back, and then you can do what you like with me. I'll go and spend summer with mother and you in the country. I'll tell you stories, I'll set you laughing. Please give me a boost—I need your help with my plans; because when I think about all the harm I've done, and what a wretched situation I'm in—I don't know what to do with myself! [*He bursts into tears.*]

URBAIN [*going up to him*]: Cheer up, laddie! The bad times are over; the good ones may be about to begin!

DUKE: That's right: tell me the secret of happiness: what is it?

URBAIN: Courage.

DUKE: Do you need that yourself?

URBAIN: I need it more than you do.

DUKE: You're troubled by something?

URBAIN: Worse than that; I'm guilty of something—almost criminally guilty. I'm not in any position to sit in judgment on you.

DUKE: Well, what is it? Can you tell me?

URBAIN: I'd like to tell you; then you'd see that you can still do something good—if only to me, living without any friends; my heart is too full, and too shut up.

DUKE: Well, go on, Urbain; speak out; my own heart has just been scrubbed clean, so it can listen to your worries. What has happened to you? What's the matter?

URBAIN: A very simple matter. I've been in love.

DUKE: Just as I thought. And did she love you?

URBAIN: No.

DUKE: What do you mean, "no"?

URBAIN: She was a married woman; it hurt her even to look at me.

DUKE: Which is exactly how a married woman ought to love. You wouldn't know what to do with them otherwise. So you took her seriously?

URBAIN: That's how I take everything.

DUKE: And, naturally, she broke it off, right?

URBAIN: She . . . died.

DUKE: Oh, dash it, that's a different matter. So when did she die?

URBAIN: Three years ago.

DUKE: One passion, I see, has filled your entire life. But after all, if you've mourned her for three years, that's enough, that's quite satisfactory.

URBAIN: Stop it, Gaétan—I was the death of her.

DUKE: You're imagining it; is anyone ever the death of women? When they do die, it's only because they've run out of other things to do.

URBAIN: Please don't make fun of it; there's no cure for my pain, because there's no excuse for the harm I've done. I used my whole will and mind, the whole force of my soul—not to fight against my passion, but to inspire another man with it—a poor creature that she crushed. I'll tell you the whole story—but not today; I can't. The memory of it is stifling me. . . . It's killing me, Gaétan!

DUKE: You? You're still in love with her?

URBAIN: I can't be sorry that my life has been full of struggle and torment; but I can't love any more—that's my punishment.

DUKE: All because of one little affair? Don't be silly! Look at me; it can hardly be possible to have been in love more often than I have, can it? Why, before I've been out of town for three months . . .

URBAIN: Oh, you! You're one of the hardy perennials that flower again every season. But look, I don't want to depress you; just remember that, at some point, I may have to ask you to render me a service of great importance.

DUKE: Well, tell me now.

URBAIN: No, let's drop the subject. I'll go and collect your bills, and you can do whatever you like with them.

DUKE: I'll have them framed.

URBAIN: It's up to you.

DUKE: And one day I'll show them to your offspring and tell them, "Take a good look at those things—never have anything to do with them."

URBAIN: Now then, no more misunderstandings between us! [*He goes out at rear. Benoît enters.*]

Scene 8

[*Benoît and the Duke; later, Pierre.*]

DUKE [*sitting at left*]: Well, you've come like the dove to the ark![9] I haven't had anything today except my cocoa.

BENOÎT: I haven't forgotten Monsieur's little habits. [*He goes to the table, on which he has left a plate with madeira and biscuits.*]

DUKE: You're an angel.

BENOÎT: Monsieur is flattering me. Monsieur's valet is outside; he wishes to have his instructions.

DUKE [*eating and drinking*]: Show him in. [*Benoît gestures to Pierre to enter, then leaves at rear.—To Pierre.*] Have you called in at my place?

PIERRE: Yes, Monsieur.

DUKE: No letters?

PIERRE: Only cards.

DUKE: Hand them over. [*Aside, reading the cards.*] Cards from the very tradesmen that were prosecuting me—now they're asking for my custom again! How far will society go? [*To Pierre.*] Thanks, that's all.

PIERRE: Monsieur has no instructions? . . .

DUKE: No.

PIERRE: Where should I wait for Monsieur?

DUKE: My place.

PIERRE: At what time does Monsieur wish to be woken?

DUKE: You'll let me sleep in.

PIERRE: Monsieur knows it isn't Sunday tomorrow?

DUKE: Yes, my friend, I do. I've completed my survey of the local countryside, I'm going to have a rest, and I'd strongly advise you to do the same. Off you go, Pierre; you've well and truly earned it. [*Pierre moves upstage, stops short in surprise when he sees Caroline enter, then leaves.*]

Scene 9

[*Caroline and the Duke, seated.*]

CAROLINE [*coming in from the right; seeing the Duke, she starts to leave*]: Excuse me, Monsieur; I thought the Marquise was in the drawing room.

DUKE [*rising*]: She'll be back in a moment. [*Caroline curtseys and again goes to leave.*] Am I frightening you, Mademoiselle?

CAROLINE: No, Monsieur; but . . .

DUKE: But . . . you wouldn't be inconveniencing me, seeing I'm alone and we're both members of the household; because . . . unless I'm mistaken, you're the successor to Mademoiselle Artémise.

CAROLINE: Yes, Monsieur, I've replaced her.

DUKE: Just as springtime replaces winter—it puts it out of memory. Oh! You didn't know Artémise! She was harsher than a December gale; I'm sure she was the cause of my first dose of rheumatism.

CAROLINE: Well, anyhow, have you got over it now, Monsieur?

DUKE: Yes.

CAROLINE: I'm very glad to hear it.

DUKE: Aha! One can talk with you! . . . You didn't know her?

CAROLINE: Mademoiselle Artémise? No, Monsieur.

DUKE: Have you ever seen an albatross?

CAROLINE: Never.

DUKE: Not even stuffed?

CAROLINE: Not even stuffed.

DUKE: You should see them; they're at the Zoo. They're very interesting creatures.

CAROLINE [*suppressing a smile*]: I know they're sea birds.

DUKE: They are indeed—with a great big beak ending in a hook. They eat all day long. They have a back that is half black and half brown, and flippers. Well now, Mademoiselle Artémise . . . [*Caroline bursts out laughing.*] Well, well, you actually do laugh! At long last, we're going to have some laughter in this place! By the way, would it be an impertinence to inquire your name? I guessed Artémise's. There are some faces like that—they proclaim their own name. Wait a minute and I'll come up with yours. . . . Marie? . . . Blanche? . . .

CAROLINE: No.

DUKE: Louise? . . . Charlotte? . . .

CAROLINE: Getting warmer.

DUKE: Caroline?

CAROLINE: That's it.

DUKE: And you're here from the provinces?

CAROLINE: From the country.

DUKE: Well, why don't you have red hands, if you've just come from the country?

CAROLINE: Because I was brought up in Paris.

DUKE: And you're not going to get bored here?

CAROLINE: I never get bored.

DUKE: Never ever?

CAROLINE: Never.

DUKE: You're lucky—very! And you were introduced here by Madame d'Arglade?

CAROLINE: Yes.

DUKE: So, the pecan pie[10] is known to you, is she?

CAROLINE: What did you call her?

DUKE: Pecan pie.

CAROLINE: What does that mean?

DUKE: It's a new term, derived from goodness knows what, and highly respectable, in my opinion; it means half-crazy.

CAROLINE: What! Do you think Léonie . . . ?

DUKE: Hmm . . . perhaps you haven't set eyes on her for some time. But hang on, we're expecting her now. Just you watch her: she'll tread on my feet without even seeing me, and when I cry out, she'll shed real tears—unless she bursts out laughing and addresses me as "poor Benoît," or keels over in a faint because she thinks I'm my mother. I'm told she's reached the stage of confessing to other people's misdeeds, and saddling other people with the responsibility for her own.... [*Caroline starts to protest.*] These are, undoubtedly, calumnies. But anyway, tell me, how does a rational human being come to know Madame d'Arglade?

CAROLINE: You know her very well yourself.

DUKE: Ah, but I'm not rational. No matter. Would you like to shake hands with me?

CAROLINE: Why?

DUKE: Because an impulse of the best and most respectable kind impels me to ask it of you. Come on! [*Caroline gives him her hand.*] Thank you! Take good care of my mother.

CAROLINE: So you're the Marquis?

DUKE: No, I'm his brother.

CAROLINE: The Marquise only mentioned one son.

DUKE [*with feeling*]: That does happen to her occasionally. It's my own fault.

Scene 10

[*Caroline, Léonie, and the Duke.*]

LÉONIE [*entering at rear*]: Here I am!

CAROLINE [*running to her*]: Oh, Léonie dear! As you can see, I came on my own.

LÉONIE: I know. I didn't get anyone to announce me, because I wanted to see if you'd still recognize me.

CAROLINE: You haven't changed.

LÉONIE: And you're beautifuller than ever... amazing! Have you seen the Marquise?

CAROLINE: Yes; the Marquise is adorable, and here I am settled in.

LÉONIE: That's just marvelous. Listen, I've been running around all day on a rather serious and rather delicate errand. A good friend of mine, getting on in years a little, was being forced to take her daughter to the ball—the father insisted; he's a bit despotic, the dear fellow—he thought the young lady was old enough to make an appearance in society, whereas the mother thought she was too old—I mean too young. They chose me to arbitrate, I set out... but on the way, I changed my mind.

DUKE [*having bowed ironically to Léonie several times*]: I'm over here, Baroness, if you happen to notice—ready to present my compliments the first time a comma happens to slip in. . . . But don't trouble yourself, I can wait.

LÉONIE: I thought I shook hands with you as I came in.

DUKE: Not today, that was on your last visit.

LÉONIE: Oh! Should we start all over again?

DUKE: No; my mother asked me to do the honors, and I'm doing them—by letting you talk with Mademoiselle. Does that suit your wishes?

LÉONIE: A friend from school; I've just met her again. . . .

DUKE: Will it take you two hours? It's just that once you start talking . . . Tell me, Baroness, what day is it today?

LÉONIE: Today?

DUKE: Yes.

LÉONIE: It's Monday or Tuesday. . . . No, I'm an idiot, it's Sunday!

DUKE: It's Thursday.

LÉONIE: Yes, that's right.

DUKE: Baroness—

LÉONIE: Yes?

DUKE: Shut your eyes.

LÉONIE: Is this another joke?

DUKE: I don't joke. Shut your eyes.

LÉONIE: Done.

DUKE: What color is your dress? No cheating!

LÉONIE: It's green.

DUKE: It's gray; you forgot, you're in half mourning.

LÉONIE: How can I tell? I didn't dress myself.

DUKE: There's logic for you.

LÉONIE [*to Caroline*]: There's the Duke's eternal teasing for you! Well, yes, I am absentminded about things that don't matter. What do I care what day it is, or the whichth of what month? I don't have any bills to pay! I don't forget my friends—that's the important thing.

DUKE: In that case, Baroness, do keep us in mind, and take good care to remember that you're going to dine today—Monday, Tuesday, or Sunday, the sixth or fifteenth of November, April, or January—in your blue, gray, or green dress—with us, them, or some other people. [*He leaves at rear.*]

Scene 11

[*Léonie and Caroline.*]

LÉONIE [*going to sit at left*]: Mad as ever—but such a comedian! [*Mysteriously.*] All the same, watch out for him.

CAROLINE: Why?

LÉONIE: The Duke is pretty sharp, believe me! There isn't a woman alive that he doesn't compromise.

CAROLINE: Has . . . ?

LÉONIE: Me? No. But I ought, as a good friend, to warn you about certain matters that I couldn't put in writing.

CAROLINE: It's an excellent time to do so.

BENOÎT [*entering from left*]: The Marquise requests Baroness d'Arglade and Mademoiselle de Saint-Geneix to be so kind as to come to her.

LÉONIE: In a moment. [*Benoît leaves.*] I was saying to you . . .

CAROLINE: Is it so very urgent? We don't have time just now.

LÉONIE [*rising*]: Oh but we do. Very briefly. Let's see—first and foremost, before I forget, a terribly brutal question: you're poor, I'm rich—do you need any money?

CAROLINE: No, thanks!

LÉONIE: You're sure?

CAROLINE: Very sure!

LÉONIE: You're not angry with me?

CAROLINE: Don't be silly!

LÉONIE: In that case, let's rely on each other. Now, here's my advice: the Marquise has another son.

CAROLINE: She told me—the Marquis.

LÉONIE: He's a scholar, a thinker. His mother wants to marry him off to a young girl I know . . . or very soon shall know. She's . . .

CAROLINE: Yes but, Léonie dear, none of this is any of my business.

LÉONIE: It's more of your business than you realize. The Marquis is sensitive, you're still pretty—if you turn his head . . . Oh, don't start protesting, you can never help these things.

CAROLINE: But one can help oneself!

LÉONIE: That all depends. Where was I? Well now, the Marquise would never forgive you if her son's marriage came to nothing

because of you. . . . Let me speak! Now, as for the Duke, he's
bankrupt, he has to marry for money, and I fancy I've got his
business in hand.

CAROLINE: Really? Are you a matchmaker?

LÉONIE: What can I do! The Marquise tortures me about it—he's
so difficult to place, the Duke! Your help wouldn't exactly go
amiss; can I rely on you?

CAROLINE: Why, Léonie, whatever are you thinking? I'm in no
position to have any influence here; nobody is going to ask for
my advice—you can be sure of that.

LÉONIE: Your position could become a very delicate one.

CAROLINE: I'm not afraid of it, now that you've warned me.

LÉONIE: And at all times—however delicate—I'll still have your
trust and friendship?

CAROLINE: I'd be very ungrateful if things were otherwise.

LÉONIE [*kissing her*]: Oh! I am so fond of you—and you well deserve it, too. Let's go to the Marquise. [*Benoît opens the door.*]
Here we are. [*They enter the Marquise's apartment.—Pierre appears
at rear, and follows Caroline with his eyes.*]

Scene 12

[*Benoît and Pierre.*]

PIERRE: Monsieur Benoît—

BENOÎT [*straightening the chairs*]: Monsieur Pierre?

PIERRE: Who is that young lady that just went in with Madame
d'Arglade?

BENOÎT: It's Madame's new companion—Mademoiselle de Saint-
Geneix.

PIERRE [*aside*]: Companion! . . . [*Aloud.*] Monsieur Benoît, I've made
up my mind: I do want to take your place.

BENOÎT: Very good; when?

PIERRE: Soon as the Duke can do without me. Well, good-bye,
Monsieur Benoît.

BENOÎT: Good-bye, Monsieur Pierre.

Act 2

Décor as for Act 1.

Scene 1[11]

[*Caroline, the Marquise, Urbain.*

Urbain is seated by the fireplace looking at Caroline, who is seated at the table with a newspaper that she has just been reading. The Marquise is seated at the other side of the table, near the fireplace.]

MARQUISE [*absently*]: Goodness! It's more than a week after Pentecost!

URBAIN: How does that affect you, mother?

MARQUISE: Not at all. . . . Caroline, did you ask about Madame de Dunières this morning?

CAROLINE: Yes, Madame; her doctor won't allow her to go out yet, but she's doing very well.

MARQUISE: You ought to have gone there, Urbain!

URBAIN: I left my card the day before yesterday; she wasn't seeing anyone.

MARQUISE [*to Caroline*]: Put away those papers, dear; they're a bore.

CAROLINE [*rising and taking the papers upstage*]: Shall I read you something else?

MARQUISE: No, you've been reading for a good hour.

CAROLINE: I'm not tired.

URBAIN: If you were, Mademoiselle, I'm at my mother's disposal this morning.

MARQUISE: Today too? You're spoiling me, my boy! Let's have a talk. [*Caroline comes back and sits down.*] I'd much prefer that. For the last month, ever since dear good Caroline has been here, I've had delightful mornings—and all because of you two. She reads so well! And when the two of you talk, it invigorates and relaxes me at one and the same time. Both of you are so full of ideas that I don't try to be clever any more; you've taught me to listen, and at times that's a very good thing.

CAROLINE: That's how I feel when you're talking with Monsieur de Villemer.

URBAIN: And that's how I feel when my mother is talking with you, Mademoiselle de Saint-Geneix.

MARQUISE: Well then, we're all very cosy and contented with one another! But the best of it is, we really do mean what we say—and how rare that is, in this world! Caroline, you've kept your word; you're perfect for me—conscientious but not intrusive, cheerful but not noisy, active but not fussy; and above all, you don't ever seem to tire of me.

CAROLINE: Can anyone ever tire of being happy?

URBAIN [*blithely*]: Just tell us that you're happy too, mother, and we'll be "obliged to you for life," as the good folks say.

MARQUISE: Yes—I am happy... with the hope of being still more so, if...

URBAIN: I know what you're going to say. Still, let me remind you that the better is the enemy of the good; now, where marriage is concerned... [*Caroline rises and goes left.*]

MARQUISE [*to Caroline*]: Where are you going?

CAROLINE: Just seeing if the clock is getting slow.

MARQUISE [*smiling*]: No, child, it's keeping perfect time. Well now, my boy, you were saying?... [*Caroline goes upstage left.*]

URBAIN: That when a man is advised to hang himself for the good of his health, he'd do well to think twice about it.

MARQUISE: Who is giving you any advice of that kind?

URBAIN: Certain people who advise me to get married for the sake of getting married, even though I know nothing at all about the person....

MARQUISE: But one does know oneself—unless one refuses to know oneself.

URBAIN: Ah, but how does one go about it? We know perfectly well how marriages are made in high society. You're introduced to a young person who is supposed to know nothing about your intentions; she examines you despondently or quizzically, while pretending to take no notice of you whatsoever, and she says to herself: "I'll try to get used to this fellow's face; but I would have preferred him to be different!" You see each other again two or three times. If you saw each other any more than that, it would be too late to change your mind. So, you get married without knowing each other; after which, you fit in with each other if you can.

MARQUISE: I quite agree with you; you deserve better than a random pairing of that kind, and it's up to me to find someone whom you could confidently accept. Trust your mother, Urbain!

URBAIN [*he sits on the chair that Caroline was occupying; she sits left and cuts the pages of a book*[12]]: Parents, my dear mother, always have wondrous hopes for us, because they have such exquisite illusions about us. It was a fond mother who said, rather naïvely:

"My children are such dears,
Fine, strong, and prettier than all their peers."

You're setting up an impossible ideal for me.

MARQUISE: No; I'm imagining. . . .

URBAIN [*looking at Caroline, who takes no notice*]: The things we imagine never materialize. Why not be content with the things that are right in front of our eyes?

MARQUISE: Do you know anybody, then? . . .

URBAIN: I'm talking in general terms, mother dear. I'm saying that moral perfection deserves to be honored, and that we may come across it without having to search for it. You, on the other hand, want to find it combined with other less important things, so you wander far away into your fantasyland, and all to no purpose.

MARQUISE: No, Urbain, you're wrong. What do I want for you? A young girl of excellent birth . . .

URBAIN: Pretty, pleasant . . .

MARQUISE: Yes; and virtuous, clever . . .

URBAIN: Well-educated, kindhearted . . .

MARQUISE: Yes; talented, well-bred . . .

URBAIN: And very rich?

MARQUISE: And very rich; but above all, from a most respectable family.

URBAIN: And without any ambition or vanity?

MARQUISE [*laughing*]: I want her to be perfect, that's the truth of the matter!

URBAIN [*rising*]: You see the point, mother! . . . Well now, that's easy enough; Madame d'Arglade will find it for you one day or another.

BENOÎT [*entering upstage*]: The Baroness d'Arglade wishes to know if Madame is alone.

MARQUISE: Oh, I know! She's bringing me news of the Dunières! Show her into my apartment. [*Benoît leaves.*]

URBAIN: She's thoroughly installed in the Dunières household, then?

MARQUISE: They did have some prejudices against her; but they've overcome them. [*She rises.*]

URBAIN: I'll leave you; I don't want to put you out. I'll tell them to show her in here. [*He goes out left. Caroline moves right.*]

MARQUISE: Stay here, please, Caroline!

CAROLINE: But what about your letters, Madame? You know that I have rather a number of them to write today.

MARQUISE: That's true. Off you go then. We're finally going to discover if the Dunières... I might need you; come back as soon as you can. [*Caroline leaves at right. Enter Léonie at left.*]

Scene 2

[*Léonie, the Marquise.*]

MARQUISE: Well, Baroness?

LÉONIE: I've conquered Madame de Dunières's hesitations; she is so prim and proper where her godchild is concerned. I was persuasive—eloquent, even! One does feel inspired when one is acting in your service. [*At the Marquise's invitation, she sits down next to her.*] I even made Madame de Dunières laugh; and you know how easy that is! In short, Monsieur de Dunières and his ward will be here in half an hour.

MARQUISE: Dear Léonie, it's so kind of you; I'm so happy!

LÉONIE: Tell me, though—will the Duke be present at the meeting?

MARQUISE: I've no idea; he doesn't come every day.

LÉONIE: Has he really turned over a new leaf?

MARQUISE: My dear, I have no idea how Urbain worked that miracle; the Duke is charming, and I honestly think he isn't doing foolish things any more.

LÉONIE: So you think that if he did happen to be here, he wouldn't say anything out of place?

MARQUISE: He? Never. He knows his place. [*They both rise.*] But he isn't the one in question.... Oh, I'm so excited! As long as the Marquis doesn't go out—I'll ask them to tell him.... [*She goes to ring the bell.*]

LÉONIE: No; I've asked Benoît to keep an eye on him; he's working in his room. Do please relax, Madame! [*She helps the Marquise back to her armchair at right.*]

MARQUISE [*sitting down*]: It's true; I am tiring myself, and I shall have to be agreeable very soon! Tell me, Baroness; my thoughts are so confused—you did say that Madame de Dunières...?

LÉONIE [*sitting down*]: She is a little afraid of the Duke! He's been in such bad company—and perhaps still is....

MARQUISE: No; Urbain assures me he isn't.

LÉONIE: Now, I'm merely saying what people have said to me, what everyone says: you ought to think about getting the Duke married.

MARQUISE [*absently*]: Oh, nonsense!

LÉONIE: Once that was done, the Marquis would make more of an effort to get himself established, and the thing would be easier to manage. You see, he's afraid of leaving his brother to his own devices, in a situation ... that isn't a happy one whichever way you consider it. [*The Marquise falls asleep.—The Duke enters upstage and goes behind the Marquise.—Léonie continues without seeing him.*] The poor Duke—he hasn't anything left; he isn't young any more, and his wit is pretty commonplace by now—not what it used to be. Now, I know one can always retrieve one's losses when one isn't too particular. But you wouldn't consider a banker's daughter, and he wouldn't consider a noble young lady if she was ugly or deformed. What he needs is somebody who, simply out of her devotion to you, and without looking too closely at his liabilities ...

DUKE [*continuing Léonie's sentence*]: ... would agree to marry this no-hoper who is no longer either young or handsome, whose wit is just about burnt out, and who doesn't know which nail to hang himself on any more ... but who still has a fine name, a genuine title, and would secure me a footing at court... in Fairyland! Don't go to so much effort; she's asleep.

LÉONIE: She's asleep?

DUKE: Best thing she could do. A real success, don't you think? You might have added—because, after all, one has to point out the true merits of the merchandise—"I'm thirty, but I don't look a day over ... twenty-nine; I'm still good-looking; I come from an industrial background, not that there's anything wrong with that, but, well, I'm silly enough to be ashamed of it...."

LÉONIE [*rising*]: I've never been ashamed of it!

DUKE [*stepping in front of his mother, and going up to her*]: Oh but you have! When you married dear Monsieur d'Arglade, you did it with a motive.

LÉONIE: What motive?

DUKE: The desire to be a baroness. But he was too sharp for you. You were rich, pretty, smart; he was poor, boring, far from attractive, and not really a baron at all.

LÉONIE: Oh, Duke—how can you say such bad things to me about my husband? He was the best man in the world.

DUKE: He's better still nowadays! Anyhow, it can't have been hard for him to die; his birth was so doubtful in the first place.

LÉONIE: That's beyond a joke.

DUKE: You can be witty enough sometimes—do please retaliate! When my mother falls asleep at the sound of conversation, the only thing that wakes her up again is silence.

LÉONIE: Let's suppose, Duke, that everything you've said about me is true: that I am thirty years old, that I am ambitious, and that I've had the intention . . . Why would it be such a misfortune for you to marry a woman who is universally supposed to be twenty-two—whom you yourself must have thought pretty, since you did court her—whom you know to be virtuous, since she wouldn't listen to you—and who would let her own money, laboriously acquired by her honest parents, fall into the chasm that has already swallowed the fortune you inherited from your illustrious ancestors? Do you think the mere fancy for a title could motivate such a sacrifice? That would be a very foolish misjudgment for so profound a thinker to make. You'll have to admit either that this pseudoidiot is a genuine madwoman, or else that this pseudobaroness is capable of genuine feelings.

DUKE: Not a bad answer, for you! [*Léonie turns her back on him brusquely.*] You're leaving, then? [*Léonie goes into the Marquise's apartment at left; the Marquise wakes up, and the Duke goes to her and kisses her hand.*]

Scene 3

[*The Duke and the Marquise.*]

MARQUISE [*waking up*]: You were saying, Baroness? Oh, is that you, Gaétan?

DUKE: Yes. I was just having a quarrel with the Baroness. I teased her a bit too strongly; but she doesn't get angry at anything.

MARQUISE: I've been asleep then? I didn't hear a thing. Where is she?

DUKE [*indicating the Marquise's apartment*]: Oh, she isn't far away; she doesn't simply walk out like that, our dear Baroness.

MARQUISE [*rising*]: Let's go to her.

Scene 4

[*The Duke, the Marquise, Caroline.*]

CAROLINE [*entering from right*]: Would the Marquise please give me five minutes' hearing about a small domestic matter?

DUKE: Should I be off, Mister Prime Minister?

CAROLINE: No, Mister Duke; because presumably you know what it's about. It's a note that I've just received. [*She gives it to him.*]

DUKE [*reading*]: "Pierre wishes to transfer his services from the Duke to the Marquise, as a replacement for Benoît. Pierre wishes to place himself under the protection of Mademoiselle de Saint-Geneix." [*Aside.*] Well, well! He's leaving me? Doesn't he like the forest of Fontainebleau any more?

MARQUISE [*with feeling*]: Caroline dear, I would strongly advise you not to give him your protection. One of the Duke's servants? . . . No, thank you!

DUKE [*laughing*]: But mother . . .

MARQUISE: No, I tell you; I don't need any Figaro in my household.[13]

DUKE: Mother, you're miles off! Pierre is leaving me because I'm scandalizing him. He's a strict Protestant, a veritable Puritan, an antique philosopher! I'm not even sure that he isn't a bronze statue.

MARQUISE: Still, he's been an accomplice in your escapades?

DUKE: Yes—but only the way a good dog is a thief's accomplice, out of instinctive devotion to duty.

MARQUISE [*to Caroline*]: What does he look like?

CAROLINE: I haven't seen him; I know he's out there.

MARQUISE: Well then, see him, darling, and if he does inspire you with confidence, take him on; I shall leave the matter to you. [*The Duke goes up to Caroline and gives her back the letter.—To the Duke.*] I'm taking you with me.

DUKE: You think Mademoiselle de Saint-Geneix shouldn't be alone with me for a single moment?

MARQUISE: What an idiot you are! I simply want to reconcile you with the Baroness; she has some good news for us.

DUKE [*offering her his arm*]: Real news, or news of her own invention?

MARQUISE: You'll see.

DUKE [*on his way out*]: Mademoiselle de Saint-Geneix, I do recommend Pierre to you; he's a real treasure. [*He leaves with his mother to the left.*]

Scene 5

[*Benoît, Caroline.*]

BENOÎT [*entering upstage*]: You're alone, Mademoiselle? Pierre is here.

CAROLINE: Very good; show him in.

BENOÎT [*leaving*]: Come in, Monsieur Pierre.

PIERRE [*entering, half-aloud*]: Much obliged, Monsieur Benoît.

Scene 6

[*Pierre, Caroline.*]

CAROLINE: Monsieur Pierre, I've been asked to find out... Good heavens—Peyraque! [*She runs up to him.*]

PIERRE: Yes, miss.

CAROLINE: Why didn't you sign yourself...?

PIERRE: The Duke didn't like my name. I'm known as Pierre nowadays.

CAROLINE: Oh, Peyraque, you good old thing! I'm so glad to see you again! How's my nurse?

PIERRE: She's in the country, my wife is; she's doing fine.

CAROLINE: And your daughter?

PIERRE: In the country too; she's married now—not a bad match, either.

CAROLINE: You're a long way from them, here in Paris; and you're still a servant, when I thought...

PIERRE: Monsieur de Saint-Geneix was helping me. He gave me some business advice; he thought it was good advice.... His and mine, they both went up in smoke together.

CAROLINE: Oh, my poor friends! And you didn't tell me about it!

PIERRE: You had enough troubles as it was. I said to my wife, "I'll keep on being servant another ten years, that's all." I go and see her every year. In three years, I'll have finished my work, and I'll go back home for good then.

CAROLINE: And you had the bright idea of coming here?

PIERRE: Yes, soon as I found out you were here.

CAROLINE: The Duke has told his mother no end of good things about you; and I know you better still—why, I was born in your wife's arms, I saw how devoted both of you were to my father, how good and decent.... Oh, don't worry about a thing, Peyraque, I'll answer for you; you're going to be very happy here.

PIERRE [*simply*]: Thank you, miss.

Scene 7

[*The Duke, Pierre, Caroline.*]

DUKE [*entering from left, busy*]: Excuse me, Mademoiselle—[*Pierre leaves*]—Monsieur de Dunières isn't here?

CAROLINE: No, Monsieur.

DUKE: Where the deuce has he got to? I saw his carriage arriving.

CAROLINE: Here he is, Monsieur. [*Dunières enters upstage.—Caroline goes out at right.*]

Scene 8

[*The Duke, Dunières.*]

DUNIÈRES [*seeing Caroline depart*]: Am I scaring anyone away?... She's very charming, isn't she? [*Seriously.*] Is there ...?

DUKE: I jolly well wish there were, Dunières my friend; but, you know how it is, mother never surrounds herself with anyone that isn't either frightfully ugly or frightfully virtuous. Anyway, come on; mother dear is desperately impatient to see you....

DUNIÈRES: She's more settled now.

DUKE: Your ward has come to see her?

DUNIÈRES [*indicating the anteroom*]: Yes; I've just shown her in there.

DUKE: Why the mystery?... Don't you want me to set eyes on her?

DUNIÈRES: It isn't that; it's just that she's a timid lass, and ... Oh, so you know ...?

DUKE: I've just this minute been let in on the secret of the grand scheme; I'm delighted with it.

DUNIÈRES: Now I want you to take me to your brother.... Admittedly, he might not want to put in an appearance; do you think he suspects...?

DUKE: I think he has guessed and is on his guard; still, if your ward is pretty... Is she pretty?

DUNIÈRES: Not bad.

DUKE: "Not bad"? Come now, you must remember I knew her in the Midi when she was little. She was an absolute angel....

DUNIÈRES: She's changed a lot.

DUKE: Really?

DUNIÈRES: Yes, she's grown up.

DUKE: Oh, is that all? You had me worried, but if that's all it is! [*Seriously.*] All the same, I see another problem: I believe she's very rich?

DUNIÈRES: You think that's a disadvantage?

DUKE: It's just that... I must tell you a secret—a secret my mother hasn't the slightest idea about.... Look, is Mademoiselle Diane very very rich?

DUNIÈRES: Yes indeed, more so than your brother, and he has...

DUKE: Oh no! My brother hasn't anything any more.

DUNIÈRES: What about his fortune?

DUKE: I gobbled it up.

DUNIÈRES: His too?

DUKE: Unintentionally. He paid my debts without telling me.

DUNIÈRES: Splendid thing to do! Well, it was his duty.

DUKE: Oh, you mustn't say that, Dunières; it isn't true.

DUNIÈRES: Why did he do it then?

DUKE: Because he's fond of me.

DUNIÈRES: That's better still.

DUKE: Yes, it's better still, but it's crazy. He's letting an excellent marriage—maybe even a happy marriage—just slip through his fingers. He'll miss out on any chance of marriage if he doesn't watch out.

DUNIÈRES: Hold on, let's not jump to conclusions. Has he really lost every last thing?

DUKE: The way I carried on, I should think he ought to have.

DUNIÈRES: All right, give me a hug; you've just been the making of the marriage!

DUKE: I'll give you a hug a little later, thanks—when I see what you're driving at.

DUNIÈRES: You need to realize, Mademoiselle de Saintrailles is . . . how can I put it? . . . a chivalrous soul, a heroine . . . a legendary heroine, that's the word! She couldn't dream of anything better than marrying a man who had lost all his money . . . lost it by some noble sacrifice. This is just the thing for her!

DUKE: Well, in that case, it isn't you I should be hugging, it's Mademoiselle de Saintrailles.

DUNIÈRES: Oh! . . .

DUKE [*crossing right*]: Let me talk nonsense for a moment. You've made me feel so much better! . . . So then, by ruining my brother, I've enriched him?

DUNIÈRES: Probably! But I shouldn't try to do it again, if I were you.

DUKE: Oh, nowadays, unless I were to be really dishonest . . .

DUNIÈRES: Good; no cause for alarm, then. Now hurry up and bring Urbain here under some pretext or other.

DUKE: No pretext is needed! Once I tell him about the young lady's character, he'll certainly want to set eyes on her.

DUNIÈRES: Off you go then.

DUKE: Haste I shall make! You've no idea how happy I am, though! [*Stopping short.*] You know, Dunières, people always say it's a life of virtue that brings happiness.

DUNIÈRES: Well, you're the living proof of it. But run along now; here come the ladies. [*The Duke leaves upstage.—The Marquise and Diane enter left.*]

Scene 9

[*The Marquise, Diane, Dunières; later, Léonie and Caroline.*]

DUNIÈRES: The Baroness has left?

MARQUISE: No, she's gone to look for Mademoiselle de Saint-Geneix, whom I want to introduce to your ward.

DUNIÈRES [*to Diane*]: Well now, have you got to know one another?

DIANE: Oh yes—right away.

DUNIÈRES: You were so nervous about meeting Madame de Villemer. You can see now that she's perfectly nice!

DIANE: Oh, I believe you; I haven't known Madame for fifteen minutes, and already I'm as fond of her as I could possibly be!

MARQUISE: Really?

DIANE: Really! Since I've been with you, one thing keeps bothering me.

MARQUISE: What's that?

DIANE: When my guardian introduced me to you, you didn't kiss me; and they told me you would.

MARQUISE: Darling child! [*She kisses her.*] I didn't dare, that's all. A kiss is an act of charity when someone of your age grants it to someone of mine. [*They go and sit at right.*]

DIANE: It's a great honor for me, Madame, and a pleasure too. My godmother has taught me to be fond of you. [*Léonie and Caroline enter right.*]

MARQUISE [*to Dunières, who is behind her armchair*]: She's utterly delightful!

DUNIÈRES: Isn't she? A born angel.

MARQUISE: Ah, here's Mademoiselle de Saint-Geneix now.

DIANE [*rising and holding out both hands to Caroline*]: Hello, Mademoiselle de Saint-Geneix. I don't know if I'm a good judge or not, but you look as though one could be friends with you from the very first moment.

CAROLINE [*having come downstage left*]: Well, I do think I'm something of a judge, Mademoiselle de Saintrailles, and I'd say that's how you look yourself.

DIANE: Really? Thank you—that's very kind! Madame d'Arglade was quite right; she said we'd get on well together. She told me all about you. I do want us to be friends.

CAROLINE [*frankly*]: Oh, that's what I want too!

DIANE: I'm not just being polite when I say that. I like really unselfish people; I want to be one myself... magnificently unselfish! But, well, I haven't yet found the opportunity.

CAROLINE: You'll find it; it's what you deserve.

LÉONIE [*sitting at extreme left*]: And you'll seize it with both hands—you're so big hearted!

MARQUISE [*sotto voce to Dunières*]: Well, isn't my son coming down? [*The Duke and Urbain enter upstage.—Diane goes and sits next to the Marquise.*]

DUNIÈRES: Oh yes he is—here he is now.

Scene Ten

[*As above; the Duke, Urbain.*]

MARQUISE [*to Diane*]: Here are my sons; allow me to introduce them to you.

DIANE [*in a low voice to the Marquise, after curtseying a little awkwardly*]: Oh, do please present the gentlemen to me, Madame— you can see I haven't learnt to curtsey yet, and I've no idea how to talk to men. They don't teach us that at convent.

MARQUISE: But there's no reason for you to be afraid of these men! My sons are your born friends.

DUNIÈRES: Yes, of course they are, certainly!

DIANE: Very well then. Especially as I've met one of them already, or so I'm told; though I don't remember, and I couldn't say which one.

DUKE: Then, Mademoiselle, you'll have to try and guess.

DIANE [*rising*]: Just a minute—don't give me any clues! The one I've met is the Duke; and the Duke [*indicating Urbain*] is this gentleman.

URBAIN [*smiling*]: Well done!

DIANE [*to the Duke*]: You, now you're the Marquis de Villemer.

DUKE: Perfect!

LÉONIE: Why do you think that?

DIANE: Because . . . I don't know exactly. . . . Am I wrong? [*Reaction from the others.*]

URBAIN: May I ask everyone a favor? Nobody say anything to Mademoiselle de Saintrailles. One of us two had the honor, I believe, of presenting her with her first doll. He deserves to be thanked for that; but since we're too brotherly to fight over it, we'll leave it to her to decide between us.

DUNIÈRES [*to Diane, who has placed herself between the two brothers*]: Look closely, now!

DIANE: Well—no, I'm not sure any more. I thought Monsieur de Villemer would look more like this gentleman [*indicating the Duke*]; but on the other hand, this gentleman [*indicating Urbain*] does look a bit serious to be giving dolls.

URBAIN: That wouldn't be any obstacle.

DIANE [*to Urbain*]: No? Well, in that case, Monsieur Duke, I thank you for my doll. [*Caroline goes upstage, and then comes downstage to stand at the extreme right.*] I may have forgotten the giver, but the gift itself is still preserved here. [*She touches her forehead.*] It had a lovely pink dress and all frizzy blonde hair. [*She goes back to sit by the Marquise.*]

LÉONIE: However ...

DUKE [*sotto voce*]: Quiet! Don't you see?—the more reassuring one is the giver of the doll. Leave the gift to my brother, for today.

CAROLINE [*to Diane*]: You *will* come to the country.

DIANE: And we'll see a lot of each other. Don't you love the country!

DUKE: What—only the country?

DIANE: Oh, I do like Paris too ... and I'd really like to travel, as well. I like anything that isn't the convent!

URBAIN: Why do young ladies hate convents?

DUKE: Because they're locked up there.

DIANE: Yes, that's right. Certainly we have more freedom there than we do with our families, we mess around more and make a lot more noise; but you must admit, when you can feel a great big wall between you and ... the unknown, it isn't natural.

LÉONIE: Now I, on the other hand, look back on that time of my life as a glorious dream!

DUKE [*sotto voce to Léonie*]: Possibly because it is already somewhat remote. [*Aloud.*] At Mademoiselle de Saintrailles' age, to pine for one's prison would be an absurdity.

DIANE: Oh that's right, isn't it!

DUKE: Undoubtedly. Your present age is the April of life. Everything is grace and perfume, smiles and promises. You see a whole world of flowers around you, and ahead of you lies summer—in other words, a world of yet richer and yet more fragrant flowers. Winter is so far away—you don't think about it much, you hardly even believe in it! You have every right to deny it and put your faith in the eternal youth of the things you can grasp, when you're youth and sunshine yourself!

DUNIÈRES: That's very neatly put; but your brother ...

DUKE: My brother would put it better. I am a mere amateur in matters of poetry; he is a real artist. He knows, where I can only feel; I am a mere instinct, he is a source of light!

LÉONIE: That's right; the M ...

DUKE: He was telling me the other day about the appearance ... the composition ... [*To Urbain.*] What was it? It was so lucid, so exquisitely put. ...

URBAIN [*slightly irritated*]: Oh, it was nothing at all. [*He goes upstage to the piano.*]

DUKE: Yes it was! it was all about . . . stars—yes; he showed me how every constellation has its own expression, its own emotion, its own particular contour—bold or threatening or kindly; how . . . Yes!

DIANE: I'm afraid that's a bit too deep for me; I'd prefer to admire all the stars indiscriminately, like a golden rain falling down above my head.

MARQUISE: She's delightful! [*To Diane.*] Well now, tell us about your plans. I'm not very fond of the country myself; how do you propose to pass the time there?

DIANE: Oh! I have plenty of things to do!

DUKE [*going to an armchair near Diane and sitting in it*]: Really?

DIANE: Yes—but you'll have to guess what they are. It's my turn to puzzle you now.

DUKE: Do we have to unravel enigmas? That's very hard; it wouldn't go amiss if we put both our heads together. [*He locates Urbain and gets him to sit where he was before.*] Let's try!

URBAIN [*seated*]: You want me to help you?

DUKE: No, I'll help you; go ahead.

URBAIN: Goodness . . . Mademoiselle is just out of convent; for a start, she'll stay up very late and get up likewise.

DIANE: Well, that's not bad. . . . But what am I going to do in the evenings?

URBAIN: You'll fall asleep in the drawing room, probably.

DIANE: No, not at all.

DUKE: Well, what, then?

DIANE: I'm not going to tell you; you'll have to find out.

DUKE [*to Urbain*]: Speak up! I'm all at sea, myself!

URBAIN: Well then, Mademoiselle will go and contemplate the stars . . . all the stars indiscriminately.

DIANE: Oh, that's naughty! That's the kind of thing my guardian would say!

DUNIÈRES: Pardon? . . .

DIANE: Oh, nothing. So that's my evenings occupied, then! Now, what about the daytime?

URBAIN [*teasingly*]: That's easier. You'll have breakfast, for a start.

DIANE [*nettled*]: What do I usually have?

URBAIN: A cutlet.

DIANE: Excuse me, but I have two. After that? . . .

URBAIN: After that? . . . Since it's important to keep changing one's clothes all the time, you'll put on a riding habit and go out to dazzle the multitudes.

DIANE [*nettled*]: On a donkey, I suppose?

URBAIN: No—on the wildest horse imaginable.

DIANE: No.

DUKE: On a mule that's plumed and shod with silver. Now that's a very pretty thing.

DIANE [*laughing and remembering*]: No—better than that!

DUKE [*starting to remember*]: That's true, there is something better than that.

DIANE: What is it? Go on, tell us!

DUKE: There's the proudest, most elegant, most capricious animal in the whole of creation—heraldic creation, that is! There's . . .

DIANE: Go on!

DUKE: The white unicorn!

DIANE [*rising impulsively*]: You are the Duke d'Aléria!

DUKE: Why?

DIANE: You came to our old Saintrailles château once. There were huge white unicorns . . . in a tapestry. And I wanted to have a live unicorn. People told me they didn't exist, but you—you promised to find me one: well, I'm still waiting for it!

DUKE: I'll go and find one for you.

DIANE: Where?

DUKE: Just a stone's throw away!

DIANE: Hurry up!

DUKE: I'll be back on it. [*He goes to Urbain.*] I'm escaping to your room; I don't want to be made friends with instead of you.

URBAIN: Oh, I can't manage small talk. I don't have any wit; I'll be off too.

DUKE: No, don't; mother will be dreadfully upset! Stay here, display yourself, entertain, conquer, marry! On with it, now! She's a delight—and you do like children. [*He slips off through the door upstage.*]

DIANE [*to Caroline, looking at Urbain*]: So that's really the Marquis? . . . Is he nice?

CAROLINE: Much nicer than his brother.

DIANE [*sadly*]: You think so? [*Léonie goes and sits next to the Marquise.*]

MARQUISE [*to Dunières*]: Dunières dear, do please make something of my son.

DUNIÈRES [*going to Urbain and bringing him back to the group*]: Well now, Urbain, are you happy with your new agricultural machinery?

URBAIN [*teasingly*]: Very happy indeed! It's work made perfect.

DUNIÈRES: Emancipation of the laborer.

URBAIN: Reduction in cost prices.

DUNIÈRES: Increase in net gain.

URBAIN: In short, prosperity!

DUNIÈRES: That's true! Thirty years ago, we didn't know what progress was!

DIANE [*sotto voce to the Marquise*]: Listen to this, Madame. Monsieur de Dunières has just got onto his favorite topic; he's going to talk about his fertilizers.

MARQUISE: Dunières!

DUNIÈRES: I'll be right with you, Madame! [*To Urbain.*] Personally, I've found that vegetable fertilizers have given me some quite exceptional results.

DIANE [*to the Marquise*]: I told you so!

DUNIÈRES: At the present time, they're putting in my September crop of horse beans. I think they may do even better than my white lupins of two years ago, which I sowed at the rate of two hectoliters per hectare and . . . [*Diane rises and goes up to Léonie.*]

MARQUISE: Dunières!

DUNIÈRES: I'll be right with you. [*To Urbain.*] Try it!

URBAIN [*sotto voce*]: No; I'm selling my lands.

DUNIÈRES: I know why; but . . .

URBAIN: Not a word to my mother, though. . . . She'll find it out all too soon as it is.

DUNIÈRES: Fine lad!

MARQUISE [*impatiently*]: Dunières! I criticize the country to you, and you're off into your horse beans and lupins! Let's talk about art instead, or architecture.

LÉONIE: Oh, the Marquis knows everything.

URBAIN [*coldly*]: Are you sure, Madame?

DIANE [*to Léonie*]: He sounds as though he's cross with you.

LÉONIE: No, not at all. Go and talk with him!

DIANE [*approaching Urbain a little*]: Me? I shouldn't dare—he makes me feel so self-conscious. [*Léonie encourages her; Diane moves further forward; Urbain crosses in front of Dunières and goes to the extreme left; the Marquise signals to Dunières, who signals back that Urbain is absorbed in a brochure.—Everyone falls silent.*] Ssh! Listen! . . . It's an angel passing, as they say at the convent. [*Despairing gesture from the Marquise.*]

DUNIÈRES: Marquise, we'll be leaving you now.

MARQUISE: Already?

DUNIÈRES: Yes; Madame de Dunières . . .

DIANE: What about my unicorn?

DUNIÈRES: Some other day!

DIANE [*disappointed*]: Oh! . . . It's fun! [*Léonie rejoins Caroline upstage right.*]

DUNIÈRES: We'll look for one at Séval.

DIANE [*to the Marquise*]: Do you wish me to come and visit you over there?

MARQUISE: As a matter of fact, if you don't come to us, I'll have to go and get you.

LÉONIE [*returning to Diane*]: Come and put your hat on. . . .

DIANE [*to the Marquise*]: Madame . . . [*She goes out to the left with Léonie.*]

MARQUISE: We'll follow you. [*To Dunières.*] Ah, well, Dunières, there's a missed opportunity! It's the first time I can ever remember the conversation falling flat in my drawing room!

DUNIÈRES: It's your own fault, Marquise! I was getting on very nicely, and you cut me short! . . . Anyhow, first meetings are always like that . . . Good-bye, Urbain! [*He goes out to the left with the Marquise.*]

URBAIN [*to Caroline, who is about to follow the Marquise*]: Mademoiselle de Saint-Geneix, may I talk with you for a moment?

CAROLINE: I am at your service, Monsieur.

Scene 11

[*Urbain, Caroline.*]

URBAIN: Mademoiselle de Saint-Geneix, I have a great favor to ask of you. You can prepare my mother today for some bad news that I shall have to tell her at the first opportunity; circumstances compel me. The marriage they're trying to set up for me is out of the question.

CAROLINE: I understand, Monsieur. . . . Your brother didn't hide his gratitude so well that I remained ignorant of your sacrifice. That's one more reason why you deserve to be respected; if

Mademoiselle de Saintrailles has a heart, and I am convinced she has, your brotherly devotion will be a real attraction in her eyes.

URBAIN: Mademoiselle de Saintrailles is a child.

CAROLINE: Children have an instinct for truth. You can trust Mademoiselle Diane's seventeen years.

URBAIN: I don't know Mademoiselle Diane, and I detest being married off by Madame d'Arglade.

CAROLINE: Letting that pass, I must say I don't see any need to inflict two sorrows on your mother at a single time—the announcement of your ruin and the announcement of your aversion to marriage.

URBAIN: My aversion . . . has existed for a long time, I must admit. But I've always kept it from my mother.

CAROLINE: You've done the right thing; you've felt that you didn't have any right to destroy all the family's hopes.

URBAIN [*with spirit*]: Yet have I made any fixed decision? Even if I refused to marry someone who doesn't know me and can't love me, would I have no right to form wiser and dearer attachments? Don't judge me as other people do; don't take me for an eccentric. I'm shy and dissatisfied with myself, that's all. I know that my serious tastes are a disadvantage in the world's eyes—because the world doesn't want us to prefer anything else to it—and therefore I don't hope or wish to interest a woman of the world. That would only be vain and futile. I've always been far from happy, Mademoiselle de Saint-Geneix! It's my own fault, most definitely; I don't have any complaint about other people, or life in general . . . but I suffer from my isolation, and I can't escape it by my own efforts. I must find some generous and noble soul who will tolerate me as I am; who will have the kind of affection for me that changes lives, and who will inspire the same feeling in me. That isn't what I'm being offered. My mother has ambitions arising from her class and her own personal ideas . . . I'd rather not say her personal prejudices. I've been able to dispose of my money for her and my brother; that wasn't difficult! But this [*tapping his heart*]—this deep feeling, which is my own personal property and isn't accountable to anyone but God—this solid reliable love and trust and faith and life-breath . . . Nobody can ask me for that, and I don't believe it can be dragged out of me except by death itself!

CAROLINE: Monsieur, you're virtually compelling me to give you some advice. . . .

URBAIN: Yes, I'm asking for it, I'm calling for it . . . or rather, I'm setting you up as judge of my destiny.

CAROLINE: Well then, I can only look for that judgment—that advice—in my own experience. Remember, I saw my father die of despair because he lost the fortune he meant me to have. I'm sure you see that the Marquise de Villemer would be in a similar position if she realized that your money had been irreparably lost. I couldn't do anything about my father's unhappiness—right up to the last moment, he hid the cause of it from me—but, if I'd had the opportunity of curing it by sacrificing my future, my instincts, my tastes, my ideas, my affections . . . I know perfectly well that I wouldn't have hesitated for an instant. Don't wait till your mother becomes troubled and loses her strength; be careful! Whatever you may decide today or some other day, always remember this: when the parents we love are gone, everything we might possibly have done to make their lives happier or longer becomes cruelly obvious! The tiniest failings become major crimes then. When your mother is no longer alive, the very thought of having inflicted such a great sorrow on her will never allow you a moment's peace.

URBAIN: You're right, Mademoiselle de Saint-Geneix—with the terrible rightness of someone who never has loved and never will love! [*He collapses onto the armchair at left.*]

CAROLINE [*approaching him*]: There is nothing here that I love more than your mother, Marquis. You're asking me to give her her deathstroke. . . . Well, I don't have the courage, not unless you can tell me to leave her with some hope at the same time. . . . Do please think about it. [*She curtseys and goes out to the right.*]

Scene 12

[*Urbain, the Duke.*]

DUKE [*entering upstage*]: Well now, what are you dreaming about? I've been lying in wait in your room till Dunières left, in the hope of seeing you out on the steps offering your arm to your charming fiancée—and you're in here? Is that how you treat a matter of such importance that is going so smoothly?

URBAIN: You think it's going smoothly?

DUKE: Of course! A fine-spirited girl who would like you to have lost your money!

URBAIN: Mademoiselle de Saintrailles is very good! But when her whim has been satisfied . . . ?

DUKE: The whim will turn into love and become a virtue.

URBAIN [*bitterly*]: In that case, everything is for the best, and all I need do is prepare for the great event! So then . . . listen.

DUKE: I'm listening.

URBAIN: I told you I'd be asking you to do me a good turn.

DUKE: Right you are . . . out with it!

URBAIN: As a result of the unfortunate association I told you about, I'm left with . . . a son!

DUKE: Well, I did suspect it—all those mysterious trips. . . . You're fond of him?

URBAIN: Oh yes! Without him. . . .

DUKE: You've acknowledged him?

URBAIN: Out of the question! The husband gone a long time, the mother under suspicion . . . proud enough of her reputation to die for it . . .

DUKE: What do you mean?

URBAIN: Yes—she tried to keep the birth hidden—she reappeared in public too soon. . . . I did tell you that I'd killed her!

DUKE: Don't be so upset. . . . Your son, now . . . you rescued him . . . brought him up?

URBAIN: Yes.

DUKE: Another of my financial victims!

URBAIN [*with feeling*]: Oh, in my opinion, that's all the better for him!

DUKE: Still, it's no reason for him to do without a father. There's a way of arranging that—I've got it!

URBAIN: What?

DUKE: The husband doesn't know me.

URBAIN: No.

DUKE: He wouldn't suspect me.

URBAIN: So?

DUKE: So, I acknowledge your son as mine. There's nothing surprising in the notion that I'd have a son left from my past life; the

surprising thing, really, would be that there was only one. I take
him with me, I bring him up, you become his uncle in the
world's eyes, and if he doesn't have any mother any more, he's
got two fathers—it's a kind of compensation. I've always wanted
to have a child. One that you passed on to me would probably
be better quality than one that I'd perpetrated myself.

URBAIN: Dear Gaétan, you're dreaming. Doesn't your name belong
to you?

DUKE: Yes, it does. Up till now, my name has only helped me to do
stupid things; it's about time it helped me to do a good deed for
once. I've smashed my life, let me at least make use of the pieces.
This child is an impediment to your marriage? I suppress the
impediment. My mother grumbles at first, we show her the child,
she finds him to be delightful (as he must be), she forgives, you
marry, legitimate offspring ensue, everything's sorted out.

URBAIN: Thank you, Gaétan!

DUKE: You agree?

URBAIN: No, I don't—I can't. A name, you see, is an enslavement;
I want my son to be free. He's being brought up in the mountains by peasants—he's starting to gain some physical
strength. . . . Later, I'll give him some moral strength! Can people
have that, in this ridiculous world where you and I are living—
and if they have it, can they use it? No; we belong to a caste—
to a rock that's forever crushing down on our chest. Aristocratic duties, social conventions—with such words people as-
sault our feelings and pervert our ideas! I want my son to be
free of all those frustrating and childish ties. I want his work to
be a lever in his hand, not a ball and chain bruising his ankle.
I want him to feel that he's shaping his own future and controlling his own life. And if and when he develops a serious attachment, I want him to be able to marry a peasant girl—a servant
girl, if he wants—without anyone coming and saying to him,
"Stop it! The blood of the Villemers is flowing in your veins—
you have to unite two escutcheons, and not two souls!"—and
without the beloved woman turning a deaf ear to his cries and
insisting that her honor and virtue must drive him away! . . .
No, let me finish! Even if I need to marry an heiress, I could
still die before it happens. We ought to make some provision
for my son. Here are my arrangements for his present and his
future. Here's his name—his address—the title that will enable

you to lay claim to him, if ... Put those papers in a safe place, and I'll be quite at ease.

DUKE: No, you'll still be very mixed up; but you can rely on me. [*He puts the papers away.*] This is something sacred.

URBAIN: Thank you!

DUKE: Come along and see my mother; she's recriminating herself too, I dare say! [*He goes upstage.*]

URBAIN: I'll follow you.

DUKE [*returning*]: Wait a moment, tell me then, is there some other affection ... ?

URBAIN: Me? Out of the question! The question is whether to wait for the slavery of matrimonial charity—or to depart first into eternal freedom!

DUKE: You're hoping to die, then? Why?

URBAIN: Oh, Gaétan, I can feel it—once passion dies, life dies too. . . .

DUKE: Oh, yes, passion, yes indeed—by heaven, that's one thing that never dies! Come now, I'm older than you, I've had some experience of the matter, you can believe what I'm saying. Mark my words: if you're feeling so discouraged, you must surely be just about due to revive, and soon you'll be saying as I do, "*L'amour* is dead—long live *l'amour!*"[14]

Act 3

The Château de Séval.—A large room in the style of Louis XV. Large door upstage, leading to an anteroom opening onto a garden. Door upstage left, opening into a gallery. Door upstage right, leading to the Marquis's apartment. Large side windows downstage left and right. Library on the walls. Settee at right. Large writing desk at left. Chairs, armchairs. A chess set on a console at left, near the window. Console at right, opposite; on it, a plate, glass of water, carafe, small decanter.

Scene 1

[*Caroline, the Duke.*

Caroline is examining some of the books on the shelves and making notes in a small notebook; then she writes in a register on the writing desk at left.—The Duke enters upstage, holding a newspaper; he is smoking. He drops onto the settee at right.]

DUKE: Oof! [*Seeing Caroline.*] Oh, excuse me, Mademoiselle de Saint-Geneix, I just came here for a smoke. . . . I didn't see you.

CAROLINE [*who has just sat down near the writing desk*]: Smoke away, Monsieur.

DUKE: No, the cigar's no good. [*He throws it out the window at right, returns, and leans on the back of Caroline's chair.*] Am I putting you out?

CAROLINE [*rising and going upstage right*]: Not at all, Duke.

DUKE [*following her*]: You're still calling me Duke? . . . In the country!

CAROLINE: What should I be calling you?

DUKE: Oh, well, I don't know. . . . Monsieur—er . . .

CAROLINE [*returning to the desk*]: Stop groping for what doesn't exist; you're the Duke at Séval just as much as in Paris. [*She goes upstage left.*]

DUKE: That's absolutely right! [*He goes up to her.*] It's very nice, the country, isn't it?

CAROLINE: It's wonderful. Aren't you taking advantage of this lovely evening? [*She goes to sit at the desk, and finds the Duke sitting there.*]

DUKE: No, it's too hot, and the sun hurts one's eyes. It's all very well for you women—you have sunshades, and we have to carry them around for you . . . in the shade. Now, since I don't care to act as pageboy to Madame d'Arglade, I've come in. . . . [*She is consulting the register; he takes it out of her hands, draws it close to him, and puts his elbows on it.*] Didn't she concoct enough stories for us at dinnertime!

CAROLINE: Concoct? . . . No, Léonie has one virtue to which your mother does full justice: she never tells lies.

DUKE: That's true. [*Caroline goes upstage right.*] It's just that, when she's thoroughly defended someone's innocence, she leaves room for only one opinion about them.

CAROLINE: That being . . . ?

DUKE: That they ought to be hanged.

CAROLINE: Oh, well, her judgment may be faulty, but her heart is sincere!

DUKE [*rising*]: Sincere, sincere! . . . If it comes to that, the heart of any self-respecting crocodile is sincere! [*Seeing that Caroline isn't listening to him, he sits on the settee.*] Mademoiselle de Saint-Geneix!

CAROLINE: Yes, Duke?

DUKE: How preoccupied you are! Do you work like this after dinner? Don't you ever rest? Your stamina is . . . nerve-shattering!

CAROLINE [*cheerfully, going up to the Duke*]: You want to have a nap here, Monsieur, and my noise is disturbing you, I suppose? Never mind; it's the last day; tomorrow the inventory will be finished, and you won't be pestered any more by my presence at siesta time.

DUKE [*rising quickly*]: Ah, that means, "You're spread out on the sofa, while I have to stand."

CAROLINE [*sitting at left*]: I wasn't thinking that at all!

Scene 2

[*Caroline, the Duke, Urbain.*]

URBAIN [*entering at right, and acting surprised*]: Hello, you're here, are you?

DUKE: Yes, I'm fleeing from a certain person of whom no evil may be spoken in the presence of Mademoiselle de Saint-Geneix.

URBAIN [*dryly, going past Caroline*]: Oh, Mademoiselle doesn't want ...

CAROLINE [*smiling*]: Mademoiselle wants to make use of the only right she claims in this place: the right to be silent.

DUKE [*to Urbain*]: That's aimed at you, that is! We mustn't be jealous. [*Urbain goes upstage right and takes a book.*] Don't you think Mademoiselle de Saint-Geneix treats us two rather harshly? I'll tell Mama about it; she wants us to live like brother and sister. [*He drops onto the settee again.*]

URBAIN [*showing Caroline a book*]: This one ought to be put on the list too, Mademoiselle de Saint-Geneix; it's a valuable work—almost unique.

CAROLINE: No, Monsieur, you couldn't do without it.

URBAIN [*coldly*]: Oh but excuse me—

DUKE [*agitated*]: Ah!

URBAIN [*going up to the Duke*]: What's wrong with you?

DUKE: Nothing's wrong with me, I'm just cross! [*He goes upstage.*]

URBAIN: You were saying something to me? ... Well, what do you expect? It's a great nuisance, having busy people around!

DUKE [*coming downstage*]: It isn't that. I'm just angry that your books are going to Paris.

URBAIN: What is that to you?

DUKE: A fine question, that is! As if I didn't know that you're selling them!

URBAIN: Not at all!

DUKE: Yes at all! It's a complete and universal liquidation! One of these days you'll sell the château itself—the only luxury you can still give your mother!

URBAIN: My mother is like you; she doesn't care for the country.

DUKE: But *you* care for it; Mademoiselle de Saint-Geneix cares for it too, and I care for it with the three of you in it. All this is my doing! It's simply horrifying to sit and watch the disaster I've caused!

URBAIN: You're mad! This is one of your black moods. Go and ride a horse; it'll amuse you.

DUKE: I don't have any horses left.

URBAIN: That's right; you lent them to Defresnes.

DUKE: I sold them.

URBAIN: Why?

DUKE: Well, good heavens, because you're selling your books.

URBAIN: All right. . . . Let's resign ourselves to the inevitable. Let's each make our own little sacrifice and smile about it. My mother is happy; Mademoiselle de Saint-Geneix has resigned herself to being her factotum; I have more than enough to do—that suits me; and you . . .

DUKE: Yes, well, I'll watch you—when I ought to be saving you the trouble! Look, give me something to do. [*Caroline goes upstage left.—Urbain sits on the settee.*] Mademoiselle de Saint-Geneix, please give me some job to do. [*He goes upstage next to her.*]

CAROLINE: Would you like to tell me whether the set of Bayle's Dictionary[15] is complete? Up there on the sixth shelf; you can count the volumes.

DUKE [*standing on a chair*]: It's pretty high up—it ought to be complete. [*He counts.*] Twenty-three volumes! [*He gets down.*] Ha! I don't take long, do I?

CAROLINE [*laughing*]: Oh, now that's too complete!

DUKE [*standing on the chair again*]: Hold on, you're right, there are only sixteen. I counted two sets as one. It's the binding's fault. [*He gets down.*] A nice start! . . . What next? . . .

URBAIN: Useless! Just have a rest.

DUKE: I'm no good for anything, am I?

CAROLINE: Oh but you are. You have the job of keeping your mother happy—keeping her spirits up; and since that's in everybody's interest, it's very good and very important.

DUKE: Keep talking. . . .

CAROLINE [*sitting at the writing desk*]: That's all.

DUKE: What a pity! You can be perfectly charming when you want to be! [*Going up to Urbain.*] Doesn't she know how to put things. . . . And very pretty, too! [*Caroline rises and goes upstage.*]

URBAIN: You're dreaming! She isn't pretty!

DUKE: You're right: she's beautiful! What a face! What charm! Such an air of intelligent candor. . . . Oh, she's a delightful creature!

URBAIN: Please, not so loud.

DUKE: Ah well, she won't hear anything, and she wouldn't take any notice anyway! There isn't an ounce of coquettishness in her; she's the only woman like that!

URBAIN: You've said that about a fair number of others!

CAROLINE [*at left*]: I've kept the Raffets[16] for Madame.

URBAIN: No, my mother prefers my brother's drawings.

CAROLINE [*ingenuously*]: Really?

DUKE: "Really!" So then, my mother doesn't know what she's talking about?

CAROLINE: That isn't what I said, Monsieur.

DUKE: Have you actually seen my drawings? [*He goes to get one from a portfolio on the table at right.*]

CAROLINE: I haven't taken the liberty of looking at them.

DUKE [*showing her one*]: Here's one!

CAROLINE: A landscape! Very nice.

DUKE: You think so?

CAROLINE: Yes; but it would look better with a little boat.

DUKE: Where?

CAROLINE: On that stream running through the trees.

DUKE: That isn't a stream, it's a path.

CAROLINE: I'm sorry; it does look like a stream.

DUKE: Ouch! [*He takes the drawing back.*] But I do have others with boats in. [*Caroline moves off to the left.*] Don't you want to . . . ? Sentence has been passed! . . . [*To Urbain.*] So, are you going to Dunières this evening? At least you've still got a horse.

URBAIN [*rising*]: He's lame.

DUKE: Yes, from lack of exercise.

URBAIN: Why don't you take him and go instead of me? [*Caroline closes the door at right.*]

DUKE: Yet again? If I always return the visits that you're supposed to make, nothing will ever be accomplished. . . . I really don't understand why you're so hesitant about marriage.

URBAIN: I thought you were hesitant about it yourself, seeing . . .
[*He moves off to the left.*]

DUKE: Me? Now that all depends. I could do absolutely anything,
even marry for love and be faithful to my wife—who knows? . . .
Mademoiselle de Saint-Geneix!

CAROLINE [*backstage right*]: Yes, Duke?

DUKE: Come and have a talk with us.

CAROLINE: Just a moment, I'm just finishing. . . . [*The Duke goes to
get her, and brings her center stage.*] Now, you were asking me? . . .

URBAIN: My brother was talking about marriage; that isn't of much
interest to you?

DUKE: Well, why not? Have you taken the pledge?

CAROLINE: There's no question of me, I trust?

DUKE: Well, no; but . . . since we're talking in general terms . . .
what is your view of marriage?

CAROLINE: Oh, I think people ought to get married.

URBAIN: Yes; Mademoiselle de Saint-Geneix has theories about that.

DUKE: So, she's expecting to get married herself?

CAROLINE: Oh now, that's different; I'm not free. [*She tries to withdraw.*]

DUKE [*stopping her*]: Wait on, why not? Have you any commitments? . . .

CAROLINE: Worse than that: I have ties. I've got four children.

DUKE [*laughing*]: What—already?

CAROLINE: And when I say four . . . really I've got five, because their
mother is my child too—even though she's older than I am.
Now, if I were to marry, I'd want to gather the whole brood
around me, and can you picture some happy mortal burdened
with the task of nourishing and cherishing all that!

DUKE: But by failing to marry, you're separated from your beloved
brood, so I don't really see what you're gaining by it.

URBAIN [*to Caroline*]: How do you propose to answer that one?

CAROLINE: You want me to keep talking about myself? It's hardly a
very interesting subject!

DUKE: Oh but it is!

CAROLINE: Well now, my dream is to get together something for my
youngest nephew; the others will be settled in a few years' time,
but the youngest—the weakest . . . Oh, if you knew what he's
like! He's a darling! He's so tender and kind and funny! [*She
is on the verge of tears.*] But men don't understand that—the way
a child can take full possession of a woman's heart and life;
they don't believe in it.

URBAIN [*touched*]: Forgive me, Mademoiselle de Saint-Geneix, but I do think I can understand.

DUKE: So, you're encouraging Mademoiselle de Saint-Geneix not to think of marriage, are you?

URBAIN [*quietly*]: We're being tactless; we've opened a wound—that's unkind! Well now, how about coming to my room?

DUKE [*likewise*]: No; she's upset. I want to have a talk with her.

URBAIN: What about?

DUKE: You'll see! . . . Mademoiselle de Saint-Geneix . . . after what you've just been saying . . .

URBAIN [*businesslike*]: Mademoiselle de Saint-Geneix, have you had an opportunity to do the accounts for the month?

CAROLINE: Not quite, Monsieur. Do you want them?

URBAIN: They'll be needed tonight.

DUKE: Why, no—tomorrow!

CAROLINE: No, they can be done right away. I'll get them together and bring them to you, Marquis. [*She goes out via the gallery at left.*]

Scene 3

[*The Duke, Urbain, on the settee.*]

DUKE: My word, you order her around like a servant.

URBAIN: I never order anyone around.

DUKE: Call it whatever you like, it was offensive to me—what you just did.

URBAIN: Why?

DUKE: Because it was the right moment; I wanted to tell her openly. . . .

URBAIN: What?

DUKE: Well, what I was telling you privately: that she's adorable!

URBAIN: Do you realize what you're saying?

DUKE: I should jolly well think so! Can't you see it for yourself? No false hair, no rice powder . . . A natural woman—how rare that is! Wit, grace . . . Ah!

URBAIN: Head over heels in love, are you?

DUKE: I suppose I am, since I'm being so awkward! . . .

URBAIN: What about your promise to our mother?

DUKE: I never promised her to be stone blind. Mademoiselle de Saint-Geneix fascinates me—enchants me—enraptures me! It isn't my fault. I can see that she's much cleverer than I am;

well, I'm delighted to submit to her superiority; what do you
expect me to do?

URBAIN: So then . . . you were going to propose marriage to her
just a moment ago?

DUKE: Yes, but I did it so clumsily—she didn't understand.

URBAIN [*rising*]: She reminded herself, I imagine, that our mother
would be opposed. . . .

DUKE: Never fear! My mother hasn't any grand and glorious hopes
for me—not now. Whether you like it or not, you're the one who
must satisfy her ambition for a splendid marriage. Oh, that's the
way it is; you'll come to accept it; it's your duty! You see, Urbain,
you've leapfrogged into position as head of the household; you've
become the firstborn son, the family's hope and future. I, on the
other hand, have to wipe out my turpitudes by disappearing
from public view. I shall get married humbly and make a good
end—the credit for which will revert to you.

URBAIN: To me?

DUKE: Yes, you ungrateful thing! But for you, I'd still be underneath my tree, dreaming of little hussies and catching rheumatism! And look at the difference now: a thatched cottage and
a human heart—because I'll have a thatched cottage just over
there at the edge of the grounds. I can live as a peasant—I have
the means. Why, I might become a farmer, I don't know; it
could be fun; it shouldn't be too difficult. In short, I'm going
to become a wise old man; and any time you need advice, I
hope you'll come and look me up.

URBAIN: That's very pleasant! So, you're sure Mademoiselle de
Saint-Geneix will accept you?

DUKE: Well, dash it, I'm going to be so lovable! What's more, I'm
counting on you to boost her confidence in me.

URBAIN: What—in the next fifteen minutes?

DUKE: She's known us for three months. The world was made in
seven days; and that was a lot more complicated.

URBAIN: And in less time than that, you'll have changed your mind
again.

DUKE: I'm not going to change my mind again.

URBAIN: Never?

DUKE: Never! . . . Never! . . . Well, one can't really answer that. The
questions you put to me! . . . But at any rate, it'll be my fixed
position for a jolly good while.

URBAIN: All right; for a start, we need to talk to our mother.

DUKE: No, not that! She has no sense of the way to go about the preliminaries—she makes everything so solemn; that's why your own courtship isn't making any progress. I want mine to go ahead under my own steam. I'll start by getting Caroline to take an interest in me; once she's in love with me, I'll let you know, and you're the one who will have the task of saying to her, "Mademoiselle de Saint-Geneix, you like the countryside, the simple life; how would you like to be a simple duchess in the countryside?" It's no more complicated than that!

URBAIN: Well, God help Mademoiselle de Saint-Geneix!

DUKE: Don't you have any confidence in me? That's ridiculous!

PIERRE [*entering upstage*]: Madame wishes the Duke and the Marquis to know that Monsieur de Dunières has just arrived. [*He waits upstage.*]

DUKE: Damn! I shan't get a chance this evening!

URBAIN: All the better. A good night's rest will restore you to your senses.

DUKE: Yes, but what if they're not the senses I want? Look, are you coming?

URBAIN: To see Dunières? Yes, I'll be right behind you.

DUKE: Hurry up, then. [*To Pierre.*] In the garden?

PIERRE: In the drawing room, Monsieur. [*The Duke leaves upstage.*]

URBAIN: Pierre, I did ask Mademoiselle de Saint-Geneix . . . [*Caroline enters via the gallery.—Pierre leaves upstage.*]

Scene 4

[*Caroline, Urbain.*]

CAROLINE: Here are the accounts, Monsieur. [*She puts them on the table and starts to leave.*]

URBAIN: Thank you, Mademoiselle. Would you mind if I asked you a question?

CAROLINE: Not at all, Monsieur.

URBAIN: You were talking a moment ago about plans. . . . You're not thinking of leaving my mother?

CAROLINE: Not in the near future . . . not unless . . .

URBAIN: Unless what?

CAROLINE: Unless she grows tired of my services ... or they're no longer deemed to be necessary.

URBAIN: Or unless something else happens ... unless someone in the vicinity makes the situation unpleasant for you.

CAROLINE [*coming downstage*]: Of course; but up till now, everyone has been good to me.

URBAIN: Except me, perhaps?

CAROLINE: I haven't noticed. ...

URBAIN: My brother is certainly much pleasanter—you trust him more. ...

CAROLINE: I trust everyone, Monsieur; I don't have any secrets.

URBAIN: Yes, but what if you had?

CAROLINE: I shan't have.

URBAIN: But supposing ... in spite of yourself ... someone told you such a secret?

CAROLINE: I'd keep it.

URBAIN: To yourself?

CAROLINE: Yes, Monsieur.

URBAIN: And ... if it happened to concern you in some way ... and made you regret that you had come here?

CAROLINE: I'd leave.

URBAIN: Without saying anything to my mother.

CAROLINE: I don't want to be a cause of trouble or distress to anyone—least of all to her.

URBAIN: What about to me?

CAROLINE: To you, Marquis?

URBAIN [*with an effort*]: Yes. Look, let's be frank. Suppose my brother, who is sincere and well-meaning, but rather impulsive and scatterbrained, came to embarrass you by a certain familiarity.

CAROLINE [*crossing right*]: That won't happen, Monsieur; the Duke is, I believe, a gentleman, and I know that he is good company, even at his liveliest.

URBAIN [*with animation*]: But ... even without failing to respect you as you deserve, he could make you apprehensive in certain ways ... certain surprising ways, where my advice and support might be of use to you. We were closer in Paris than we are here, Mademoiselle de Saint-Geneix. I took the liberty sometimes of asking your advice, and I thought I might sometimes deserve the same trust from you; but here, work, business ... and your reserve, which seems to increase—perhaps I can guess the reason. . . . [*Caroline looks astonished.*] Yes; my brother has unwittingly made you cautious, even fearful, and sad at times, unless I'm mistaken! Well now, I'm fond of him, I have some influence over him, he's an excellent man. Tell me frankly what you think of what he says and does, and I can promise you . . .

CAROLINE: Thank you, Marquis; but I can assure you that I should never wish to be the cause of even the slightest ill-feeling, or the most insignificant disagreement, between your brother and yourself. So, even if I did have any complaints about him, nobody would know.

URBAIN: Even if he gave you very serious grounds for complaint?

CAROLINE: You're imagining the impossible.

URBAIN [*carried away*]: Then let's imagine the impossible! You'd leave?

CAROLINE: Please let me believe that I must be the judge of my own actions.

URBAIN: Very well, Mademoiselle de Saint-Geneix, I hope your prudence can match your presumption! [*Aside.*] She's in love with him! [*He goes into his apartment, at right.*]

Scene 5

[*Pierre, Caroline.*]

PIERRE [*holding a large notebook, and coming in via the gallery*]: Here's the cadastral survey that Mademoiselle was looking for.

CAROLINE [*starting*]: Thank you, Pierre. Take it to the Marquis, please. [*She goes to the casement at right.*]

PIERRE: Mademoiselle isn't well?

CAROLINE: I'm fine, thank you, Pierre.

PIERRE: Is Mademoiselle sad?

CAROLINE: It'll pass.

PIERRE: It isn't the Duke?

CAROLINE: The Duke? He's an excellent man!

PIERRE: What about the other one? [*Caroline sits on the settee.*] The Marquis isn't always good to you; he talks to you harshly.

CAROLINE: Oh, he doesn't talk to me much at all.

PIERRE: Are you unhappy here?

CAROLINE: No. But sometimes I do think about the past. It's so good to be at home! You're loved, respected—whatever you say and do. Strangers aren't so tolerant; they pass judgment on you, and if they're bored or in a bad mood, they take it out on you without even realizing.—And then you yourself don't always understand them; you're afraid of taking more interest in them than they want, and if you try to be discreet, they accuse you.of ingratitude. But after all, that's what we're here for—to put up with annoyances! [*She rises.*]

PIERRE: I am, yes. But you were never brought up to do that. If it gets out of hand, I'll take you away.

CAROLINE: You, Peyraque?

PIERRE: I'd tell you, "It has to be done!"

CAROLINE: Very good; and where would you take me?

PIERRE: Home with us. My wife would find some work for you; you said you're always better off at home than with strangers.

CAROLINE: And would I be at home in your house? [*Going up to him.*] Thank you—you're very kind! But I do have to stay here.

PIERRE: Why?

CAROLINE: I know Monsieur de Villemer has been making arrangements for my nephews' schooling—not that he's said anything to me. I want to serve his mother as long as I can, in return.

PIERRE: Yes, but what if he's treating you badly?

CAROLINE: Oh ... if I should happen, for some reason, to upset anyone, I hope they'll be frank enough to tell me so.—Here, take this note. [*Pierre starts to go out to the right; he sees that Caroline has sat down in tears at the writing desk; he comes back to her.*]

PIERRE: Miss Caroline—excuse me, that's how I called you when you were little; I wasn't much good at entertaining you, but I was a comfort to you sometimes. If my wife was here, she would say to you ... Oh, I can't put things into words!

CAROLINE [*taking his hand*]: Doesn't matter—just talk to me, Peyraque; I haven't a father any more ... really I don't have anyone in the world to give me advice and look after me. . . .

PIERRE: Oh, I'm only a servant, I can't stand up for you! But when I think about your parents, how they were so proud, how people used to respect them so much ... You shouldn't let anyone make you unhappy. Nobody has the right to do that, you understand? Nobody! A man that can't marry you shouldn't even look at you, and ... the Marquis looks at you too much!

CAROLINE [*quickly, rising*]: No—you're making a mistake!

PIERRE [*severely*]: And you, you're just trying to fool yourself. . . . It won't get you anywhere.

CAROLINE [*collapsing back on the chair, in tears*]: Pierre . . . You're being so cruel to me!

PIERRE: Yes, I can see that, but it's my duty!

CAROLINE [*energetically*]: Well, I know mine; I'll do it to the bitter end. [*She rises and crosses right.*] I'm going to support this marriage that's being arranged—I'm going to work towards it as hard as I can. You needn't worry, I shan't be a disgrace to my father, and if ever you see me weakening, just scold me, please— I'd be grateful for it! There now, give me a glass of water please. [*Pierre goes to get one and brings it to her.*]

PIERRE: Yes, that's the way; now, pull yourself together.

CAROLINE: Thank you! [*She drinks a little, moistens her handkerchief and wipes her eyes with it.*] It's over—see?

PIERRE: Chin up, miss!

CAROLINE: Yes, Peyraque! [*The Duke enters via the gallery; Pierre leaves upstage.*]

Scene 6

[*The Duke, Diane, Caroline.*]

DUKE: Ssh! Here's Mademoiselle de Saintrailles!

DIANE [*entering cheerily*]: Here I am! [*She kisses Caroline.*]

CAROLINE: You were here?

DUKE: Absolutely. Now, kiss each other, and let's have a serious talk. Mademoiselle de Saint-Geneix, we need you. [*To Diane.*] Speak up!

DIANE: No, you first.

DUKE: All right, this is serious business—listen carefully. Mademoiselle Caroline, do you admit that a girl who is pretty, good, rich, from a good family—like Mademoiselle de Saintrailles here—has the right to want to marry a lad who is charming, virtuous, and nobly impoverished—like the Marquis de Villemer, in fact? Give us your answer!

CAROLINE: I admire Mademoiselle de Saintrailles, and I respect her all the more for it.

DIANE: Really? Is that the truth?

CAROLINE: As true as the fact that I'm fond of you.

DIANE [*to the Duke*]: Go on then; tell us your opinion too.

DUKE: Going on, then, my opinion is that when—out of modesty, or pride, maybe—the impoverished lad is a bit reticent, it's up to the rich girl to press forward and conquer.

CAROLINE: And what can I do to help?

DUKE: This. I've sent Urbain a message asking him to meet Monsieur de Dunières in the drawing room. On the way, he'll pass through here; you'll detain him on some pretext, and I myself, using some other pretext, will take you away, so that Mademoiselle and he will be left alone and will at last be able to have an honest-to-goodness talk with one another.

CAROLINE: All right, there's nothing to it; we'll say that . . .

DUKE: Why, what's wrong with you?

CAROLINE: Me? Nothing.

DUKE: Yes: you're pale.

DIANE: And her hands are frozen!

DUKE: Mademoiselle de Saint-Geneix isn't very strong. [*They sit Caroline down on the settee.*]

CAROLINE: Excuse me, Duke, but I'm extremely strong.

DUKE [*to Diane*]: Don't believe a word of it; she's strong only in willpower.

DIANE [*aside*]: Poor girl!

DUKE: She works too hard; she ought to go for a walk, she . . . Aha! an idea! Here's the pretext!

DIANE: Well, tell us.

DUKE [*crossing left*]: Yes, here it is. [*To Caroline.*] Can you ride a horse?

CAROLINE: Hardly.

DUKE: In that case, you need to learn. I'm going to have Jacquot saddled. [*He goes upstage.*]

DIANE: What's Jacquot?

DUKE [*coming downstage*]: He's a pedestrian pony, a garden beetle, a goat with a mane! [*He goes back upstage.*]

CAROLINE: But I haven't the slightest desire to go horse riding this evening. It's getting dark.

DUKE: No, not at all! I simply want you to have an outing that is both sensible and healthy. [*To Diane, indicating the window at right.*] Look, you were asking for Jacquot—there he is, coming back from the meadow! [*Calling out of the window.*] Hey, you chaps over there! Wait for me! [*To Diane and Caroline.*] I'm going to get him ready, this fiery beast, and coach him a little;

I'll come back and look for you, and in five minutes, the deed is done. [*He leaps out of the window.*]

Scene 7

[*Caroline, Diane.*]

DIANE: Well now!... What a shame he's so childish—he's very nice, isn't he! [*The Marquis enters right.*]

CAROLINE: Here's the Marquis.

DIANE [*to Urbain, who is heading for the gallery*]: Marquis!

Scene 8

[*Urbain, Diane, Caroline.*]

URBAIN: Oh! I'm extremely sorry... Mademoiselle de Saintrailles... I didn't know.... Monsieur de Dunières was asking for me.

DIANE: No, Monsieur, I was. Would you like to give me an audience?

URBAIN: Audience? That's a delightful word, Mademoiselle!

DIANE: No, it's really stupid. Afraid of being tactless, that's all. [*Sotto voce to Caroline.*] Please help me out, Caroline.

CAROLINE: Monsieur, Mademoiselle de Saintrailles wants to learn about... botany. She knows you have some books on the subject, and some specimens. I told her that you'd be delighted to lend them to her.

URBAIN: Do you want to take them all this evening, Mademoiselle?

DIANE: Oh no, I'm just at the ABC stage! You'd have to pick something I can cope with, if you'd be so kind.

URBAIN [*going upstage right*]: I'll do that right away.

DIANE: Oh, it isn't as urgent as all that.

Scene 9

[*As above; the Duke.*]

DUKE [*entering upstage*]: Jacquot is saddled, Mademoiselle de Saint-Geneix! Seize the day—what's left of it. Come on!

URBAIN [*to Caroline*]: You're going horse riding?

CAROLINE: Yes, Monsieur.

URBAIN: I didn't know... You haven't ever ridden, I think?

DUKE: Mademoiselle de Saint-Geneix can do anything. Anyway, I'll be there.

URBAIN: Oh! You're the teacher?

DUKE: None other.

URBAIN [*going to the casement at right*]: But I can only see one horse.

DUKE: Well, that's to be expected; yours is lame, and mine is sold!
Unless we ride one of the draft horses. [*To Caroline.*] Would you
prefer that? It suits me either way; I'm easy.

CAROLINE: But . . . I thought I was going alone, Duke.

URBAIN: Of course; why don't you stay here! You can help me to
choose books for . . .

DUKE: Later. I don't want Mademoiselle de Saint-Geneix to be
exposed to Jacquot's little quirks on her own; who knows what
he might do! [*To Caroline.*] Come on, I'll take him along by the
bridle, and you can have a grand tour of the lawn.

URBAIN [*acidly*]: I'd suggest a grand tour of the hunting ground,
rather.

DUKE: Why?

URBAIN [*restraining himself*]: It's more sheltered . . . and more enjoyable.

DUKE: Yes, of course, you're right! [*He goes out upstage with Caroline.*]

Scene 10

[*Diane, Urbain.*]

DIANE: Is botany a very difficult subject to learn?

URBAIN [*absentmindedly, looking out the casement*]: Yes, it's delightful!

DIANE [*aside*]: Well, that's a fine answer! [*Aloud.*] But could we
make notes on the specimens?

URBAIN: You'll have them readymade.

DIANE: You'd go to all that trouble?

URBAIN [*absentmindedly*]: It's an opportunity. . . .

DIANE: To do a good deed?

URBAIN: Yes, Mademoiselle.

DIANE [*sitting at left*]: Monsieur de Villemer, you're not listening to
me. [*Urbain closes the casement.*]

URBAIN: Have you something to ask?

DIANE: Yes—I'm asking you to listen to me.

URBAIN [*going up to her*]: I'm listening, Mademoiselle.

DIANE: Monsieur de Villemer, I want your advice.

URBAIN: Well now, Mademoiselle, when botany is applied to agriculture . . .

DIANE [*rising and going to sit on the settee at right*]: Yet again? . . . Monsieur de Villemer, I have the greatest respect for agriculture, but I have no passion for it at all.

URBAIN: Well then, from the point of view of . . .

DIANE: Look, I'd prefer to have your advice about something else; such as, for instance, how I should make use of my time and my opportunities, and my money and my independence and my future.

URBAIN: Oh? Nothing more than that?

DIANE: You think it's a lot?

URBAIN: Yes, indeed! It's the easiest problem to solve, though.

DIANE: All right, let's have it—in brief.

URBAIN: In brief, then: be on your guard.

DIANE: Against other people, or myself?

URBAIN: Against other people, and against yourself.

DIANE: That seems to me even more difficult than botany.

URBAIN: Much more difficult. It's so easy to be taken in.

DIANE: Why, you're suspicious—perhaps even envious! And you're supposed to be such a good person!

URBAIN: An undeserved reputation, Mademoiselle. There are some days when I feel positively evil and vindictive.

DIANE: Is this one of them?

URBAIN: Maybe.

DIANE [*rising*]: Well then, I'll come back some other day, because I only like kindness; and personally, I think it's a very good thing to make other people happy!

URBAIN: You think it's easy?

DIANE: I'm not interested in easy things.

URBAIN: You're full of boldness and bravery, then? Be careful; you'll have many troubles.

DIANE: Won't people be grateful?

URBAIN: Oh, certainly not.

DIANE: Even if I give up my freedom and money—and my life— to help them?

URBAIN: Mademoiselle de Saintrailles, don't give up all that except to a man who is passionately in love with you.

DIANE: And such a man would be grateful?

URBAIN: Not necessarily; but at least he wouldn't have been a coward when he accepted your sacrifices. [*He moves away a little to the left.*]

DIANE: Monsieur de Villemer, I do thank you for being so frank; but I am meant to live in the world, and I don't see it quite as black as you paint it. Self-sacrifice is my goal, my ideal, my dream—everyone has their own! I wanted to choose the best one—and I shall do it. I'm not afraid of the future; maybe I'm simply a force that God is intending to use! I'll turn neither to the right nor to the left; I'll do exactly what my heart tells me; I'll care for other people's needs, and I'll be happy, because I want to be good. Goodnight, Monsieur de Villemer. Thank you for your specimens; I'll expect them tomorrow.

URBAN [*going to Diane*]: And you'll have them. Forgive me for saying unpleasant things and showing you how misanthropic I am. You have to say things as they are, even if they're unpleasant.

DIANE: Very well, I shall have the task of converting you.

URBAN [*disconcerted*]: Why... how do you propose to do that?

DIANE: That's my secret; you won't be able to guess it, so don't try. Now, I have something to say to the Duke d'Aléria. Do you think he has gone very far with Mademoiselle de Saint-Geneix?

URBAN [*promptly*]: I'll go and see. [*He goes upstage.*]

DIANE: That's right, off you go! [*Aside.*] Poor fellow, he's so glad to get away from me!

Scene 11

[*As above; Dunières, the Marquise.*]

DUNIÈRES [*entering via the gallery, and seeing Urbain leaving*]: Hello, Urbain. Oh, you were in here with my ward? I was looking for her. Well, where are you going in such a hurry?

URBAN: I'm going on an errand for her. [*He goes out upstage.*]

Scene 12

[*Dunières, the Marquise, Diane.*]

MARQUISE: Where are you sending him?

DIANE [*smiling*]: To pick some flowers for me.

MARQUISE: You weren't talking about something else?

DIANE: Oh yes we were.

DUNIÈRES: Well?

DIANE: I'll tell you in a minute. [*The Duke enters upstage.*] Here's the Duke. He doesn't waste any time, does he!

Scene 13

[*As above; the Duke.*]

DUKE: So you've been waiting for me, have you?

DIANE: Didn't your brother remember to tell you?

DUKE: I haven't run into him.

DIANE: You and Mademoiselle de Saint-Geneix have come back?

DUKE: I came back so fast that I never went.

DIANE: What about her?

DUKE: She's out in the grounds with Pierre.

DIANE: Pierre?

DUKE: The husband of her nurse.

DIANE: Oh, I know. Caroline told me about that. A very devoted man.

MARQUISE: Extremely devoted.

DIANE: Wonderful! I like him very much!

DUKE: Aha, you like him, do you?

DIANE: That's how I feel.

DUNIÈRES: What's that? What's she talking about?

DIANE [*approaching the Marquise*]: Oh, well, you know—little girls, they have all kinds of silly notions in their head. [*Seriously.*] Not that this is a silly notion. [*To the Duke.*] I want to have a talk with you.

DUNIÈRES: Oh now, that's a different matter!

DIANE [*to the Duke*]: On your own—I like tête-à-têtes, they're fun.

DUNIÈRES [*going up to Diane*]: With the Duke? Oh, I should say not.

DUKE: Why, what difference does that make to you? Whether it's my brother or me, isn't it the same thing?

DUNIÈRES: It isn't the same thing at all.

DIANE [*to the Duke*]: Papa Dunières is absolutely right. I want to have a talk with you, and I don't want to be heard.

MARQUISE [*to Dunières*]: Very well, my friend, let's be off!

DUNIÈRES: No, let's stay!

DIANE: But you don't have to go away. [*To Dunières.*] You won't listen, will you?

DUNIÈRES: Oh yes I will!

MARQUISE: Nonsense. We're going to have a game of chess; that will keep you occupied. [*Sotto voce to Dunières.*] And you'll pretend to play. [*She sets up the chess set on the writing desk.*]

DUNIÈRES [*going to the writing desk*]: Since you wish, Marquise—and since Madame de Dunières will never find out about it . . . [*He sits down opposite the Marquise, at left.*]

DUKE [*to Diane*]: Well now, what is this secret?

DIANE: Did I say it was a secret?

DUKE: I thought you did.

DIANE [*taking him to the extreme right*]: All right. Well then, I do really love your brother.

DUKE: And you've got good reason to do so!

DIANE: You think so?

DUKE: Naturally!

DIANE: You sound so serious.

DUKE: Oh yes; I'm very serious, myself, when I set my mind to it.

DIANE: Do you often set your mind to it?

DUKE: Whenever it's a matter of Urbain.

DIANE: So then, you approve of my choosing your brother?

DUKE: I approve of you, and I admire you.

DIANE: But don't you admire him too?

DUKE: Oh, well, I don't take any credit for that. I couldn't do otherwise. You needed to find him out; I already knew him.

DIANE: So then, supposing I didn't rank him clear above you and any other man, I wouldn't have any sense? But listen.

DUNIÈRES: I *am* listening!

DUKE: Oho! Dunières! . . .

MARQUISE [*sotto voce to Dunières*]: Not a word! I'm listening too.

DIANE [*to the Duke*]: He said one thing that gave me something to think about: "Never marry a man unless he's passionately in love with you." Maybe that's another way of saying, "I myself am not in love with you at all."

DUKE: Or else, "I'm waiting for passion to overcome pride."

DIANE: Still, in all the romances . . .

DUKE: Oh, in all the romances, the ladies have some fairy godmother who makes people fall in love with them at first sight; whereas in the sad world where we live, a woman has to rely on her own powers of enchantment. Yours are real and first-rate— use them. When you're faced with a young and generous soul, don't waver. You're only going to make the attempt once in your life, so make it sure—my brother deserves it.

DUNIÈRES [*carried away*]: Very good!

DIANE: Oh, so you've been listening? That's not at all nice!

DUNIÈRES: Maybe, but what he was saying was very good. [*He rises and goes over to the Duke.*] Duke, you are a delightful man!

DUKE: Well, what did I tell you!

DUNIÈRES [*to Diane*]: On this note, let's be off; nobody can see anything any more, and the chess game is suffering the effects. [*Pierre comes in with a lighted lamp, and puts it on the table.*]

DIANE: Oh! Mademoiselle de Saint-Geneix has come back?

PIERRE: Yes, Mademoiselle. [*He closes the casement at right and leaves upstage.*]

DUNIÈRES: Right, let's go!

DIANE: No, just wait a minute for me to sum everything up. [*To the Duke.*] Could you go and call for the carriage yourself?

DUKE: In other words, you have no further need of me here. [*He goes upstage, then returns.*] Do I have to harness the horses myself?

DIANE: That won't be necessary—they're so clever they do their own harnessing. [*The Duke leaves upstage.*]

Scene 14

[*The Marquise, Diane, Dunières; later, the Duke and Urbain.*]

MARQUISE: Well now, my angel, let's hear the grand summing-up.

DIANE: Oh, I'll tell you tomorrow. I need to have a talk with my godmother tonight.

DUNIÈRES: Ah! You haven't made up your mind yet?

DIANE: I've made up my mind about one thing: here is the best mother in the world, and I want to be her daughter.

MARQUISE [*kissing her*]: Dearest Diane! [*Urbain enters upstage.*]

DIANE [*quietly*]: Ssh! Not a word till tomorrow!

URBAIN: You're leaving?

DUNIÈRES: Yes. Where have you come from all out of breath?

URBAIN: I went looking for my brother, at Mademoiselle's request. I followed the tracks of a pair of horses, but . . . [*He goes to the extreme right.*]

DIANE: But you didn't find him? It doesn't matter.

DUKE [*coming in via the gallery*]: Mademoiselle de Saintrailles's carriage is ready.

DIANE: Goodnight, Marquis!

DUNIÈRES [*to the Marquise*]: Don't see us out.

MARQUISE: Oh but I will. Coming, Gaétan?

URBAIN: Excuse me, mother, I have to say a word or two to my brother. . . . [*Diane, the Marquise and Dunières leave via the gallery upstage left.*]

Scene 15

[*The Duke, Urbain.*]

DUKE: Before I listen to what you're going to tell me, let me congratulate you. . . .

URBAIN: All in good time; but first, tell me . . .

DUKE: Tell you? Well, well—twice in one evening! What's wrong?

URBAIN: What's wrong is that I want some clarification of your intentions as regards Mademoiselle de Saint-Geneix. If we are all to continue living in the one household, that lady should take your name; neither my mother nor my wife could possibly remain under the same roof as your . . . inamorata.

DUKE: Well, at least you didn't say "mistress"; I must thank you, on Mademoiselle de Saint-Geneix's behalf, for that piece of tact! Really, brother, you're insane!

URBAIN: Quite possibly; but I do need to have this sorted out. If I get married and you don't, I become the head of the household; you said so yourself. If you get married too, you preserve your rights as the older son, in public opinion.

DUKE: How you do jump to conclusions! I have to get married tomorrow then, just like that, before I even know whether she's interested in me or not?

URBAIN: That's a poor joke, and it doesn't deceive me at all.

DUKE: A joke? . . . I really don't follow you.

URBAIN: Forgive me, but you know exactly what I mean.

DUKE: Even though I say I don't?

URBAIN: I say you do!

DUKE: So, you're calling me a liar, are you?

URBAIN: You can take it however you like.

DUKE: Look here, we're way off beam. You're making me realize something I would never have believed: you're jealous!

URBAIN: Jealous of you?

DUKE: Yes, jealous of me. You're in love with Mademoiselle de Saint-Geneix—much more in love than I am, maybe. [*He sits on the settee.*]

URBAIN: Well, that wouldn't be saying very much! She or any other woman, what do you care, with your easy pleasures and varied pastimes! And you're so fond of me, too—so generous, so devoted . . . so much the noble prince! If I insisted, you'd yield up your rights to me; that's how little you care about them! What could you possibly care about—you've blithely thrown away your mother's money, and then, as a form of compensation, you've no less blithely tried to turn her household into an object of scandal and ridicule! A precious good-for-nothing you are! But none of this is of the slightest consequence; my anger is just a joke! . . . You're not the one who's in love—I am, and therefore . . . Oh, this libertine's generosity of yours is a dreadful thing—it muddies everyone who comes near you. . . . Your plans, your wishes, your very glances contaminate a woman, and if I had been in love with the woman we're talking about, I would certainly cease to be in love with her, the moment she had been outraged by your thoughts! [*It is now quite dark outside.*]

DUKE [*rising*]: All right, that's enough, that's more than enough—you'd try the patience of an ox! Go to the devil, Mister Pedant! That's just like you virtuous hypocrites. You're all saints and we're all sinners, isn't that right? Well, such sinners are less pernicious than you are—we throw away other people's money, yes, but we give our souls, we'd give our very lives if need be, in return for a good deed. We love, we have feelings, we're alive—and that's why we can hope to be loved, whereas people like you have to be worked out and understood and worshipped as gods! And when a woman doesn't pay enough attention to you, you start to suspect her, you start to hate her! Oh yes, you do hate Caroline—it isn't my looks and thoughts that are contaminating her, it's your talk—your talk is what is sullying her! Why? Because she yawns when she's with you and laughs when she's with me! And that's all it takes for you to talk about turning her out of your house in disgrace! . . . But I'm here in your house too! . . . Oh, I jolly well wish I could walk out of it and throw your charity back in your face! But I do have one thing left: thanks to you, I have the chance to live here and devote my life to my mother. Keep the merit of it for yourself; I don't want anything more from you. I'll be a workman, a beggar, a lackey . . . yes, a lackey, sooner than put up with the disgrace and disgust of being in your debt for one day longer! [*He goes out upstage and slams the door behind him.*]

Scene 16

URBAIN [*alone*]: Oh, how dreadful! . . . My own brother! . . . Where
am I? [*He goes upstage.*] I can't see any more. . . . My son! . . .
[*He leans on the back of the settee.*] Am I dying? . . . I can't breathe!
[*He tries to open the casement.*] I can't! . . . God, give me some air!
[*He smashes a windowpane with his fist and falls unconscious near
the settee. Rapid footsteps are heard; Caroline enters via the gallery.*]

Scene 17

[*Caroline; Urbain unconscious.*]

CAROLINE: What's wrong? . . . Who was shouting? . . . What a
noise! . . . It was here all right. [*She sees Urbain stretched out.*]
Marquis! [*She lifts him energetically and puts him on the settee; she
removes his cravat.*] My God! He's bleeding! [*She wraps his hand
in her handkerchief.*]

Scene 18

[*The Duke, Caroline, Urbain.*]

DUKE [*entering upstage*]: Come on, brother, this is quite absurd! . . .
[*Seeing Urbain.*] Urbain! . . . Urbain! . . . [*He goes to the head of the
settee.*] I was wrong, do forgive me! . . . Urbain! [*Frightened, to
Caroline.*] Is he . . . ?
CAROLINE: No, no, just fainted! . . . We need some air! Open the
windows wide! Quick! . . . Get me some water! . . . There—open
that bottle!
DUKE [*rapidly carrying out her instructions*]: What about the blood?
CAROLINE [*holding the injured hand*]: It's nothing, just a cut.
DUKE: Good God, what are we going to do?
CAROLINE: Nothing for the moment; later on, the doctor can tell
us. . . .
DUKE: The doctor? I'll run and get him! [*He goes upstage.*]
CAROLINE: Right; off you go!
DUKE: But it's a long way, and no horses. . . . I'll go on foot. . . . In
the meantime . . .

CAROLINE: I'll handle everything, I'll stay here! . . . His heart is beating better. . . . And he's breathing. . . .

DUKE: If my mother finds out . . .

CAROLINE: She mustn't!

DUKE: She's going to be asking for you!

CAROLINE: Call on her, tell her I'm tired; keep calm.

DUKE: We can rely on Pierre; I'll send him to you.

CAROLINE: Yes, you send him.

DUKE: But what about you—you'll be exhausted!

CAROLINE: Don't worry about anything.

DUKE: Oh—Urbain! My poor brother!

CAROLINE: Yes, yes, just hurry up and go! [*The Duke leaves upstage and closes the door.—Caroline unfolds the screen and places it partly around the settee. She feels Urbain's hands and lowers the window blind; she comes back to him and watches his breathing.*] He's asleep! [*She goes to the desk, turns the lamp down*[17] *and prepares for her vigil.*]

Act 4

Décor as for act 3.

Scene 1

[*Pierre, Caroline, Urbain.*

As the curtain rises, Caroline is writing by lamplight. Urbain is sleeping on the settee. The blinds of the two windows are lowered. It is dark. When the door at rear is opened, daylight is visible outside.]

PIERRE [*entering at rear, speaking and moving cautiously*]: He's still asleep?

CAROLINE: Yes, he's quite peaceful.

PIERRE: You haven't slept, and you've been in here nearly eight hours!

CAROLINE: Is it that long? I've written some letters—to my sister, to your wife; you can send them off. [*She gives them to him and rises.*]

PIERRE: Yes, Miss. Thanks for writing to my wife. [*He goes upstage.*] You ought to get some rest!

CAROLINE: No, I want to see the doctor.

PIERRE: There's nothing wrong with the Marquis except tiredness. Three nights, maybe, he's done nothing but pace around in his

room. And on top of that, he's been writing all day. . . . Less
than that would be enough to make anyone sick.

CAROLINE [*going up to the settee*]: Pierre . . . do you think . . . he's
suffering from a nervous shock?

PIERRE [*meaningfully*]: That, Miss, is something that only concerns
the members of the family.

CAROLINE: You're right; it's none of our business! You mustn't say
anything to his mother, you understand?

PIERRE: I know; she's likely to panic.

CAROLINE: Listen! . . . I think there's someone walking in the
gallery.

PIERRE [*going to the gallery door*]: Yes, I heard it already.

CAROLINE: Is it the Duke?

PIERRE: No.

CAROLINE: All the same, you ought to meet him on the way; we
must make sure nobody hears him coming back. [*Pierre leaves
upstage and meets the Duke at the door; he talks to him quietly.—
Caroline goes back and sits by the writing desk.*]

Scene 2

[*Caroline, the Duke, Urbain.*]

DUKE [*quietly*]: So, he's doing better, is he?

CAROLINE: Don't wake him; he's doing very nicely.

DUKE: Thank God for that!

CAROLINE: What about the doctor?

DUKE: No doctor. I've been running around all night for nothing.
He's off on his rounds; he won't be back till this evening.

CAROLINE: All right; I trust he'll find the patient cured.

DUKE: I do hope you're right. It isn't very serious then?

CAROLINE: If it's only fatigue, which is what Pierre thinks . . .

DUKE: Yes, but what if it's a nervous breakdown?

URBAIN [*in a weak voice*]: Gaétan! . . .

CAROLINE: He's waking up!

URBAIN [*louder*]: Gaétan!

DUKE [*going to the head of the settee*]: Here I am! How are you feeling?

URBAIN: Fine. I've been sleeping here, have I? What's the time
now? [*Caroline opens the shutters of the casement at left, the Duke
those of the casement at right.*]

DUKE: It's broad daylight. [*The stage is growing brighter.*]

URBAIN: Then ... I don't understand. ...

DUKE: Don't try to think back. Have some more rest.

URBAIN: No! I have rested ... and I distinctly remember... But what's wrong with my hand? ... This handkerchief ... You haven't been here on your own? ... Who were you talking to just now?

DUKE: I've just arrived, and I was asking after you—asking the person who spent the night here with you.

URBAIN [*agitated; trying to rise*]: What person ... ? I want to know. ...

CAROLINE [*going up to Urbain*]: Don't trouble yourself, Marquis; I was the person. Last night I happened to be going past in the gallery; I thought I heard somebody calling; I found you unconscious; I put you over there. The Duke went for the doctor but didn't find him. He kept the accident from your mother; you don't need to worry, she won't know anything about it. I've been writing some letters here while you've been asleep. You haven't been feverish, and I think it's time you had something for breakfast. Everything is quite straightforward, and there's no need for the slightest concern. [*She leaves via the gallery, taking the lamp, which she has extinguished.*]

Scene 3

[*Urbain, the Duke.*]

DUKE: Well, aren't you going to say anything to her? Aren't you going to call her back? Haven't you understood?

URBAIN [*clinging to him*]: Brother, you must marry her!

DUKE: Marry her—when you're the one who's in love with her?

URBAIN: I never said ...

DUKE: What you emitted just now was a genuine cry of self-sacrificing love—you can't deny it any longer! I've been upsetting you without meaning to—without even suspecting ... I do apologize; I should have realized sooner.

URBAIN: Gaétan, I've been horrible. I was mad—delirious. ... Oh, I'm in such a wretched state! [*He bursts into tears and collapses into the chair at left.*]

DUKE [*near him*]: Come on, none of this weakness—chin up! A brave lad like you!

URBAIN: Let me be weak. I've been acting strong for such a long time!

DUKE: Quite right—go ahead and have a cry, you'll feel all the better for it; but let's try to talk sense. Point number one, it was Pierre who accompanied Mademoiselle de Saint-Geneix on her outing last night. [*Urbain rises.*] You thought I was setting up a tête-à-tête for myself. . . . That's just ridiculous. Put it out of your head once and for all. Personally, since I'm determined to avoid further misunderstandings, I hereby declare and swear to you once and for all that I shall not entertain the slightest amorous and/or marital impulse toward Mademoiselle de Saint-Geneix.

URBAIN: What's the point of such a sacrifice, when . . . ?

DUKE: It will prevent you from suffering and our friendship from being disturbed. You see, personally speaking, I can't bear any more of last night's anguish. It's too much for me; it'd drive me positively insane! The sacrifice, in any case, isn't very heroic, because Mademoiselle de Saint-Geneix never even grasped that I was taking an interest in her. And then again, as you yourself said—and you were right—I'm not the inconsolable type; tenacity is not my strong point. If I set my mind to it, and with a bit of help from on high, I'll be in love with someone else before the week is out.

URBAIN: No, no; marry Caroline. I'll rise above it, this jealousy— it's disgraceful, it's selfish. She won't ever suspect that I've been in love with her; I'll get rid of it, I'll burn it to ashes, I swear it. My dear brother, Caroline has to be loved seriously and forever; she deserves to bear your name; she'll provide our mother with care and happiness; she'll settle you down; she's strong, and she's affectionate; she's remarkably intelligent, uncommonly knowledgeable; she has immense reserves of good sense; and on top of that, she's so delightfully unpretentious. She's active, energetic, devoted, generous. . . . In short . . .

DUKE: In short, you positively adore her, and for that reason I have to marry her! This is insanity! Do you want me to tell you something? As of yesterday, I've come to think she's in love with you.

URBAIN: Oh, you couldn't be more wrong about that!

DUKE: All the same, in Paris . . .

URBAIN: In Paris she respected me, that was all; and since then, she's been . . . almost painfully cold to me.

DUKE: Yes, because she's realized that you love her, and, being proud and loyal, she's wanted to drive you towards Mademoiselle de Saintrailles.

URBAIN [*promptly*]: Oh, if only that were the case! . . .

PIERRE [*entering upstage*]: Monsieur de Dunières is in the drawing room, and wishes to speak with the Duke.

DUKE: The devil he does! At this unearthly hour! [*To Pierre.*] I'm coming. [*Pierre closes the screen and leaves upstage.*] You see what it's like: one is under such pressure to cure the world's problems that one never gets any rest. [*He goes upstage and comes back.*] Come now, if I were in your shoes, I shouldn't have much to complain about! Loved by two charming young ladies at the same time! But you can't marry both of them; it's a defect in the national legislation, but still, that's the way things are. What am I to answer when good old Dunières questions me?

URBAIN: That I can't marry Mademoiselle de Saintrailles, because I'm in love with someone else.

DUKE: Come now! As bluntly as that? Can't be done!

URBAIN: Well then, find out what he wants, and if necessary . . . I'll explain the situation to him myself!

DUKE: Do have a think about it, though.

URBAIN [*seeing Caroline approaching*]: I have thought about it; just go away. [*The Duke leaves upstage.*]

Scene 4

[*Caroline, Urbain.*]

CAROLINE [*coming in via the gallery*]: Well, Marquis, your breakfast? . . .

URBAIN: What about you yourself? Aren't you going to think of some rest?

CAROLINE: After a perfectly quiet night's vigil? That's nothing, Marquis. I'm used to it.

URBAIN: Don't you want me to thank you, then? . . .

CAROLINE: Thank me for what?

URBAIN: For what you would have done for anyone else, whoever it might have been—yes, I know. You're most generous, but I . . .

CAROLINE: Pierre is waiting to serve you. . . . [*She starts to leave.*]

URBAIN: Mademoiselle de Saint-Geneix, do stay, please! I have some very serious things to say to you.

CAROLINE [*coming downstage*]: In that case, give me your instructions, Marquis.

URBAIN: Don't take that tone; you're doing me a great injustice. For some time I've been very abrupt, almost impolite, possibly even bitter and hurtful to you.

CAROLINE: I haven't noticed it, Marquis.

URBAIN: In other words you don't want to forgive me.

CAROLINE: Or else I haven't taken your abruptness to heart.

URBAIN: I've been very ungrateful; because you have given me the only really enjoyable times I've had in this miserable life of mine. In Paris, with my mother, when we were so close, it was pure and delightful; you gave me a new spirit—you brought out a new feeling in me: a feeling of self-confidence. We talked about the really important things, the things that are good for the soul—and your soul was so true that it helped to clarify mine. Now that you were making me really live for the first time in my life, I couldn't help feeling a deep sense of gratitude and respect and genuine friendship. But since then, my state of weakness—I hid it, but it betrayed itself in front of you yesterday—prevented me from being open towards you. You had the compassion to forgive my misfortune, but I do want you to voice that forgiveness aloud. My conscience has quite enough burdens already; don't leave it with the remorse of having offended a heart as generous as yours, and having possibly misunderstood a human being so noble that I felt overwhelmed by her. . . . I've been very guilty toward you. . . . Let me take the blame and offer you the reparation I owe you!

CAROLINE [crossing right]: But I don't want you to take any blame, Marquis. Even if you may have misjudged me now and then, I don't wish to know about it. Nothing serious ever happened, and I could always comfort myself in whatever ways were necessary.

URBAIN: You comforted yourself . . . ?

CAROLINE: By recalling that I was a stranger among you, and that people had been very quick to treat me with respect and confidence—which only time could show whether I deserved.

URBAIN: You . . . a stranger here! You . . .

CAROLINE: A good sick nurse if you like, and one who is obliged to you all the more, since you've been a good patient—a much too grateful one. [She goes upstage.]

URBAIN [bewildered]: Caroline, listen to me—you must!

CAROLINE [with an effort]: No, you need some peace and quiet; and I . . . since you insist . . . need some rest too. [She goes upstage left.]

DUKE [offstage]: Urbain! Urbain!

Scene 5

[*Caroline, the Duke, Urbain.*]

DUKE [*entering upstage, and bringing back Caroline, who has been trying to leave*]: What's all this? Sulking? Saying farewell? Come now! That's a fine thing to do, you childish and faithless philosophers! Listen to me.... Victory has been won! We needed a miracle to bring you together.... Well now, this miracle ... has been accomplished!

CAROLINE: Duke ...

DUKE: Please let me talk, Mademoiselle de Saint-Geneix; you don't have the floor at present.

URBAIN: Hurry up and say it then!

DUKE: Yes ... but I'm so out of breath! Would you please let me hop around the room a bit so I can calm down? [*He crosses right.*] No, you're getting impatient! Well then, let me tell you some news—the most ... Madame de Sévigné herself would be lost for words![18] [*He returns to center stage.*] Dunières is out there, along with his ward, and along with my mother, who is seventy-five percent out of her wits with astonishment and delight!

URBAIN: Why astonishment?

DUKE: Oh, but don't you understand? ...

URBAIN: No, of course not!

DUKE: I am the one!

URBAIN: You are the one?

DUKE: Yes: I am the one who is chosen, I am the one who is approved, I am the one who is regarded as charming, I am the one who gave the doll, I am the one who is beloved, I, in short, am the one who is going to marry Diane de Saintrailles! [*He drops onto the carpet.*]

URBAIN [*ecstatically*]: Oh, brother, I'm so happy to hear it!

DUKE: So am I, as it happens. Still, it's a funny thing! Honestly, I must have been born with a silver spoon in my mouth. You see how much justice there is in this world! Here am I, penniless, decrepit ... [*He rises.*] Yet who said so? I'm young, I'm dapper, I'm nimble, I'm dazzling! Try as I may to disguise myself and veil myself and keep myself in my little corner, there's something inside me that makes everything work out all right—so that after I've squandered everything, what do I find but a delightful girl, a veritable spring flower, a pure and generous soul, with a great name and a great fortune that is exalting her still further, since she's using it to save me from dishonor!

URBAIN: How?

DUKE: Can't you guess, my dear creditor? [*Urbain reacts.*] There's no question of refusal; my honor is my wife's honor. She wanted to reimburse my mother too, but my mother wouldn't let her. Darling mother! What a splendid life the three of us are going to give her! . . . And as for you and all your self-sacrifice, alas! we can ask nothing more than for you to go and be happy.— Mademoiselle de Saint-Geneix, everyone here loves and admires you; the only thing that is missing, for you to be truly the daughter of my mother, is to become the wife of her son. And as for her son, you know perfectly well, my dear sister, that he worships the ground you tread on. Say but a word, simply put out your hand to him, and here are two fine fair marriages settled within fifteen minutes.

CAROLINE: But . . . I declare . . . I . . .

DUKE: What?

URBAIN: Oh Gaétan, you see how it is! It's my own doing—I haven't been able to make myself loved!

CAROLINE [*bewildered*]: Loved! . . . [*Recovering.*] No, this is a dream! You don't love me, you can't love me!

DUKE: Mademoiselle de Saint-Geneix, please don't tell a fib for the first time in your life. I myself was blind, I admit, but no woman could possibly have been—not to that extent, anyway. You may not have wished to notice my brother's passion; a pure soul like you would no doubt fight against the evidence for a long time; but you must, in spite of yourself, have smelled love in the air around you. And now that there isn't any obstacle left between you, open your eyes and let your heart speak.

CAROLINE: But I tell you . . .

URBAIN: You see, she's adamant!

DUKE: Oh well, if she doesn't yet love you, by Jove, she will love you! She must love you; she has to!

URBAIN: Gaétan!

DUKE: Don't interrupt me! She is immensely fond of my mother, at any rate; she will be no less fond of . . . a person she hasn't yet got acquainted with—your son!

CAROLINE [*coming nearer*]: His son?

URBAIN [*to the Duke*]: That's right, go right ahead; tell her about my son; tell her everything.

DUKE: That won't take long: an elopement, three years of bereavement, a splendid, delightful boy—an orphan who can now be adopted, and of whom you will become the mother. You can see perfectly well that it suits you—given that you live only to make people happy!

CAROLINE [*almost beaten, in tears, falling onto the chair at left*]: Good heavens!

URBAIN: Caroline—in the name of my son—for him, if not for me, and out of compassion, if not love!

CAROLINE: Oh, leave me alone—you'll be the death of me! It's impossible!

URBAIN: Caroline, I'm lost without you—that's right, lost! You don't know what aspirations and disappointments I've had. Everything you could imagine—sins and atonements, sacrifices and duties, evil and good, storms and tempests! Till I knew you, I'd only been in love once—and it had been bad. The fault may not have been mine alone, but I don't wish to soften it. Don't you see, I can't tell any lies, even if they would lead you to trust me. I can hardly dare tell you that my whole life will be devoted to making you happy—yet I know that I still have the power to make you proud and happy, if only you'll care enough for my heart to try to heal it. Say something—don't leave me in despair—ever since last night I've been suffocating! I don't have enough air to breathe any more; I don't have enough light to see where I'm going. I realize I've hurt you, even though I love you, and I know I don't deserve to go on living! If you do hate me, it would have been a thousand times kinder to have left me to die last night!

CAROLINE: Hate you! . . . Why should you say such cruel things to someone who is in torment enough already? Oh! Your affection is a bitter thing—and it's so hard not to irritate it! Come now—do have some consideration for me. Don't you care how much harm you do me? Am I nothing, or nobody?

DUKE: So you do love him?

URBAIN: Go on, tell him!

DUKE: Yes, tell me!

URBAIN: Tell him!

CAROLINE [*to the Duke*]: All right . . . if he deserves to be loved as
he demands . . . let him prove it! Let him stop being selfish, let
him stop choosing a wife that his mother would never accept
without making an immense sacrifice.

URBAIN: But my mother . . .

CAROLINE [*rising*]:[19] Monsieur de Villemer, you and I are not a pair
of children; so let's not have any illusions. The Marquise de
Villemer will never be able to forget that she has paid for my
services. So then, let us part today, and for good. I know you'll
think about me, and I'm afraid it may hurt you,[20] but you'll
recall what you owe me, after what you've dared to tell me and
what you've made me tell you in return. [*The Duke goes upstage.*]
Wait a minute! We do have one comfort left: you have a son—
let me look after him. I'll be able to bring him up and teach
him. I can go and live where he is; you can see him quite often,
as long as you don't see me; I'll give him all the love I can't give
you, and when I return him to you, we can shake hands and
tell ourselves without any uneasiness that we could have been
happy together, but we preferred duty to happiness and heal-
ing friendship to fatal passion. [*She drops back on the chair.*]

DUKE [*coming down center stage*]: Now that, my dear Caroline, is
utterly noble, utterly sincere, and utterly impossible! To meet
again only years and years hence—to avoid each other consci-
entiously in the meantime—with this child linking the two of
you together? A fine fantasy that is! You poor well-meaning
child—what about your reputation?

CAROLINE [*rising*]: That, Monsieur, is my business; seeing I've been
able to preserve it intact, I surely have the right to sacrifice it.
[*She moves off to the left.*]

URBAIN: Caroline! . . .

DUKE: You can see how she loves you—the generous girl! But how
can you hope to make such a sacrifice without driving him out
of his wits—when he's the object of it? Come now, you're a
saint, but you have no idea where lofty schemes can lead noble-
minded people. I'll have none of that, thank you kindly—either for you or for him! The pair of you could be happy and
honored in the broad light of day; I won't have you weeping . . . or blushing . . . in the darkness. What needs to be done
before you can marry my brother? Something very simple: my
mother has to open her arms and say, "Please, daughter!" All

right, she will say it, and very soon, too—because here she is with my beloved fiancée, who is going to help us persuade the two of you.

Scene 6

[*As above; the Marquise, Diane.*]

MARQUISE [*entering via the gallery with Diane, whose arm she is holding*]: So we have to come and hunt you out, do we, children? Oh—you've been telling Caroline . . . The dear little thing, she can join in our happiness! [*She holds out her arms to her*].

DUKE [*to Caroline*]: See?

CAROLINE [*kissing the Marquise's hand emotionally*]: Madame! . . .

DUKE: That's enough! . . . Mademoiselle Diane, since you've come here to work miracles, lend us your help. . . . In other words take Mademoiselle Caroline away and keep your eye on her while the two of us tell our mother something that you'll find out about immediately afterwards. [*In a low voice.*] Oh, it's something big—and it will happen, if you set your mind to it!

DIANE: You're not going to discuss anything serious, are you? If it was your brother, there'd be no problem. But you . . . aren't you a bit green?

DUKE: Good Lord! Do you have to tell me that at a time when I need to be sensible!

DIANE [*going to Urbain and holding out her hand to him*]: Monsieur Urbain, I do have eyes in my head, and I am all on your side. Come along, Caroline, off we go!

CAROLINE: But . . .

DUKE: Now then, there's nothing more to be said. I'm in charge here. [*He sees Caroline and Diane out, and shuts the door upstage.*]

Scene 7

[*Marquise, the Duke, Urbain.*]

DUKE [*placing a chair near the settee*]: Seat yourself there, please. [*Urbain sits down. The Duke kisses his mother, who laughs. He offers her his arm.*] No laughter now, mother! You'll see! [*He gets her to sit on the settee, then takes a cushion, puts it on the floor in front of her, and kneels on it.*]

MARQUISE: What a big baby you are!

DUKE: Mother dearest, since you see the two of us both at your feet, you've probably guessed that we have some whopping great confession to make to you.

MARQUISE [*looking at Urbain*]: The two of you?

DUKE: Yes; me first. The day before yesterday... in fact even yesterday, I was in love, oh, seriously in love, with Mademoiselle de Saint-Geneix, and I was on the point of asking you to let me tell her so.

MARQUISE: Oh yes? Are you sure you didn't tell her so?

DUKE: Well, maybe a little, but she didn't understand, which amounts to the same thing.

MARQUISE: And after that?

DUKE: After that—or rather before that, a very long time before, because it started when Caroline first came to us—my brother, the gentleman you see here saying nothing and just holding your hand, was, like myself... or in fact much more than myself, in love with her.

MARQUISE: What do you mean?

DUKE: I mean that, ever since Caroline...

MARQUISE: You, Urbain?

URBAIN: Yes, mother.

DUKE: Well, what do you expect? Couldn't possibly have been otherwise. If you'd had ten sons, all ten of them would have been in love with Mademoiselle de Saint-Geneix, and we'd all ten of us be here at the moment, on our knees, like this, in a circle around you, arranged in order of age.... Couldn't you have foreseen that?

MARQUISE: True enough! I should have foreseen it; but... she doesn't know?

DUKE: She knows everything.

MARQUISE [*rising*]: What?

DUKE: I myself told her, just now, just a moment ago.

MARQUISE [*to Urbain*]: So you intend to marry her?

DUKE: He does intend to marry her. So did I, at one stage.

URBAIN [*rising*]: What other intention could I possibly have, with a woman that I admire and you yourself respect?

MARQUISE [*crossing left*]: True enough. Good heavens, children, here I am so happy, and you have to strike me down in the middle of it!

DUKE: But why? Quite the contrary—we're bringing you one more reason to be happy. Do you think you can do without Caroline? This way, she's yours for life.

MARQUISE: It's not a question of me; don't talk about me. [*She goes between them.*] Your brother needs a better marriage than that— a marriage like yours.

DUKE: Mother dearest, my brother needs the marriage that will stop him being the miserable, wretched, suffering creature you've seen for the past three years. [*Urbain signals to the Duke not to upset his mother.*]

MARQUISE [*alarmed, turning to Urbain*]: Suffering? You've been ill, Urbain? I knew it.

URBAIN: No, mother . . . in my conscience, yes, I must admit. But that trouble would be wiped out for ever if you convinced Mademoiselle de Saint-Geneix to share my life.

MARQUISE: She's resisting, then? Does she understand . . . ?

URBAIN: She thinks you have ideas . . . that I could never hope to change—not that I've ever contested or challenged them, mother. Whatever my own views might be, I would still treat yours as sacred. So I don't mean to defend a cause; I want you to make a sacrifice—a great and serious sacrifice—out of your love for me.

MARQUISE: Urbain . . . what a thing you're asking of me!

DUKE: A sacrifice that both of you are making out to be much greater than it is. This isn't a case for reasoning, mother darling; it's a case for remembering.

MARQUISE: Remembering what?

DUKE: That you were young once. [*The Marquise reacts.*] Oh, I'm familiar with the touching story of your own early days. Some recollections are stamped forever in children's minds, because they're stamped in their hearts. I can remember how my noble relatives, a great assemblage of hidalgos, every one of them a direct and lineal descendant of the Cid himself,[21] didn't consider the Marquis de Villemer's title sufficient for him to become my stepfather. And yet he was the only father I ever knew, and he made you the happiest woman in the world. Well now, supposing, among his ancestors, there had been two or three fewer generals and one more gentleman of the legal profession—would your marriage have been any the less respectable, your love any the less permissible, your happiness any the less complete? I don't believe so; and, if you'll allow me to say so, it wouldn't have altered your affection for a man who was worthy of you and whose marriage to you gave me the best years of my life and the best brother in the world.

MARQUISE [*in tears*]: He does love Caroline then? [*To Urbain.*] She's the only one who can make you happy?

URBAIN: Yes, mother; and if I've ever shown you that I do care about you . . .

MARQUISE: If you've ever shown me! But what about her? Does she love you?

URBAIN: Ah, who knows?

MARQUISE: Go and get her.

URBAIN: What are you going to say to her?

MARQUISE: That if she doesn't love you, she's out of her mind. [*Urbain utters a cry of happiness, kisses his mother and leaves upstage.*]

Scene 8

[*The Marquise, the Duke; later, Léonie.*]

DUKE: Well, what about me?

MARQUISE: You? You've such a tongue, such a memory, such an audacity. . . . You're the devil incarnate. . . . But you're not such a bad devil! [*She kisses him.—Léonie enters via the gallery.*]

DUKE: Thank you, mother!

LÉONIE: Am I intruding? [*The Marquise crosses to far right.*]

DUKE [*going to her*]: No, not this time. [*The Marquise makes a reproachful gesture.*] I mean, of course, not ever—do excuse me! You'll know by now, Baroness, what has happened, and you've come to congratulate me?

LÉONIE: No. [*The Duke reacts.*] I meant, of course, yes—do excuse me!

DUKE: Now that was a slip.

LÉONIE: So was yours. [*Going to the Marquise.*] Madame darling, I've come to say good-bye to you. I'm expected at Baden, you know, and although I hate to leave you, I must go as soon as the horses are here. . . .

DUKE: Really? Oh, that's too bad. I was just getting used to your company.

LÉONIE: And I was just getting used to your conversation.

DUKE: The devil you were! How will you manage without it?

LÉONIE: I'll listen to other people instead.

DUKE: Other chatterers?

LÉONIE: Anybody at all. All the people you borrowed your best speeches from.

DUKE: Oh now . . . you do say that in such a way! . . . Is my happiness getting on your nerves a little, Baroness?

LÉONIE: Your happiness? No, I don't believe so.

MARQUISE: Yes, it's like a dream, isn't it?—everything that's happened today . . .

DUKE: A bad dream for the Baroness, who had predicted that I was going to meet the same end as Don Giovanni, and considers that heaven is being unjust! Go on, mother, why don't you tell her that I am adorable and faultless, and pay her back for all the bad things she tells you about me . . . when you're asleep.

LÉONIE: Be careful, now! You're going to use up all your brainpower. What are you going to have left for your own household?

DUKE: Now that you're leaving us, I shan't need anything any more. I shall have the happiness . . . I mean the regret of seeing you to your carriage. [*He goes upstage.*]

MARQUISE: Where are you off to?

DUKE: I'm going to tell Diane guess-what. [*He leaves upstage.*]

Scene 9

[*Léonie, the Marquise.*]

MARQUISE: Why the war between you? It's ridiculous, Baroness. On your side, it looks like spite. The Duke hasn't been courting you, has he? I would have noticed it.

LÉONIE: I wouldn't have stood for it.

MARQUISE [*smiling*]: Oh!

LÉONIE: I really should hope to respect the man I chose.

MARQUISE: There, Madame d'Arglade, you're going a little too far.

LÉONIE: Anyhow, I'm off.

MARQUISE: And in a huff—why? I don't understand; but the Duke will tell me.

LÉONIE: Does he tell you everything?

MARQUISE: Everything that can be said to his mother.

LÉONIE: He's a good son.

MARQUISE [*sitting on the settee*]: But of course he is. Come, Baroness, admit it: you're jealous of someone here.

LÉONIE [*laughing and sitting on a chair near the settee*]: Jealous? Me? And of whom, in heaven's name? Mademoiselle de Saintrailles, or Caroline?

MARQUISE: Why bring poor Caroline into this?

LÉONIE: I thought the Duke told you everything!

MARQUISE: Well?

LÉONIE: Well, don't you know that the Duke is in love with Caroline?

MARQUISE [*after a moment's hesitation*]: I know that the Duke has been very taken with Mademoiselle de Saint-Geneix; he told me so just a short while ago.

LÉONIE: Ah!

MARQUISE: Yes; he even said that he'd seriously wanted to marry her.

LÉONIE: Why is he marrying somebody else, then?

MARQUISE: Because Caroline didn't give him any hope.

LÉONIE: That hope, no doubt, was what he was trying to regain last night?

MARQUISE [*surprised, controlling herself*]: Last night?

LÉONIE: I'm just saying that, if the Duke spent the whole of last night closeted with Caroline, no doubt he was simply hoping to overcome her obstinate resistance.

MARQUISE [*coldly*]: How do you know that?

LÉONIE: You didn't know about it, then?

MARQUISE [*severely*]: I'm merely asking how you know it.

LÉONIE: Very simply indeed. All night the doors of their apartments remained open. I was worried about Caroline—I thought she might be sick, so I went to look for her. She was here in this room, locked in with somebody. They were talking very softly indeed. The Duke didn't return to his own apartment till morning.

MARQUISE: Who saw him?

LÉONIE: I did, and so did Pierre—if he wanted to see him.

MARQUISE: You swear to this?

LÉONIE: I do.

MARQUISE [*rising and crossing left*]: Very well, Baroness. I've been questioning you like this to convince myself of something I don't like to admit: that you'll use any means to grasp at a secret where you can't obtain it in confidence.

Léonie [*rising*]: It was the merest chance. . . .

Marquise: Chances of that kind, in sufficient number, would justify the things that people say about you.

Léonie: Nobody can accuse me of telling lies.

Marquise: People are aware of that; that's why they regard you as a menace: you make use of what is true to present what is false.

Léonie: So . . .

Pierre [*entering upstage*]: Mademoiselle de Saint-Geneix wishes to know if Madame is alone.

Marquise: In a moment; ask her to wait, please. [*Pierre removes the chair that is near the settee, and then leaves.*] Very briefly, I am obliged to tell you that, if the Duke was indeed making an appeal to Caroline, it was probably not for himself, but . . .

Léonie: For whom, then? His brother?

Marquise: I haven't said that. I'm simply telling you that you are incriminating. . . .

Léonie: No indeed, I'm not doing any incriminating; but I may be permitted to think that Caroline is secretly in love with the Duke and will not marry anyone else.

Marquise: That . . . that's possible; I want to . . . and I am going to find out. [*She rings the bell.*]

Léonie: You will forgive me?

Marquise [*sitting at left*]: For what? Oh yes—chance. I've told you what conclusions might be drawn on that score. Give it some thought. Good-bye, Baroness. [*Caroline enters upstage.*]

Léonie: Good-bye, Marquise. [*She goes upstage and says to Caroline, who is on her way in:*] Now, just tell the whole truth; whatever the consequences may be, you can rely on me. [*She leaves upstage.*]

Scene 10

[*The Marquise, seated at left; Caroline.*]

Caroline [*worried*]: Madame . . .

Marquise: Well, Mademoiselle de Saint-Geneix? . . . Well?

Caroline: Must I be the first to speak, Madame?

Marquise: Well, I do think so.

CAROLINE: I shouldn't have thought so myself. Madame must understand that I am being put through a most painful and delicate trial.

MARQUISE: Nobody who is truthful can ever experience such a trial. My son the Marquis has asked me for permission to offer you his name. I want to know, first of all, whether you really love him.

CAROLINE: Even if I did love him, would you approve of my telling him so?

MARQUISE: No; but you might have told his brother, who seems to have asked you about it often enough.

CAROLINE: I don't think the Duke would have kept a secret of mine concerning his brother.

MARQUISE: And yet you do trust him?

CAROLINE: Yes, in every other respect.

MARQUISE: You surprise me a little. Didn't you allow him to be rather pressing . . . yesterday evening?

CAROLINE: No, Madame; yesterday evening, I didn't know anything. It was only this morning that the Duke told me about the Marquis's intentions.

MARQUISE: Oh? I thought you were somewhat disturbed . . . last night! As you didn't come and spend the evening with me . . . You did ask the Duke to tell me that you were unwell? . . .

CAROLINE: I was a little unwell.

MARQUISE: You need to take care of yourself. I imagine you went to bed late, as usual?

CAROLINE: I did have a lot of letters to write.

MARQUISE: So, you worked . . . in your room?

CAROLINE: No, Madame, I wrote here.

MARQUISE: Here? Why?

CAROLINE [*embarrassed*]: I can't really say; I was here.

MARQUISE: And were you writing long?

CAROLINE: I think so.

MARQUISE: Till daybreak, possibly?

CAROLINE: It wouldn't be the first time—one simply forgets oneself.

MARQUISE [*rising and crossing right; dryly*]: One mustn't forget oneself! You don't have anything to tell me about the reflections or uncertainties of this long sleepless night? You were thinking about the Marquis, perhaps?

CAROLINE: Good heavens, Madame, why are you interrogating me? God himself doesn't ask us to give an account for thoughts that we don't linger over. You have no right to ask me about anything except the acts I have committed of my own free will. I see you're afraid that I may have been encouraging a plan you disliked. I can tell you that I have no such offense on my conscience. And I have enough pride to believe that that is all you need to know.

MARQUISE: Yes, it is all I need to know, but I have to justify my respect for you—I have to remove all the Marquis's hopes. Only a romantic attraction of the deepest possible kind could justify the sacrifice that a Marquis de Villemer would make, if he were to forget what he owes the world and what his social position requires of him. Now, you're certainly not ambitious or scheming; so if you don't return his love, you needn't hesitate to tell him. . . .

CAROLINE: It's a question of my own dignity, Madame; please allow me to choose the method. First of all, I have to leave.

MARQUISE: What good would that do? He would follow you.

CAROLINE [*going upstage*]: That would be disrespectful to me; I haven't deserved that.

MARQUISE: Passion is never rational. He has to be discouraged in advance. Take a strong line! Tell him that you're in love with someone else.

CAROLINE: Tell a lie? I couldn't do it.

MARQUISE [*severely*]: Tell a lie! . . . Caroline, you're not trusting me; that isn't right.

CAROLINE: I don't understand you, Madame.

MARQUISE: I understand you even less. You're not in love with Urbain, yet you don't want him to know it. That shows a lack of honesty.

CAROLINE [*bursting out*]: Oh, I knew perfectly well I'd be accused of some disgraceful intention or other!

MARQUISE: If the accusation is unfair, prove it.

CAROLINE: What am I to prove? Oh, I understand, Madame. You want Monsieur de Villemer's unhappiness to come from me alone—isn't that so? Very well; tell him, tell both your sons, that I'll never forgive them for putting me in such a shameful position toward you.

MARQUISE: Mademoiselle de Saint-Geneix, I have the right to see into the very depths of your heart. I can still take an interest in you, protect you, defend you . . . and perhaps satisfy you.

CAROLINE: I'm not asking you for anything, am I?

MARQUISE: Ah! . . . That's enough, Mademoiselle de Saint-Geneix. I wanted to know your true feelings; I will find them out. [*She rings the bell.*] Go and wait for me in my room. I owe it to myself to ask you for this act of obedience.

CAROLINE: It will be the last one, Madame. [*Pierre enters. She speaks quietly with Pierre and leaves via the gallery.*]

MARQUISE [*crossing right*]: Ask the Duke to come here immediately.

PIERRE: But here is the Marquis.

MARQUISE: That doesn't matter! Do as I tell you, quickly! [*Urbain enters and Pierre leaves via the gallery.*]

Scene 11

[*Urbain, the Marquise.*]

URBAIN: Mother, where's Caroline?

MARQUISE: In my room; she's waiting for me.

URBAIN: You haven't convinced her?

MARQUISE: No.

URBAIN: Oh, she doesn't have anything—she doesn't feel anything for me!

MARQUISE: Urbain, my dear son, do calm down.

URBAIN [*explosively*]: I can't—not any more! I must see her again!

MARQUISE: No! Give her some time to examine her conscience— give her the whole day! Come now, you mustn't let the whole world see. . . . You're weeping over a woman—you! . . . I never saw you weak in your life.

URBAIN [*crossing right*]: Mother, I don't understand you, I don't seem to have my head on my shoulders today! Tell me that she's going to love me, that you're going to convince her. . . . That's what I need to be told, or nothing.

MARQUISE: You're being very unkind to me, Urbain!

URBAIN: Excuse me, mother; I know I'm beside myself! But please give me some hope.

MARQUISE [*going up to him*]: Someone's coming; in heaven's name, do be quiet!

Scene 12

[*As above, Dunières; later, the Duke and Diane.*]

DUNIÈRES: Well, Marquise, I hear some good news! Two marriages at once?

MARQUISE: Please be quiet, Dunières.

DUNIÈRES: Why? We're all one family from now on! Our bridal couple ... [*he indicates the Duke and Diane, who are entering upstage*] want Mademoiselle de Saint-Geneix included. It surprised me at first, but, when I come to think about it, ... I believe I recall hearing that there were two Saint-Geneix at Fontenoy.

DUKE: You've miscounted, Dunières; there were four. But I don't see Mademoiselle de Saint-Geneix here.

URBAIN: That's because she won't listen to us.

DUKE: Because we haven't been eloquent enough! We'll get off to a fresh start. [*Calling out.*] Pierre! Pierre!

MARQUISE: My son!

DUKE: Pierre! He'll hear the bell. [*He rings the bell.*]

MARQUISE: Don't be in such a rush, my boy. Mademoiselle de Saint-Geneix wants to think; and I must ask you to do some thinking too—hasn't anyone told you ... ?

DUKE [*ringing again*]: Nobody has told me anything; should anyone be thinking today? Everyone should be feverish, delirious, enraptured! [*He rings the bell and calls out.*] Pierre! Here's someone else who is going to be happy! Pierre!

Scene 13

[*As above; Pierre.*]

DUKE [*blithely*]: Pierre, my friend, go and tell Mademoiselle de Saint-Geneix that we are all expecting her here.

PIERRE: Monsieur, Mademoiselle de Saint-Geneix has left.

URBAIN [*leaping up*]: Left!

DUKE: Since when?

PIERRE: She isn't in the house.

URBAIN: She'll be gone ... for some days?

PIERRE: For good, Monsieur. [*Urbain collapses onto the settee.*]

MARQUISE: She told you so?

PIERRE: Yes, Madame.

DUNIÈRES: Why?

PIERRE: I don't know, Monsieur.

DUKE: How did she go?

PIERRE: I don't know, Monsieur.

URBAIN: Where has she gone?

PIERRE: I don't know, Monsieur.

DIANE: She didn't tell even you?

PIERRE: I didn't allow myself the liberty of asking her, Mademoiselle.

MARQUISE: That's enough, Pierre; you may go. [*Pierre starts to leave.*]

DUKE: Pierre! . . . Excuse me, mother, I have an order to give him—you'll allow me? Wait here, Pierre.

PIERRE: Forgive me, Monsieur, but I'm leaving Madame's service, and from now on . . .

DUKE: You're not taking orders any more? That's reasonable. All right, Monsieur Pierre, we have a favor to ask of you.

PIERRE [*coming downstage*]: I'm listening, Monsieur.

DUKE: Monsieur Pierre, Mademoiselle de Saint-Geneix was here less than fifteen minutes ago. She isn't with us any more, but she can't be far away. You're too devoted to let her go off on her own; therefore, she must be waiting for you. You won't say where she is, because you have promised not to say and your conscience is inflexible. Am I right?

PIERRE: Yes, Monsieur.

DUKE: Well now, Monsieur Pierre, would you kindly undertake to carry an open letter to Mademoiselle de Saint-Geneix, please?

PIERRE: Yes, if Monsieur will give me his word of honor that nobody is going to follow me.

DUKE: You have it. [*He writes.*] Nobody will move an inch from here till we receive the reply to this letter. [*Pierre takes the letter and leaves upstage.*]

MARQUISE: Gaétan, may we know what you have just written?

DUKE: Three words: "You're being slandered."

URBAIN [*elatedly, rising*]: She'll come!

MARQUISE: You're sure, my son? Let's wait.

URBAIN: But who is slandering her? And to whom?

DUKE: You want to know? Would the Marquise de Villemer have broken her promise [*the Marquise reacts*] and let Mademoiselle de Saint-Geneix go, unless someone had succeeded in convincing her that she wasn't worthy of you?

URBAIN: Who could have had the infamous hide . . . ?

DUKE: Oh no, it's nobody here. . . .

DUNIÈRES: It must have been the Baroness, then?

DIANE: Oh, that's impossible!

URBAIN: Say something, mother.

DUKE: If my mother has promised not to answer any questions, she won't say a word.

URBAIN [*fervently*]: No! My mother won't have listened to a lie without trying to find out the truth.

DUKE: And yet Mademoiselle de Saint-Geneix has left. Urbain, if our mother has been prepared to break your heart, she can't have done it simply out of disappointed ambition. [*The Marquise reacts.*] She's too generous! . . . She's not saying a word. Caroline has to come, and she will come.

DUNIÈRES: Yes, but she isn't coming.

DIANE [*going towards the rear*]: Perhaps she's already too far away.

PIERRE [*announcing*]: Mademoiselle de Saint-Geneix.

Scene 14

[*As above; Caroline.*]

URBAIN [*rushing up to Caroline*]: Mademoiselle de Saint-Geneix, you've been the victim of the most iniquitous perfidy; crush it beneath your feet; speak!

CAROLINE [*pale and cold*]: I don't know who is accusing me, or what I am being accused of. I'm waiting to be questioned; and I have the right to insist on it.

URBAIN: You hear her, mother!

MARQUISE: Yes; I see the crisis is inevitable. I had hoped to soften it by trusting to the secrecy of some and relying on the discretion of others; but "disappointed ambition" is the term being used to describe my distaste for a blow that will break all our hearts and destroy all our hopes [*she approaches Caroline*], so I shall have to be bold and explain myself to you all, since my hand is being forced. And, after all, why not? The Villemer family ought to have neither secrets nor false and dubious situations. [*To the Duke.*] You, Monsieur—inspired by an impulse that may have been romantic but was also, in view of its necessarily brief duration, unwise—you took it into your head to pay your respects to Mademoiselle de Saint-Geneix. I happen to know that she listened to you—and did so in secret, since she wouldn't admit it when I questioned her. No doubt she rejected your proposals, since you think yourself free; but I believe I am in a position to state that she has suffered for her sacrifice, and that it has driven her to leave. You must appreciate,

then, that I have a duty to go further and overcome your
scruples—which can, presumably, be overcome if I give my
consent. Stop deceiving this noble-minded girl [*indicating Diane*],
who believed you to be free from any ties; stop encouraging
your brother to have feelings that you couldn't understand,
and that would be the death of him; marry Mademoiselle de
Saint-Geneix. There are certain questions of delicacy, Monsieur,
that amount to reasons of honor.

DUKE [*indignantly*]: Madame! . . . Excuse me, mother! [*The Marquise returns to the extreme right.*] Really, this is a jolly cruel way
to punish me for my past! You're accusing me of something
infamous!

MARQUISE: No—of something highly irresponsible.

DUKE: Irresponsibility can lead to crime—and it would be a crime,
if I had been troubling the sleep of one decent woman yesterday, only to offer my worthless heart to another today. How can
I even start to give an answer in the presence of this angel who
condescends to put her faith in me—or this other pure-minded
creature who is standing there stupefied by these revelations of
yours! Good Lord! I believed I was absolved, purified, born all
over again; I was full of enthusiasm, sincerity, devotion, conviction; I thought I really was worthy to call one of them my wife
and the other my sister! And lo and behold, all because of a
suspicion that I can guess and that you're going to be very
sorry for, my poor mother, you've gone and ruined everything!
[*He collapses on the settee.*]

DIANE: Ruined everything? No, not at all; look. [*She kisses Caroline.*]

DUKE [*leaping up again impetuously*]: Oh how I will love you!

URBAIN [*to the Duke*]: But what about her? What has she done that
anyone should dare to put her through such an inquisition?

DUKE [*vehemently*]: I'll tell you what she's done. She's spent the
whole night here keeping an eye on you, having found you
over there, injured, unconscious, practically on the point of
dying, while I was running frantically round the countryside
for help that I couldn't find and that wouldn't have been as
good as hers anyhow! If my own word isn't enough for you,
mother dear, go and ask that honest man over there [*indicating
Pierre*]—he has every right to be there!

MARQUISE: Oh—what have I done!

DUKE: You've believed the disparagements of a creature . . .

MARQUISE: She thought she was telling the truth. [*Coming forward.*] Mademoiselle de Saint-Geneix, I never doubted your honor!

CAROLINE: Excuse me, Madame, but you did doubt my honesty.

MARQUISE: The only reparation I can offer you . . .

CAROLINE: I'm not in a position to accept any.

MARQUISE: That's a cruel thing to say, Caroline! [*She collapses on the settee.*]

CAROLINE: And has no one been cruel to me, Madame? I do appreciate that it is ungrateful for unfortunate people to utter complaints. Since so many of them have no courage and no pride, it's all the worse for those who do; in the end, they all fall under suspicion. What was my crime? I was here to work, and I did work. I never meddled with anything that wasn't my duty, and I never complained about my situation. I didn't go looking for anyone's friendship or trust. People wanted—against my will—to guess and read and pry into my heart, and trouble it and tear it apart and call on it to surrender; and when my pride was supposedly conquered, I was brought before a tribunal, interrogated, interpreted, every thought that was attributed to me was scrutinized, and I was positively flung at the head of the man I was alleged to be infatuated with—and all this, because nobody stopped to reflect that I might be doing a personal favor, or carrying out a duty, or trying to save anyone from worry! [*Bursting into tears.*] Which wouldn't have been a very difficult thing to imagine. Keep your reparations, and just give me my freedom. I'm not asking to be compensated and consoled; I'm simply asking to be forgotten.

URBAIN: Oh, your pride is perfectly justified, but it is pitiless. . . . I said all along that it was impossible to love me. [*He leans on the back of the settee, behind his mother.*]

CAROLINE: Good heavens!

MARQUISE: Mademoiselle de Saint-Geneix, you are right and I am wrong; I forgot that nothing deserves more respect than a misfortune nobly endured. I am not asking for forgiveness. But do please see how desperate my son is, and be generous. Do please sacrifice your pride for him. . . . Well, Urbain, does she want me to go down on my knees? Come and help me, then! [*She rises.*]

CAROLINE [*quickly*]:[22] No!

DUKE [*to his mother*]: No, mother, not that—you don't understand her.

MARQUISE: Caroline, my child, I beg you. [*She drops back on the settee.*]

CAROLINE [*falling at her feet*]: Oh, mother!

URBAIN: Lord Almighty!

MARQUISE [*holding Caroline in her arms*]: Tell me that you love him.

CAROLINE: Oh yes, with all my heart! [*Urbain kisses her hand, lifts her to her feet, and takes her across to Diane.*]

MARQUISE [*turning to the Duke*]: And what about you? Have I wronged you badly?

DUKE: Please don't start all that again, mother; it's adding years to my life.

DIANE: Nonsense! You're not a day over twenty.

DUKE: Indeed, that's the truth; I have to live the other twenty all over again.

DUNIÈRES: All over again?

DUKE: Quite differently this time, Dunières, quite differently.

The End

Françoise

A Comedy in Four Acts

Characters

FRANÇOISE LAURENT
HENRI DE TRÉGENEC
DOCTOR LAURENT, *Françoise's father*
JACQUES DE LA HYONNAIS
DUBUISSON
MADAME DUBUISSON [*his wife*]
CLÉONICE DUBUISSON [*their daughter*]
MARIE-JEANNE, *the doctor's maid*

Scene: in and around Bourges.

Act One

The doctor's home at Bourges.—A drawing room indicative of a simple, secure lifestyle, tasteful and orderly. At rear, a large glass door opening on a partly visible consulting room. At left, door from the anteroom. Door at right, leading to the dining room. Center stage, a pedestal table. At right, a fireplace.

Scene 1

[*Dubuisson, Marie-Jeanne, both entering.*]

DUBUISSON: So then, Marie-Jeanne, he ain't home?

MARIE-JEANNE: Oh, no, Monsieur Dubuisson; it isn't nearly time for him to come back yet.

DUBUISSON: He's got a fine practice, Doctor Laurent. Got the biggest medical business in the whole Bourges neighborhood. He must be making big money, your boss?

MARIE-JEANNE: Oh, sure, he could be a rich man if he wanted; but he treats too many of the poor people, and he doesn't charge you moneyed folk enough.

DUBUISSON [*half proud, half defensive*]: "You moneyed folk"? . . . Well now . . . I was just bringing him . . . [*He sits to the right of the table.*]

MARIE-JEANNE: The payment for his visits to your young lady last year? He did mention that to me, and to save you the trouble of having to come back, there's his bill—he left it with me this morning. Does that look right? [*She has brought the bill from the consulting room.*]

DUBUISSON [*examining the piece of paper that Marie-Jeanne has given him*]: Let's have a look. [*Aside.*] He's forgotten two house calls. [*He takes some money from his pocket and counts it out onto the table.*]

MARIE-JEANNE: So then, she's quite better now, is she, Mam'zelle Cléonice?

DUBUISSON: Too much so—she's been running off to dances all winter. Living in Paris . . . Costs you an arm and a leg!

MARIE-JEANNE [*going upstage*]: Poor fellow! Wait a bit till I hear your troubles. Tell us then, Papa Dubuisson—

DUBUISSON: What?

MARIE-JEANNE: Does that bother you maybe, when I talk to you like that?

DUBUISSON: No, not at all! You're from the same neck of the woods as me.

MARIE-JEANNE: Sure! We're born natives of the one place, both of us—or the next best thing, anyhow, 'cause you was running a pub at Cluis-Dessous when I was milkmaid at Cluis-Dessus. You've made your way in life better than what I have! I can remember how I used to say to you, "You'll go a long way, Christophe Dubuisson; you've got your finger in fifty pies—job here and a job there, getting blood out of stones all over the place; you're sure to make a packet!"

DUBUISSON [*with a sly, good-humored smile*]: Well?

MARIE-JEANNE: Well, doesn't it seem a bit funny to you, that you're the number one banker in Berry, and you've got a house in Paris, house here in town, and château in the country?

DUBUISSON: The château did kind of bother me at first; costs more than it's worth; but that was my wife's idea, so I got used to it. Now that sets me thinking... [*He rises.*] You know Monsieur Henri de Trégenec?

MARIE-JEANNE: I should think I do! It was Doctor Laurent that taught him, but really I was the one that brought him up. What do you want to know about him?

DUBUISSON: Is he a steady lad—does he look after himself?

MARIE-JEANNE: Ah, well now, having grown up with us, he hasn't been taught to be a miser.

DUBUISSON: I'm not at all keen on misers; can't stand them! ... But... does he throw his money away?

MARIE-JEANNE: Him? Well now, what does it matter to you?

DUBUISSON: Nothing! Look, aren't you going to check your money?

MARIE-JEANNE: Oh goodness no; you can count a lot better than I can. Wait a moment, somebody's ringing the bell. [*She goes out to the left.*]

DUBUISSON [*looking at the bill*]: He's forgotten two house calls, no less! ... It could be just to test me; he's a cunning fellow, the doctor is. ... All the same, he doesn't charge much, he doesn't fleece you. Besides, I can afford it. [*He adds to the money lying on the table.*]

Scene 2

[*Dubuisson, Marie-Jeanne, and Henri.*]

MARIE-JEANNE [*to Henri, as she enters*]: Yes, yes, everything's going fine here, but if you've come for lunch, it's too early.

HENRI: I can wait. [*He takes a book and sits near the fireplace.*]

DUBUISSON [*aside to Marie-Jeanne*]: So then tell me, neighbor, is that him—the young Count?

MARIE-JEANNE: Yes, that's Monsieur Henri. [*The bell rings.*] Oh, there's someone else ringing the bell. It's the same every day here, a regular public procession. [*She leaves.*]

Scene 3

[*Dubuisson, Henri.*]

DUBUISSON [*aside*]: I'd very much like to go up to him.... But these high-class people, you never know how to handle them! ... Oh, let's take the plunge. Count!

HENRI [*without getting up*]: May I help you, sir?

DUBUISSON: Count de Trégenec doesn't have the honor of knowing me, but ...

HENRI [*smiling*]: No indeed, sir; I don't believe I have that honor at all.

DUBUISSON: What I meant to say was ... never mind; I'm Dubuisson the banker.

HENRI [*shaking hands with him and offering him a chair*]: Sir ... [*Aside.*] I thought he was a bailiff. [*Aloud.*] You must excuse me, Monsieur Dubuisson, for not shaking hands right away with my own neighbor, but I spend so little time in the country ... and you've only just settled here yourself, if I'm not mistaken?

DUBUISSON [*sitting*]: Only two years, that's all, and I know you're living in Paris. My wife spends every winter there.

HENRI: I know; I've heard about the balls she gives.

DUBUISSON: Yes, she's trying to marry our daughter into society; my wife, she's a kid from the country too, just like me!

HENRI: I hear she's rather keen on titles.

DUBUISSON: Yes, she enjoys that sort of thing.

HENRI: Just a minute ... I heard some talk of a marriage between your daughter and a Portuguese nobleman, a Duke de Belver.

DUBUISSON [*laughing derisively*]: One of your friends?

HENRI: Not at all; quite the reverse!

DUBUISSON: Yes, I know.

HENRI: Oh?

DUBUISSON: Yes, yes, this man, all he's got is his name, his title and his debts, and he's after my daughter. . . .

HENRI: Oh but excuse me, he's also got his ugliness and his age! Those are considerable assets!

DUBUISSON [*laughing*]: Yes—one eye missing, and assets amounting to fifty or sixty years of age. [*Aside.*] Nice guy; he's a funny fellow, he is. [*Aloud.*] And along with it all, he's wicked as the devil. You can imagine if my daughter is going to have either hide or hair of him!

HENRI [*teasingly*]: If your daughter happens to take after you . . .

DUBUISSON: She's a lovely little thing, she is. Now me, I'm plain ugly—ugly as the Duke.

HENRI: Well now, but isn't the Duke in this neighborhood too? He's hunting hereabouts, they tell me?

DUBUISSON: Yes, that's just an excuse for wheedling his way into our place; but he's wasting his time. So happens he's mentioned you to us, though.

HENRI: He's said something bad about me, no doubt?

DUBUISSON: No, but I know he's thought it. Why, he's old, he's poor, he's nasty. . . . But he did have a nice girlfriend, and you snitched her away from him. . . .

HENRI [*rising*]: Not so loud, please, sir!

DUBUISSON [*also rising*]: Oh, of course; there's the young lady of the house here. . . . So Mademoiselle Françoise, you've been making up to her too? You seem to be something of a ladykiller.

HENRI: No, sir; I have the utmost respect and friendship for Mademoiselle Françoise, and incidents from my frivolous past mustn't profane her ears. As for the Duke's girlfriend, I can't even remember her name, and I'm sure he has no reason to miss her.

DUBUISSON: Still, he *is* kind of bitter; he says you did some silly things on account of that young lady . . . and a few other young ladies! Which means that you've got into a bit of difficulty here and there. . . . So then, you're wanting to sell your lands at Luzy, which are slap-bang next door to mine, and I wouldn't mind striking a deal on it, assuming your terms are reasonable.

HENRI [*aside*]: Aha! that's what it is. [*Aloud.*] The Duke has been talking in ignorance, Monsieur Dubuisson; I haven't expressed my intentions to anybody, but I do thank you for the offer you've been so kind as to make. [*He goes upstage.*]

DUBUISSON: My apologies! I thought you needed . . . Er . . . pardon?

HENRI [*picking up a magazine*]: I didn't say anything, sir.

DUBUISSON: Sorry, I just thought . . . It's just that, if you did want to get rid of Luzy . . . seeing how it's right in the middle of my property . . . it's up against the suburbs at one end, and I did have the idea of making a road, an avenue, from my house in town all the way to my château.

HENRI: And I'm obstructing you? . . . I'm very sorry about it, but . . .

DUBUISSON: Still, that isn't your last word; you'll think it over! Better to sell outright than find yourself forced out.

HENRI: Forced out?

DUBUISSON: Sure; could happen to anyone! Any time I can be of service to you, Count; see you later!

HENRI: Good-bye, sir! [*Dubuisson goes out to the left.*]

Scene 4

[Henri; later, Marie-Jeanne.]

HENRI: "See you later"—with that look and that wily-peasant smile—sounds like a threat . . . or at the very least, a prediction. . . . Ah well! It's high time to put an end to this stupid business of throwing away my money, my youth . . . maybe my soul! [*Seeing Marie-Jeanne, who has just entered.*] Marie-Jeanne, is Françoise up yet? No answer? Why the high-and-mighty airs? What's wrong this morning? Don't you like me any more?

MARIE-JEANNE: Oh yes, but you're coming here too often.

HENRI: You don't know what you're talking about.

MARIE-JEANNE [*annoyed*]: Thanks a lot, sir.

HENRI [*giving her a kiss*]: You're upset? Good morning, Marie-Jeanne!

MARIE-JEANNE: Naughty boy! Stealing a kiss from me—me, at his age!

HENRI [*laughing*]: Yes indeed, I do allow myself that act of larceny! Aren't you my nurse, my old friend, almost my mother? Have I ever had a mother, apart from you? I can't think of any; I never knew my real mother.

MARIE-JEANNE [*aside*]: How can you be cross at him? He's too lovable! If only he knew how to love back!

HENRI: So Françoise hasn't come down yet?

MARIE-JEANNE: No, Françoise isn't seeing anyone when her father is out.

HENRI: Very sensible of her; but I am not just anyone. I bet she's in there! [*He goes to the doctor's consulting room and returns.*] No! Who's this man?

Scene 5

[*As above; La Hyonnais, holding a magazine, comes out of the consulting room and sits upstage, near the door, without seeming to notice Henri.*]

MARIE-JEANNE [*to Henri*]: He's a gentleman that wants to consult the doctor about his health; he's been waiting in the consulting room.

HENRI: Why is he coming out of it? [*Looking offstage.*] Oh! It's because Françoise has just gone in there.

MARIE-JEANNE: He's a man that knows how to behave. He's setting you a good example; stick to it.

HENRI: He's watching her, though! He's looking at her all the time over the top of his magazine.

MARIE-JEANNE: Why should you care? . . . He's a patient!

HENRI: He looks about as sick as I am, that lad. Wait a minute, I know that face; where on earth have I seen him before? Oh yes—in Brittany. . . . What's he doing here?

MARIE-JEANNE: Well, go and talk to him, if you know him; it'll help him pass the time. He's been here so long. . . . He's looking at you too.

HENRI: And yet, as you can see, he isn't uttering a word to me. Let's see if he'll say hello to me. [*He takes a few steps upstage. La Hyonnais watches him and doesn't move.—Ironically.*] If you're sick, sir, that draught won't do you any good; you shouldn't stay in front of the door. [*La Hyonnais smiles, nods slightly, and doesn't move.—To Marie-Jeanne.*] Don't you think the fellow is being a bit impertinent?

MARIE-JEANNE: Well, so are you, I fancy.

HENRI: He seems to be defying me, and I know my father hates his very name. . . . These country political feuds . . . Well, I don't care . . . but I'd very much like to seize the opportunity, and tell him I'm sick of the very sight of him. . . . What a pity I'm not.

Scene 6

[*As above; the Doctor.*]

DOCTOR [*to Marie-Jeanne, who has gone up to him, and is telling him about La Hyonnais*]: Good, good! [*To La Hyonnais.*] Excuse me, sir; I'm late; it's the fashion here in Berry! [*He puts down his hat, his walking stick, and various papers.*] I'll be right with you. [*To Henri.*] Ah! there you are, my boy! Good morning. [*He shakes his hand.—To Marie-Jeanne.*] And my daughter?

HENRI [*indicating the consulting room*]: She's in there, tidying your books, but this dragon of a Marie-Jeanne won't let me say hello to her.

DOCTOR: I, however, *will* let you—aren't you brother and sister? After all, she's of age; her old nurserymaid is simply in the habit of treating her like a little girl at boarding school.

MARIE-JEANNE [*aside to the doctor*]: Only because of what people might say!

DOCTOR: Very sensible of you, too. Off you go, now. [*Marie-Jeanne follows Henri into the consulting room.*]

Scene 7

[*The Doctor, La Hyonnais.*]

DOCTOR: Now, sir, if you'd like to come into my room. . . .

LA HYONNAIS: No point in inconveniencing you, Doctor; I'm not sick. I merely want to talk about the fellow who was here a moment ago, Monsieur Henri de Trégenec.

DOCTOR: Ah! You know him?

LA HYONNAIS: Only by sight; but I'd like to know him better, and that's why I've come to you.

DOCTOR: Let's sit down, sir; I've been running around all morning! [*They sit at the table.*] Now, what's it about, and to whom do I have the privilege of speaking?

LA HYONNAIS: Jacques Mahé, Baron de La Hyonnais, country nobility, money enough; an unremarkable life, but a harmless one.

DOCTOR: Very good, sir! And so?

LA HYONNAIS: Sir, you're an intelligent man, and a good man. I know that because I've read a book on science and philosophy which ought to be the legal and moral guide for everyone of your profession.

DOCTOR: The only merits of my book are its honesty and simplicity. Are you involved in medicine . . . as an amateur?

LA HYONNAIS: I'm a student; I hope to get my degree this year.

DOCTOR: Oh! In spite of being a nobleman?

LA HYONNAIS: Because of being a nobleman, and even a kind of local lord of the manor. I thought I needed to make myself useful, and practice—not for money, since I have an inheritance of my own. But I'm not here to talk about myself. Let me say something about you, and you can tell me whether I'm well informed. Twenty years ago, at the request of his dying wife, the Marquis de Trégenec handed over to you his only son, Henri—who had been brought up out of his sight, on one of his farms.

DOCTOR: Yes, sir; my wife had been at convent with Madame de Trégenec, in Paris, and both of them died young. But I was fond of Henri, so I continued to look after him, and I had him brought up here.

LA HYONNAIS: You took an interest in him because of his misfortunes—his father couldn't stand him, his uncles didn't want to know of him; a sort of mysterious curse . . .

DOCTOR: That, sir, I know nothing about, and even if I did . . .

LA HYONNAIS: You wouldn't say it to the first person who came along, but perhaps I may be able to gain your confidence. It's possible, Doctor, that I could be Henri de Trégenec's brother.

DOCTOR: You? What makes you say that?

LA HYONNAIS: Oh, I'm the son of Monsieur de La Hyonnais right enough; but it isn't certain that Henri is the son of the man whose name he bears. I can't say anything definite, but six months ago, when my father was on his deathbed—and he was a kindhearted man; he was the best friend I ever had—he said to me, "Jacques, I've done my duty by your mother, I don't have any reason to blame myself there, but before I knew her, I was in love with a girl who was too rich for me. She married the Marquis de Trégenec, and after that, I saw her only once— to say good-bye to her forever. But that one visit, and the knowledge of our old romance, made the Marquis deadly jealous. Madame de Trégenec died of sorrow, and her son Henri seems to have been quietly disowned—he's been brought up with strangers, far away from his father's home. I didn't want to see him—that would only have supported people's suspicions; but I had a letter from his dying mother, putting him under my protection, and I did promise, in my heart, that I would never leave him in trouble—since he was the son of a woman who was always dear to me. I've always tried to look after him from a distance. Now, if you care anything for me, it's your turn." My father wasn't able to tell me any more. I promised . . . he gave me his blessing . . . he passed away, and I've come to keep my word.

DOCTOR [*giving him his hand*]: Monsieur de La Hyonnais, you're a fine young man! I wish I could feel that Henri is worthy of such devotion. I can't hide from you that his character is attractive rather than substantial. He's exuberant, he's flighty, hot one minute and cold the next, easily swept away by either truth or falsehood; but a serious friend like you could do him a lot of good.

LA HYONNAIS: And his position in life?

DOCTOR: Needn't concern you. He has his mother's inheritance— the Marquis put it in real estate, in our neighborhood. And anyway, he's the fellow's heir, his right to his name can't be challenged; the law will protect him on that point.

LA HYONNAIS: You know, sir, that the law can always be evaded. I understand, too, that Henri has some debts, that he has recently decided to get married, and that he has written to the Marquis to find out how he intends to provide for him. He should be getting a reply fairly soon, and that's why I've come to see you now; the reply could strike a serious blow at his plans and his prospects, and I want to prevent that.

DOCTOR: [*They both rise.*] Get married! He hasn't said a word about it to me. . . . And I did think I was in his confidence! As for his debts—I'm not sure whether they are very serious. . . .

LA HYONNAIS: Henri doesn't know anything about his mother's troubles; do you think I could spend the day at Bourges and get to know him, without surprising him too much?

DOCTOR: Nothing simpler. Let's see . . . you're on your way to Vichy[1]. . . .

LA HYONNAIS: Fine!

DOCTOR: And you've stopped here to consult me; a colleague has referred you to me.

LA HYONNAIS: What's my illness?

DOCTOR: Anything at all. . . . Migraine—doesn't everyone have headaches?

LA HYONNAIS: Not me; I wouldn't know what they are. I'm as fit as a fiddle.

DOCTOR: How about a nice dose of rheumatism then?

LA HYONNAIS: Worse still. But I'll come down with anything you like.

DOCTOR: Migraine it is, then! So then, I've got hold of you, you're my patient; you have a chat with Henri, and you'll take a liking to him, no doubt. You'll have lunch with us. . . .

LA HYONNAIS: Could I at least eat? I'm as hungry as a hunter. I could eat the hunter's horse, too.

DOCTOR [*laughing*]: We'll make that a symptom of your illness! All right, I'll find Henri and tell him the tale as briefly as I can—and I'll tell my daughter the same thing. [*He goes into the consulting room.*]

Scene 8

LA HYONNAIS [*alone*]: His daughter! . . . I thought she was the one Henri was wanting to marry. Lovely girl; talented and plenty of good qualities too, so they say. The Doctor must be fairly well-to-do; calm, healthy life—it's in the air all around you. The young fellow seems to have everything going for him—unless the world has led him too far astray.

Scene 9

[*The Doctor, Henri, La Hyonnais.*]

DOCTOR [*aside to Henri*]: Because he's asking to see you.

HENRI: Very well!

LA HYONNAIS [*to Henri*]: Monsieur de Trégenec, chance has thrown us together; so then, let me introduce myself. Our families aren't exactly in contact, even though we don't live far apart, in Brittany. Differences of opinion. . . .

HENRI: I know that, sir; my father hasn't altogether kept up with the times, but I don't go along with all his ideas. Some of my friends know you, and have a good opinion of you, and if you think of me the same way—I'm virtually unknown in Brittany. . . .

LA HYONNAIS: I have a high opinion of anyone who has been brought up by Doctor Laurent.

HENRI [*blithely*]: Oh, he's brought me up very badly! You think he knows anything about raising children? Not at all! He adores them, he pampers them, he plays games and tries to teach them, he puts up with all their frailties, he pardons all their stupidities! . . . That's why I'm an ignoramus, an idiot, an absolute spoiled brat—when I'm here; elsewhere I do behave better. I'm happy to be just another of the world's insignificant idlers. [*He goes in front of the Doctor, who is arranging some papers on the table.*]

DOCTOR: Oh, that's quite possible; and if so, I wash my hands of it. But if he isn't kind at heart even so, he's a consummate hypocrite—because I do believe [*meaningfully*] he's genuinely devoted to us. . . .

HENRI [*warmly; he has sat near the table*]: Oh, absolutely! I'm quite genuine in that respect; it's the one serious thing in my life!

DOCTOR [*aside to La Hyonnais*]: See how delightfully frank he is?

LA HYONNAIS [*likewise*]: Yes indeed; he's a delightful fellow; kindhearted too, it seems.

DOCTOR [*aloud*]: As for his education, well, I've never been able to make a scholar of him; but . . .

HENRI [*rising*]: Oh, that's right; why not say it! I've learned hardly anything—and I've remembered even less. But that's Françoise's fault.

DOCTOR: Nonsense! In what way? . . .

HENRI: She learned everything instead. When I saw she was managing it so well, why, I left her to do all the memory work; so that . . .

DOCTOR: Let's not exaggerate; Françoise is a good girl, an excellent girl. . . .

Scene 10

[*Henri, the Doctor, Françoise, La Hyonnais.*]

FRANÇOISE: Ah! you're talking about Françoise; I heard my name. So what evils have you been saying about me, you ungrateful creatures, while I've been seeing to your lunch out of the sheer goodness of my heart? [*Seeing La Hyonnais; a little abashed.*] Oh, excuse me, sir; I thought you were . . . I . . . [*Gaily and naturally.*] I make too much noise, don't I? and it must be bothering you. While you're waiting for my father to cure you, why don't you keep me quiet?

LA HYONNAIS: I think I'm getting better already, Mademoiselle, because I do have my hopes. [*Aside.*] Nice voice; and looks as honest as sunlight.

HENRI: You want to know what we were saying about you, Françoise? Well, your father was saying—in a terribly smug tone of voice—"She's a good girl!"

FRANÇOISE: Oh, certainly, it's hard to be good in his presence.

HENRI: To which I was going to add, she knows five or six languages. . . .

FRANÇOISE: I don't know anything of the kind.

HENRI: She does embroidery like a fairy. . . .

FRANÇOISE: Fairies don't do embroidery.

HENRI: She plays the organ like Saint Cecilia[2]. . . .

FRANÇOISE [*ironically*]: At the very least!

HENRI: She reads serious books. . . .

FRANÇOISE: There isn't any other sort here.

HENRI: She laughs like a child. . . . Putting it in a nutshell, she's an exceptional woman. And—most remarkably—she's also the best and most uncomplicated woman in the world.

LA HYONNAIS [*aside*]: Aha! She *is* the one he's in love with; she's the one he's going to marry. And no wonder! [*He talks with the Doctor.*]

HENRI [*to Françoise*]: So, you're not on speaking terms with me any more?

FRANÇOISE: No; if you're going to start treating me as an exceptional woman, I'm most annoyed. I suppose I have blue spectacles and black fingernails.

HENRI: You have adorable eyes and pink fingernails. You're an angel of beauty, tenderness, modesty, and devotion. In fact, I don't know why you're so perfect; it's offensive; it's enough to drive one to despair.

FRANÇOISE: So much the better—if that's what you think.

DOCTOR: Good. Is dinner ready for us, Françoise? Here's Monsieur de La Hyonnais; he . . . [*To La Hyonnais, with a smile.*] Do you have any appetite, sir?

LA HYONNAIS: Well, yes . . . just a little!

FRANÇOISE: I think everything is ready.

DOCTOR: You've had lunch already, Françoise; but you will keep us company, won't you?

FRANÇOISE: Yes, certainly; I'll wait on you hand and foot, unless Cléonice arrives too early.

HENRI: Clé . . . What kind of name is that?[3]

DOCTOR: She's the Dubuisson girl.

FRANÇOISE: It isn't her fault if her mother gave her a name like that; she's very nice.

MARIE-JEANNE [*coming in through the door at right*]: Lunch is served.

DOCTOR [*to La Hyonnais*]: Come on! [*They go out to the right.*]

MARIE-JEANNE [*to Françoise*]: And there's the Dubuisson carriage stopping at the door now. [*She follows the Doctor.*]

HENRI [*to Françoise*]: What a horrible creature your young lady is, to rob us of you like this!

FRANÇOISE: It's her first visit this year; I can't possibly avoid it. . . .

HENRI: Get rid of her quickly!

FRANÇOISE: As soon as I can. [*Henri kisses her hand and leaves; Françoise gazes after him. Cléonice enters through the door to the left; Françoise starts as if woken out of a dream.*]

Scene 11

[*Cléonice, Françoise.*]

CLÉONICE [*very stylish—too much so, for a young lady*]: Well, here I am at last! Give us a kiss, darling!

FRANÇOISE [*kissing her on the forehead*]: I shan't ask how things are; you've come back looking so pretty, so smart. . . .

CLÉONICE: Well, what about you? One does one's utmost, and one still doesn't amount to anything alongside you. Your outfit is so ravishing, and yet it's all so simple. How do you manage not to look like a country girl?

FRANÇOISE: Oh, it must be the sheer excellence of my taste, I imagine. How is your mother? [*She offers her a chair at right, and they sit.*]

CLÉONICE: Very well; she's gone on a visit to a great assortment of lawyers' wives. She wanted to drag me along with her. Just what I'd like!

FRANÇOISE: You're still being naughty then, you little imp? You're still a rebel?

CLÉONICE: Against Mummy? Oh, that's nothing. I'm much naughtier with Daddy. Mummy may be a chatterbox, but at least she's fun and enjoys life, whereas Daddy . . . Daddy, well, you see, darling, he's misery personified, he's a grouse, an eternal foe. . . . I mean, he's an absolute rainy day, Daddy is; what more can I say?

FRANÇOISE: And yet these detestable parents do keep spoiling you and loving you.

CLÉONICE: Yes—while they're waiting to offer me up as a sacrifice. Good heavens, when social climbers start picking up the bad habits of the aristocracy . . .

FRANÇOISE: What, are you still at it? . . . Are you going to the bad, young lady? You'll have to stop misbehaving yourself, you know.

CLÉONICE: No, darling, I really am going to the dogs. Can you imagine it, Mummy is mad keen to turn me into Lady Somebody-or-other. I have to be married off to a title—an idiot who happens to be a count or baron, or a one-eyed man who happens to be a duke or a prince . . . in cloud-cuckoo land!

FRANÇOISE: Duke de Belver, perhaps?

CLÉONICE: You said it—porcelain eye and everything!

FRANÇOISE: Even so, it's the best eye he has; the other one is so nasty!

CLÉONICE: Happily my father is not exactly taken with the good hidalgo; but if I listened to Mummy . . . [*Standing.*] Couldn't you possibly find me a husband with some kind of coat of arms and a reasonably human face to go with it? No, of course not; you don't see anyone at all, hardly. It must be dreadfully boring!

FRANÇOISE: Not at all; I'm quite happy. Do I look like a funeral elegy? [*She rises.*]

CLÉONICE: Nah, you're a sensible creature; it's frightening how sensible you are. Mummy keeps saying all the time, "I don't know why you should take an interest in Mademoiselle Laurent; you don't have anything in common—you're not even the same age." Now, me, I reply that your friendship is a great honor for me—you being such a meritorious person, you know. Then she says, "That's fine if it gives people the impression that you're clever and educated, which you're not exactly!" And then along comes my father and says gloomily, "It isn't for lack of paying tutors and throwing money around!"

FRANÇOISE: Still, Monsieur Dubuisson doesn't act the tyrant; he keeps giving in to you.

CLÉONICE: On the surface, yes; but at heart, never! If you'd only seen him with the poor boy that was in love with me. . . .

FRANÇOISE: Ah! the famous cousin—Monsieur Jules Dubuisson? . . . You're still thinking about him?

CLÉONICE [*with self-parody*]: Alas and alack! Not excessively, I'm afraid.

FRANÇOISE [*laughing*]: It won't be the death of you, then?

CLÉONICE [*as above*]: Who can tell?

FRANÇOISE: But still, if you'd really wanted him . . .

CLÉONICE: Oh, that's true, they would have given in. But what do you really think of him—cousin Jules?

FRANÇOISE: Just what I told you. He's too young, too . . .

CLÉONICE: Too blond? Yes, he is too blond.

FRANÇOISE: And too shortsighted.

CLÉONICE: To make matters worse, he refuses to wear glasses.

FRANÇOISE: That's his vanity.

CLÉONICE: It's funny, the only guys that ever want to marry me are guys that can't see a thing. [*Looking offstage right, towards the dining room.*] Look, who's the gent in there? And the other one? Very presentable, they are. You didn't tell me you had company, Françoise!

FRANÇOISE: One of them is a childhood friend of mine.

CLÉONICE: Oh—the young man that grew up with you! He's a marquis or count of some kind, isn't he? Let's hope Mummy doesn't see him here! She'd have me married off to him on the spot.

FRANÇOISE: Oh, don't worry about that! His father the Marquis would never let it happen . . .

CLÉONICE: Too much of a misalliance? Good for him! But then what about you? I mean, you're better bred than I am, you come from the good old local middle classes; but still, middle-class is all you are, and yet everyone says he's going to marry you.

FRANÇOISE: Henri? That's a fine story!

CLÉONICE: Well, it's high time you settled down; you're all of twenty. . . .

FRANÇOISE: Twenty-four, if you don't mind, little girl; and yet I fancy I still have time to think things over.

CLÉONICE: Unless you've got a secret passion, like me!

FRANÇOISE: Like you? Nothing of the kind!

CLÉONICE: Worse than that, is it?

FRANÇOISE: Will you listen to the little tease! What are you driving at?

CLÉONICE: This young Count . . . Well, he's very handsome; I do congratulate you! Oh, here they are, they're coming in here!

FRANÇOISE: If you don't want to see them, we can go into my room.

CLÉONICE: Not at all! I most certainly do want to see them! And what if it does make you jealous?

FRANÇOISE: Rubbish! You're absolutely crazy!

Scene 12

[As above; the Doctor, Henri, La Hyonnais; later, Madame Dubuisson.]

DOCTOR: Aha! Here's my little patient! Well, well, you're fresh as a daisy; you won't have any more need of me from now on, I trust. And how is Madame Dubuisson?

CLÉONICE: Oh, Mummy is stiflingly healthy.

DOCTOR: Why, here she is now.

MADAME DUBUIOSSON [*the Doctor and Françoise go up to her; Cléonice remains downstage right; Henri and La Hyonnais are talking upstage left*]: Yes, me it is. How you going, Monsieur Laurent? And you, Mam'zelle Françoise? Great, nice to hear it; same with me, thanks. Well now, young lady? . . . Why, you've got company!

DOCTOR [*indicating Henri*]: This young man is one of the family— Monsieur Henri de Trégenec.

MADAME DUBUIOSSON [*overpolite*]: Oh! Count de Trégenec? I've heard so much . . . [*Françoise sits her down*]: Oh, all right . . . [*To the Doctor.*] We've come to see you; we have so much gratitude to thank you for! Our very life is thanks to you! . . .

DOCTOR [*eyeing Cléonice*]: Oh, it wasn't as serious as all that! A slight touch of nerves, that's all.

MADAME DUBUISSON: Forgive me, but when a young lady isn't sleeping at night, it's *always* a serious matter.

CLÉONICE [*pulling at her sleeve*]: Mummy!

HENRI [*aside to Françoise*]: Now there's a lady who isn't at a loss for words!

MADAME DUBUIOSSON [*to the Doctor*]: Well now, I do hope you're going to come and see us a lot in our château? We want to have social company, and we're meaning to cultivate all the right people that's in the neighborhood—you especially, doctor, being so knowledgeable!

DOCTOR: Why, good heavens, what use would my knowledge be to you, ma'am, when you're in such good health?

MADAME DUBUISSON: Oh, knowledgeable people are always of interest to me, personally speaking; they're such an ornamentation to one's society! I like gifted people, and everyone recognizes that you're one . . . [*turning towards Henri*] seeing what kind of pupils you've turned out. . . .

HENRI [*astonished*]: Madame . . .

MADAME DUBUIOSSON [*responding to a significant look from her daughter*]: I'm talking about Mam'zelle Françoise: when you see a young lady so sensible and so well brought up . . . [*Aside to her daughter.*] Your hair's a real mess; you always look like a mad dog! Can't you comb it down? Well now, couldn't Doctor Laurent have done a better job of introducing us to his young man? There, look, he's turning his back on us. [*Henri has gone upstage; he comes downstage left, takes a book, and talks quietly with La Hyonnais.*]

CLÉONICE: But Mummy, he introduced you to him, he greeted us, everything's been done. You're the one that's driving him away with all your compliments.

MADAME DUBUISSON: Me? I never so much as opened my mouth. [*To Françoise.*] He doesn't look terribly impressive, that Count; mind you, I'm told he isn't exactly rolling in money.

DOCTOR: I beg your pardon, but he's very comfortably off.

MADAME DUBUISSON: Fair enough; anyone that thinks they're rich is rich, in my opinion! All depends on how you look at things. . . . But [*raising her voice*] when you're used to a life of luxury . . . I must admit, I'd feel kind of uncomfortable if I didn't have a hundred thousand a year. . . .

DOCTOR: Still, you haven't always had that much. Your husband . . .

MADAME DUBUISSON: My husband, my husband! I was brought up different. I wasn't exactly high society, I admit; but I had the feel for it—I had the taste for it. Yes, that's the truth! Even when I was just a little kid, I used to say to myself, "I must get rich somehow"—and I have!

DOCTOR: You thought it was your due?

MADAME DUBUISSON: Those that know how to spend deserve to be rich, if you ask me.

DOCTOR: In that case, you must be right. Nobody knows that better than you do.

MADAME DUBUIOSSON [*quickly and loudly*]: Now me, I like that kind of thing—nice houses, nice furniture, jewelry, lace, carriages, all the latest things, everything that's in fashion; I have artistic tastes, you see! I like to see that I'm looking nice, and my daughter too. Nothing's too expensive as far as I'm concerned! Everything smiles on me when there's money smiling in my hands. See, I got my old château, and it was pretty classy as it was, but I turned the whole thing upside down till it looked like a royal palace. I don't spare any expenditure; I get in two hundred workmen; there's noise everywhere, dust everywhere, but that's fine with me; it's my money they're shoveling around there! I've got some splendid horses: ten thousand francs each, darling! They're full of devilry, too; just now they started bolting and practically smashed everything up. It didn't worry me, though, I was just laughing; I just said to myself, "That's my money frisking around!" [*Henri goes into the consulting room with La Hyonnais.*] What, they're gone, have they?

DOCTOR: Just being polite. Seeing you were talking about your financial situation. . . .

MADAME DUBUISSON: Oh, I don't make any secret about what I've got! It's only misers and chickens that keep their money hidden! . . . All the same, they're mighty stuck-up, those fine gents of yours. You can't even tell what color their talk is.

DOCTOR: Come now, they would have had to be very skillful to have got a word in!

MADAME DUBUIOSSON [*put out*]: I daresay the Count is more talkative when one isn't around. Honest, I didn't have any idea he was going to be here; if I had, I would never have been so indiscreet. . . . [*They rise.*]

DOCTOR [*a fraction dryly*]: Indiscreet?

MADAME DUBUISSON: Oh, look, I just say whatever I think, I've got the right to do that, haven't I? I've always been thoughtful and careful about things. . . . I'm talking to Françoise. [*She goes forward; Cléonice is now behind the Doctor.*]

FRANÇOISE: Me, Madame?

MADAME DUBUISSON: Yes, love. You're a good girl, a respectable girl, I'm quite sure of it; but still, if you care about your reputation, you don't want to go seeing so much of that young man. It doesn't go down well in town. They're making insulations that he's in love with you and he's trying to marry you. . . . Well, maybe that's right. In which case, get married quick—you're old enough—because people do start talking. . . .

DOCTOR [*upset*]: Idiotically!

MADAME DUBUISSON: I dare say! Just giving you a bit of friendly advice, that's all; you'll be grateful for it in the long run.

DOCTOR: Infinitely!

CLÉONICE [*having put on her hat*]: Come on, Mummy, let's be off now! [*Aside.*] You've upset Doctor Laurent.

MADAME DUBUIOSSON [*aloud*]: Upset? Why? The idea! When I like him so much, and I'm so grateful to him for everything! You wouldn't bear a grudge, would you, Doctor? And you will come to the housewarming at the château? I want to give a party, and I really need to get busy with it. Oh, that reminds me: right next to our grounds there's a little cottage of yours—"La Chanterie" it's called; ain't that right? Well now, you really must sell it to me. I need it—we want to expand, and it suits me perfectly.

DOCTOR: Oh, I'm very sorry, but that little house is my daughter's, and it suits her very well too. [*He goes upstage.*]

MADAME DUBUISSON: But I'll pay her whatever she wants, and you can get another one.

FRANÇOISE: You don't sell memories.

MADAME DUBUISSON: We'll talk about it again! Good-bye, Doctor; see you later! No hard feelings, Françoise darling, hey?

FRANÇOISE [*after Cléonice has kissed her*]: Oh, there's no cause for that! [*She shows them out.*]

Scene 13

[*Françoise, the Doctor; later, Marie-Jeanne.*]

DOCTOR: My word, but there is cause. That woman is ridiculous!

FRANÇOISE: Treat it as a joke, Father. You're all upset!

DOCTOR: Well, yes, I am! What right has the erstwhile barmaid of the "Buisson Fleuri"[4]—just because she's converted her pub sign into a family escutcheon—to set herself up as our fairy godmother and start giving you good advice . . . you of all people!

MARIE-JEANNE [*who has come in, apparently to tidy things up, and has overheard*]: Well, I did tell you: Monsieur Henri has been coming to see us every morning for a week now. . . .

FRANÇOISE: Same as he does every year.

MARIE-JEANNE: No! The other years, he just comes three or four times, and he doesn't stay in the country.

DOCTOR: Marie-Jeanne is right; we don't call her the wisewoman for nothing! We'll have to tell Henri. . . .

FRANÇOISE [*gradually becoming more intense*]: Oh! Do you want to upset him like that? You can't think he's over-happy as he is—he hasn't any real family, he hasn't anyone who cares for him except us. Poor Henri! . . . And we're supposed to break, or loosen, our ties with him . . . after a lifetime of friendship! . . . It's out of the question, father! It's up to you, of course—I'd submit to you in what I do—but not in what I feel or believe; and for the first time in my life, I'd be obeying you against my will!

DOCTOR [*aside*]: So much feeling! . . . [*To Marie-Jeanne.*] Where is he?

MARIE-JEANNE: He's gone out to show the other gentleman around town.

DOCTOR: I'll go and join them.

FRANÇOISE: Goodness! Are you really going to tell him . . . ?

DOCTOR: To come as before; nothing more, nothing less. Why should we rock the boat? Everything was going very smoothly as it was. Come on, stop worrying! There's no reason to make a big fuss about anything. [*He kisses her; Marie-Jeanne brings him his walking stick and hat.—Aside.*] Very odd! [*Aloud.*] Good-bye! [*He leaves.*]

Scene 14

[*Françoise, Marie-Jeanne.*]

FRANÇOISE: So, you naughty creature, you had to go and . . .

MARIE-JEANNE: Oh, who cares! If Henri doesn't see how much harm he could do to you . . . well, he's just plain selfish!

FRANÇOISE: Selfish—Henri!

MARIE-JEANNE: Well, yes, a little bit—he is a bit like that!

FRANÇOISE [*hugging her*]: Go on, you wretched thing! You're the selfish one, expecting our friends to think about us all the time. [*They go upstage towards the consulting room.*]

Act 2

At La Chanterie.—A small rural living room, simple and tasteful; chintz furnishings. Door upstage, leading to a flight of steps. Window at the audience's right. In the corner, a fireplace facing the audience, with the plate-glass of a window blind. Doors downstage left and right. Gloomy weather.

Scene 1

CLÉONICE [*alone; entering furtively, leaving the door open behind her, and going to open the shutters as she speaks*]: Let's see if he's come; I'll open the window to the garden. [*She opens it.*] Nobody yet. This is a fine escapade—having a rendezvous in the doctor's cottage. Luckily he hardly ever comes here, and if Françoise finds me here . . . I'll act as if I'm looking through her music. [*She disarrays a few music scores.*] After all, that's why she gave me her key. All the same, I'm getting terrible palpitations, what with leaving the grounds. . . . But I only needed to hop over the hedge to get here, and anyhow, what's the harm in having a few words from an upstairs window? There's no other way; I just want him to give back . . . To think I was stupid enough to write to him! I mean, it was two years ago, I was just a baby then; goodness, that letter must look silly! But let's see if he's coming. Hope he can find the garden gate—he's so short-sighted! You never should make a rendezvous with shortsighted people! He's a shady customer too, or he would never have made me meet him here, when he could perfectly well have slipped me the letter at home, any time there was nobody looking. I mean, you'd think it was as big as a packing case! Is he trying to get me into trouble, maybe? Nah! He isn't smart enough. Ah, here he is at last. Well, can't he even see the house? He's going away to the pond. . . . Psst! Psst! . . . Is he deaf as well as blind? He's seen me . . . here he comes. [*In a stage whisper.*] Well, here I am; have you brought it? . . . No? He's making signals—wants me to keep quiet; has he got company out in the garden? He's writing something. [*Listening to something backstage.*] Good heavens! Who's coming from there? I'm getting out! [*She runs out the door to the right.*]

Scene 2

HENRI [*alone, entering upstage*]: The doors and windows are open, so
they must be here. But I don't see anyone. Oh! Maybe they're
in the garden! [*He goes to the window.*] Who is that fellow, and
what does he want with me? All those signals! I don't understand
his pantomimings at all. I'll go and say hello to him. [*Muttering.*]
I do have the honor. . . . So he's picking up stones to throw at
me? Is the creature a lunatic? He doesn't look very dangerous,
all the same. [*He jumps out of the way; a pebble wrapped in paper flies
through the window and lands in the middle of the stage. Henri picks
it up.*] Aha! It's something in writing—copperplate, too! Suppose
I send his rock back to him—maybe it's a special favorite of his.
No, he's running away. Well now, what's the game? [*He reads.*]
"You want to take away my only memory—the only evidence of
my happiness and your love. I believe you're going to get married. Well, you won't never have that letter without the life of he
who won't never stoop to avenge himself." There do seem to be
a few double negatives there. [*Turning the paper over.*] No address,
and the signature is "He who"! Well, it isn't for me, obviously.
Why throw it at me? Is it for Françoise then? Surely not; she isn't
here. Good Lord—here she is!

Scene 3

[*Marie-Jeanne, Françoise, Henri.*]

FRANÇOISE [*upstage*]: Oh, it's you, Henri—you've come with my
father, have you? Where is he?

HENRI: I haven't seen him. But first of all, what's this, Françoise?

FRANÇOISE [*glancing through the note*]: I don't know. Where did it
come from?

HENRI [*pointing to the window*]: Out there.

FRANÇOISE: What do you mean, out there? Is this aimed at me? I
can't think of any enemies I've got. Well, Marie-Jeanne, go and
see whose little joke this is. It's highly amusing!

HENRI: No, I'll go myself, if it's all right with you.

FRANÇOISE: It's fine with me.

MARIE-JEANNE: I'll go and you won't. That would be the finishing
touch—to be seen here taking it upon yourself. . . .

HENRI: Don't I have the right to?

MARIE-JEANNE: No indeed not! [*She goes out upstage.*]

FRANÇOISE [*holding Henri back*]: Now then . . . I think I'm beginning to understand. . . . Did you see anyone here, Henri?

HENRI [*pointing to the garden*]: I saw a little fellow out there—not exactly an ugly looking gentleman!

FRANÇOISE: He saw you, did he?

HENRI: Not very well; I'm starting to think he mistook me for a woman.

FRANÇOISE: Short and shortsighted: I know who that is! Give me the note.

HENRI: It's terribly compromising!

FRANÇOISE: That's exactly why I want it. Give it to me.

HENRI [*hesitantly*]: All right, on condition . . .

FRANÇOISE: No conditions. [*He gives her the note.*] Now then, what do you want?

HENRI: Swear to me that it wasn't written to you.

FRANÇOISE [*laughing*]: Oh, all right! I swear it. Why?

HENRI: Thank you, thank you, Françoise!

FRANÇOISE: Why the solemnity?

HENRI: Yes, yes, Françoise darling, I'll tell you. [*He gets her to sit near the table.*]

MARIE-JEANNE [*reentering*]: Nobody at all! I wonder what this is all about.

HENRI: Oh, I don't care any more.

MARIE-JEANNE [*concerned*]: Well, I do. I . . .

HENRI: Well, go and have another look, then. [*Aside to Françoise.*] Françoise, I want to talk with you.

FRANÇOISE: All right, talk.

MARIE-JEANNE: Go on, we're all ears.

HENRI: Yes, but you're in the way.

MARIE-JEANNE: Nonsense! Since when?

HENRI: Since you turned into such an infernal faultfinder!

MARIE-JEANNE: Just a minute! Do you have the master's permission to come here to La Chanterie? Didn't he tell you the day before yesterday. . . ?

HENRI: Yes, but you'll see I have every reason. . . . Françoise [*he sits her down on the left*], I mean to tell your father what I'm going to say to you. . . . You can tell him first. . . . [*He has sat next to her on a cushion.*]

FRANÇOISE: Well then, I'm listening. How excited you are! [*Aside.*]
So am I—but why?

HENRI: Well, Françoise, this is the most serious moment of my life!
I want to settle down—put an end to the silly stupid life I've
been leading for the past five years—I want to get away from
the world. I want to get married, in other words.

FRANÇOISE [*trembling*]: You?

HENRI: Does that surprise you so much?

FRANÇOISE: Yes, because . . . because . . . I don't know. [*She stops short
with a catch in her voice.*]

HENRI [*taking her hands*]: What's wrong, Françoise? You're crying!
[*Marie-Jeanne drops her knitting.*]

FRANÇOISE [*pulling herself together*]: Well, yes; because I'm fond of
you—like a sister, or a mother. And you've told me hundreds
of times that you didn't expect to get married.

HENRI: Well, you've said the same thing!

FRANÇOISE: Yes—but that was different. Anyhow, we're not talking
about me.

HENRI: Yes we are! I need your advice—I need to know what you
really think.

FRANÇOISE: Well then, don't you remember? When you used to ask
me why I wouldn't look at prospective husbands, I told you I
hadn't wasted my feelings on silly sentimental curiosities, I hadn't
played with fire as children do, I'd set up such a lofty idea of
love. . . . But why should we make such a big thing out of something so simple! I've never had any intention of marrying, not
unless I was deeply and genuinely in love. If two human souls
are to be joined together utterly and forever, why, as far as I can
see, it must be either the happiest and most sacred thing in the
world, or the utmost desolation and despair.

HENRI: And I used to reply . . .

FRANÇOISE: Oh you—what you said was this—and not so very long
ago, either, "The only real and lasting thing is the kind of
simple friendship that you and I have for each other. Love is
selfish, demanding, crazy. . . ."

HENRI [*embarrassed*]: Did I say that?

FRANÇOISE: Then you'd say, "It's perfectly obvious, Françoise, that
you don't know what love is, but I've burnt my wings looking
for it, I don't believe in it any more, I don't even want it any
more. . . ."

HENRI: I wasn't telling the truth!

FRANÇOISE [*continuing*]: "All I really want is freedom, and I've put my life into two compartments, permanently: one is for plain honest friendship, the other is for fun and games." It seemed to me you were happy like that, Henri; I thought things were going to stay that way forever. Now you tell me everything is changed. . . . You can see that I've good reason to worry about your future.

HENRI: Darling, there were obstacles between us—serious ones, so I thought. But, listen, I'm free—I wrote to my father a few days ago; I asked to go and tell him about my plans. You know how cold Monsieur de Trégenec has always been towards me. He's never done a single thing for me; it's never been necessary up till now; but now the time has come, now he needs to think about my future. What he replied, just this morning, was that your father can make the decisions and tell me where I stand; he's leaving everything in his hands. That's why I've come back to Bourges. I was going past here, I saw the door open, I thought you were working here, and here I am—here I am at your feet, Françoise, and I'm telling you that you're the one I want to marry, unless I've just imagined that I'm the only thing you really care about!

FRANÇOISE: Me?

MARIE-JEANNE [*going towards him*]: Really? Do you really mean that?

FRANÇOISE [*getting to her feet, bewildered*]: Goodness, are you in love with me—you? [*Dropping down again.*] No, it's just a daydream! You're not thinking about what you're saying, it isn't so—it's impossible!

HENRI: Oh—don't you believe me, then? You think you know me, but you don't know me really! I always pretended to be light-hearted with you . . . as though I didn't really care . . . and you believed it. But I've been in love with you since . . .

FRANÇOISE [*attentive and trembling*]: Since when?

MARIE-JEANNE: Yes, since when?

HENRI: Since always! I think I was born that way. I know you were fourteen, fifteen when your father separated us; later I saw you again. . . . I was leaving. . . .

FRANÇOISE [*still attentive and worried*]: Yes, you cried a lot; but you were glad to go all the same; you were curious, you were keen to have your freedom!

HENRI: Well, yes, that's the truth—I was laughing and crying at the same time. I was going to see my father and my home country, and I didn't know them at all. I had such a sorry reception too—I was turned away so quickly! I thought I'd come back to Luzy again and live near you. . . .

FRANÇOISE: Instead of which, you stayed in Paris for two whole years without ever thinking about us—almost without ever writing to us.

HENRI: Well, what do you expect—I was so young, I was left to my own devices; but I tired soon enough of living for pleasure, and that brought me back to you. And I felt then that you were the only one who could make me happy.

FRANÇOISE: And yet, after a very short time—you left us again. . . .

HENRI: Françoise, all these interrogations—they're chilling, they're terrible; anyone would think you were trying to deny that I love you!

FRANÇOISE: No; but I know what you're like: you're impressionable, changeable. . . . All my life I've been worrying about the things that made you unhappy.

HENRI: And now that I'm asking you to make me happy, you start worrying about yourself!

MARIE-JEANNE: Sure!

FRANÇOISE: Myself? . . . Oh no, I'm not thinking about myself! . . . Poor Henri! My friendship has always been good for you, up till now, but suppose it changed in a way that you didn't want. . . .

HENRI: Why should it change? You're so kind to your friends. . . .

FRANÇOISE: And I'd put my trust in a man I loved: I'm going to show you that. [*She goes and says a word or two to Marie-Jeanne, who goes out to the left.*] Listen, it isn't that you have any prejudices, but you do indulge in a few romantic fantasies—and when you make a promise, you make it with all the pride of a nobleman from Brittany . . . not that I mind, even if I am middle-class through and through. Well now, I want to know if the "yes" that you'd say at the altar on your wedding day would be a Christian's "yes," a gentleman's, or a man of the world's.

HENRI: How do I know? It'd be the promise of the man who loves you.

FRANÇOISE: All right, Henri, I'll believe your promise; all I ask is, think carefully before you make it. I won't make any promises myself. That would commit you to keep your word, and I want you to be still able to change your mind. Think about it for a few days, and then talk to me about it again. I'm very much afraid you're deceiving yourself . . . and I would be so unhappy if you ever regretted it! . . . I care for you so deeply, so . . . [*Aside.*] I really must go, or else he'll see that I'm out of my wits.

HENRI: Why do you think . . . ? Why, where are you going, Françoise? You're not leaving me like this?

FRANÇOISE [*Marie-Jeanne has just whispered something to her*]: My father wants me for a moment. [*She goes out to the left.*]

Scene 4

[*Marie-Jeanne, Henri.*]

HENRI: Her father! . . . You look worried, Marie-Jeanne. Let's see, who is it?

MARIE-JEANNE: You heard: it's the Doctor.

HENRI [*looking backstage*]: Oh! And he isn't alone.

Scene 5

[*Henri, La Hyonnais.*]

HENRI: You're back from Vichy already, sir? That treatment didn't take long. [*Exit Marie-Jeanne.*]

LA HYONNAIS: What kind of reception is this?

HENRI: Monsieur de La Hyonnais, how long have you known the Doctor?

LA HYONNAIS: As long as I've known you.

HENRI: And . . . his daughter?

LA HYONNAIS: Same time: two days.

HENRI: Word of honor?

LA HYONNAIS: Yes, sir, word of honor. . . . Now, tell me, why are you so suspicious?

HENRI: Suspicious! No, I like the look of you; I do feel I can trust you. I don't know why, but the day before yesterday—it was the first time I'd ever spoken to you in my life, and yet I opened up as if we'd been friends for twenty years.

LA HYONNAIS: You told me that you were in love with Mademoiselle Laurent; and I approved of your choice. She seems intelligent and kindhearted, as well as pretty.

HENRI: Well, your admiration for her went to my head.

LA HYONNAIS [*surprised*]: Went to your head?

HENRI: I mean it lifted my spirits. Naturally it did! I told you, I have two personalities inside me: one is all kindness and self-surrender, the other is all mistrust and self-assertion. Heaven and Doctor Laurent's education created the first, experience and reflection created the second. I've been so happy and spoiled and loved here! This little cottage is where I spent the most peaceful years of my life, this is where I dreamed my dreams, and when I think about it, even now, I dream them again. But the world is practical, and I've lived in the world. Françoise was my dream, reality was my waking life; and now . . .

LA HYONNAIS: Now?

HENRI: Now I'm in a position to act, and I've spoken out. . . . But instead of the delirious happiness I was expecting—because I did think I was loved, loved ardently—

MARIE-JEANNE [*bringing some flowers, which she puts into the vases*]: Oh you're a real prize idiot, you are, and no mistake!

HENRI [*losing his temper*]: Leave me alone, won't you! Look, you were part of my dream of happiness too—your kindness, your cheeriness—and for the last few days, you've been nothing but a nuisance.

MARIE-JEANNE: All right, I'm off, sir.

HENRI: No! [*She leaves.*] All right then; go to the devil! You've been spoiling my fairytale.—Well, La Hyonnais, what would you do in my place? [*He sits on the sofa at right.*]

LA HYONNAIS: I'd overcome the one of my two personalities that wasn't honest and right; I'd cultivate the one that was wise and rational.

HENRI: Oh, yes, you're a moral man, a philosopher!

LA HYONNAIS: That's very kind of you, but perhaps I'm merely an egoist who makes a better job of it than you do. Look, Henri, you're too good for this frivolous environment that you call the practical world. You're chasing illusions there. Can anything be more deceptive, or more transient, than money and the advantages it tempts us with? It's like the red and black of gambling houses: you look for systems, you devise martingales, you dream all the time of breaking the bank, and after thousands of agonizing emotions that are unworthy of a responsible man, what you break is yourself; you discover that chance can't be controlled by human forethought. Believe me, if any plan isn't based on the fundamentals of true happiness—I mean the appreciation of moral truths, love of your family, your own people, honor, and humanity—it's false, it's just a retreat into daydreams and fantasies. Nothing is under our control in our struggle with destiny; nothing is guaranteed. If we trust to the mercy of events for money, success, fame, peace, or freedom— that's childish, blind, fanciful. But if we find peace in our own conscience, independence in our own dignity, comfort in our own work, love in our own heart—which is the temple of every-day religion—that's definite, real, and practical. Can any amount of bad luck take it away from us? God himself encourages it, and he blesses it in our lives. That isn't chance; it's Providence.

HENRI [*to himself*]: Yes . . . possibly.

LA HYONNAIS [*aside*]: He's thinking it over. . . . Well, may his better spirit win! [*Enter the Doctor.*]

Scene 6

[*The Doctor, La Hyonnais, Henri.*]

DOCTOR: Ah, there you are! [*Henri remains deep in thought on the sofa.*]

LA HYONNAIS: You seem very upset. . . .

DOCTOR: I have a problem. . . .

LA HYONNAIS: A problem?

DOCTOR: Because of him. . . . His father . . . the Marquis has writ-ten to me.

LA HYONNAIS: And?

DOCTOR: I know the truth. Henri is going to be robbed of every-thing.

LA HYONNAIS: That's what I expected.

DOCTOR: How can I tell him? . . .

LA HYONNAIS: You'd be casting doubt on his mother's good name. . . .

DOCTOR: It's out of the question!

LA HYONNAIS: You have to keep him in the dark.

DOCTOR: Yes. Go and wait for me down there; I'll see you in a moment. [*La Hyonnais goes out upstage.—To Henri:*] Well, you look awfully worried.

HENRI [*coming out of his reverie*]: Doctor, I have so many things to tell you and ask you!

DOCTOR: I know what you want to say. . . . Françoise has just told me about it.

HENRI [*agitated*]: And what decision is she making? What decision are you making?

DOCTOR: Nothing as yet. I have to talk to you about your father the Marquis. . . .

HENRI: Yes, that's right. He's written to you? Let's have a look at his letter.

DOCTOR: No, there's no point; it's so callous. . . .

HENRI: Oh, I'm used to that, I don't care!

DOCTOR: I don't have it on me, but I can remember it all . . . [*aside*] as much as I can mention! [*Aloud.*] On two points it's very clear.

HENRI: The first being?

DOCTOR: "I have a great deal of respect for you, Doctor, and your daughter. Monsieur Henri is free to choose for himself."

HENRI: Laconic, isn't he? He's the same with me. And the second point?

DOCTOR: I'll tell you in a moment. First, though, you have to tell me how things stand with you.

HENRI: I thought the main thing, as far as you were concerned . . .

DOCTOR: The main thing, as far as I'm concerned, is your past and future conduct. Have you touched your mother's inheritance?

HENRI: Yes, a bit.

DOCTOR: A bit, or a lot?

HENRI: A lot.

DOCTOR: And how are you living at the moment?

HENRI: I'm living as I always do. I've done what every son and heir does—I've mortgaged my property. I'll have a very large fortune coming to me, being an only son. My creditors know I'm a gentleman, and they've treated me royally. I'll pay back the capital and the interest together; till then, I can live without any hardship or difficulty.

DOCTOR: That's the very way to ruin yourself.

HENRI: No; it's the only way to live, when your parents are too strict. They don't want you to enjoy yourself until you're too old to enjoy anything! So, you have to even it up: you have to bank on the future. It's only natural.

DOCTOR: In other words, you rob your future children of the comforts you never had yourself, so that they'll curse you just as you cursed your own parents. A fine system that is! [*He sits at left of the table.*]

HENRI: That's the way the world runs, I didn't invent it.

DOCTOR: Since you simply go along with it, you wouldn't have arranged it any better.

HENRI: Is my father refusing me the means to get started in life, then? I can't believe it!

DOCTOR: You'd better believe it, because that's how it is.

HENRI: What—nothing? Absolutely nothing?

DOCTOR: Nothing. And you yourself know how stubborn he is.

HENRI: Only too well! Well then, after he's gone . . . ?

DOCTOR [*aside*]: Here's the hard part. [*Aloud.*] After he's gone . . . you can't hope for things to be any better. He . . . he's got his debts too.

HENRI: Nonsense! Who told you that?

DOCTOR: He did. He's been speculating on the stock market. He's in debt for everything he's got; he's demonstrated it to me; it's plain, it's clear, it's a fait accompli.

HENRI [*with a forced smile*]: Really? I wouldn't have thought my good father had so much youth in him. [*He breaks a paper knife.— He is sitting at the edge of the table, facing the Doctor.*]

DOCTOR: You're very tense and pale! Look, let's have the truth: how much do you owe?

HENRI: Everything I have!

DOCTOR: You'll have to sell Luzy and clear your debts. Otherwise the interest will snowball, and the first thing you know, you'll find yourself bankrupt.

HENRI: Yes, that's what I'll do . . . and I'll go to California. . . . That's nice enough . . . it's fun. . . .

DOCTOR: And it's dubious, especially for someone like you, who hasn't the stamina for great adventures. So you're in debt for more than you have?

HENRI: Yes.

DOCTOR: How much more?

HENRI: A hundred thousand francs, maybe.

DOCTOR [*rising*]: Great heavens! . . . Very well; I'll lend it to you, without interest. [*Henri makes a gesture of refusal.*] You can pay it back to me. You've had enough education to take on a career. We'll look together; I'll help you find something. Work is the real cure for young people's mistakes, and when you've tried it, you'll see that in some respects misfortune can be a good thing!

HENRI: Yes indeed, when I've worked ten years . . . twenty years . . . when I've painfully managed to get together enough to buy back my honor, I'll find myself getting old with no security, no reward, no family. Everything seems to be crashing down on me at once. I was going to ask to be your son-in-law; I thought I was bringing you a certain degree of honor at present and a large amount of money in the future. . . . But I'm going away in utter disgrace!

DOCTOR: No; nothing of the kind. You're staying with me, I'm looking after you.

HENRI: You're forgetting that you've just about driven me away. Françoise's reputation . . .

DOCTOR: Françoise loves you as a brother; be worthy for her to love you still better. That doesn't require ten years. I'm not going to wait till my money comes back before I call you my son-in-law; all I need is to see you settled in a job for . . . let's see . . . say a year—and then hear you say that you're prepared to keep going. Then I'll have confidence in you. So, settle down, don't be so reckless, and turn over a new leaf. Think it over for fifteen minutes; I'll come back with Françoise, and if she tells you to wait and prove your merit . . . well then, my boy, you won't have too much cause to complain about things!

HENRI: Oh, Doctor, you're so kind. . . .

DOCTOR: Not a word—I know what you're like; you never talk sense when you're in trouble! . . . Wait here for me. [*He leaves to the left.*]

Scene 7

[*Henri; later, Cléonice.*]

HENRI: A fine man! But being pitied—it's a horrible thing. People are going to say, people are going to think I'm after Françoise's money to cover my losses. She might think so herself, when she sees that I have neither the courage of a hero nor the moral fibre of a saint! But are things really so desperate? My father couldn't be altogether ruined, could he? I'll go to Brittany— yes; he won't give me a warm welcome, but I'll ride out his bad temper and discover what lies in store for me. That's the thing to do—and quickly, before I see Françoise again. . . . He's given me fifteen minutes. Let's leave him a word or two—that'll save painful explanations—some reason to postpone any decision. . . . That's it. [*He sits on the sofa and writes.*]

CLÉONICE [*entering on tiptoe*]: They're all here; I can come back and make sure nobody noticed anything. [*Seeing Henri.*] Ah, there's the young Count; let's find out whether he saw my stupid cousin run away. [*She coughs.—Henri rises.*] Don't let me disturb you, sir; you're busy; I'm here to see Françoise. Is that the living room over there? [*With emphasis.*] I've never been here before, myself. [*Aside.*] Not the tiniest hint of disbelief. . . . Well then, I can relax; and anyhow, if he had seen me . . . I've changed clothes.

HENRI [*preoccupied*]: I'll go and tell Mademoiselle Laurent. . . .

CLÉONICE: No; she's busy too, so my governess says. I'll wait here. [*Henri is on the point of leaving.*] Goodness, sir, you seem very scared of having me on your hands! You've been writing? Don't put yourself out. I don't need anyone to keep me company. I like being alone. [*She picks up a book.*]

HENRI [*aside*]: Funny little girl! [*With an unsettled air he resumes writing.—Aloud.*] Since you insist. . . . It's very rude on my part . . . but . . .

CLÉONICE [*sitting at left*]: On the contrary, it shows respect, and I'm much obliged to you for it. [*Henri looks at her, astonished.*] I'm talking seriously! Most young people in these parts would seize the opportunity to flirt with the heiress. Now the only people I admire are people that don't pay me any attention.

HENRI [*aside, listening as he writes*]: Well, that isn't so very stupid!

CLÉONICE [*aside*]: He isn't even listening to me. Let's see if I can pull him out of his reverie. [*Aloud, rising.*] Ah, here's Françoise! . . . No, I was wrong; she's gone. I'm . . . [*To Henri, who has risen.*] I'm not being indiscreet, am I, coming here to see her today?

HENRI: Today? Why do you ask?

CLÉONICE: Lord, how cross you sound!

HENRI [*surprised and upset*]: Me? Why, really, Mademoiselle, you're a great tease.

CLÉONICE: Would I tease about an attachment? . . . God forbid! People are lucky when they can follow their inclinations.

HENRI: Which you can't, eh? Being rich does prevent people from being free to choose!

CLÉONICE [*aside*]: Is that a reference to . . . ? [*Aloud.*] Oh, I'm not talking about myself. There's nothing very interesting about me. As it happens, I'm so spoiled that I'd be allowed to choose anyone I felt like.

HENRI: Ah! You're as free as that? Well, no doubt you'll soon be listening to what your little heart tells you.

CLÉONICE: That's just what I want to do; but how can you listen when it never says anything? [*Aside.*] So there, you nosy thing!

HENRI [*aside*]: She's very nice . . . but . . . [*He returns to the table and picks up his letter, as if to fold it.*] Nonsense! Why should I leave right away? Françoise would be worried—maybe hurt. [*He crumples the letter and puts it in his pocket.*]

CLÉONICE: Oh, look—it really is her, this time; you can cheer up now.

Scene 8

[*As above; Françoise.*]

FRANÇOISE [*entering left and going up to Cléonice*]: I've kept you waiting for me, dear. [*Aside to Henri.*] I have to talk to you.

CLÉONICE: Oh, I'm in the way; I'll be off.

FRANÇOISE: No, of course not; what an idea!

CLÉONICE: Oh yes I am! I can hear wedding bells in the air, and they're giving me a headache. It's only natural! The very thought of marriage, ever since it appeared to me in the shape of the Duke de Belver, makes me turn green with fright.

HENRI: Ah! You said you were free to choose, and yet . . .

CLÉONICE: And yet this personage deigns to offer me his name, his heart and his eye! But I'm free to refuse him, and I do! Well, good-bye!

FRANÇOISE: But . . .

CLÉONICE: No, honestly, good-bye; I'll be back! [*Starts to leave.*] Oh, just one thing—it may be relevant. When people get married, they make settlements, don't they? My father told me to tell yours to remember . . . It's an obsession of Daddy's; he wants desperately to buy Luzy from Monsieur de Trégenec.

HENRI: Why, that's very opportune—just now I'm wanting to sell it.

CLÉONICE: If you put it like that, my father will offer you three cents for it. I can see you don't know anything about business!

FRANÇOISE: You should talk! Look what kind of an agent you are!

HENRI: I see—Mademoiselle is full of mockery!

CLÉONICE: Ah now, that isn't nice, when it's a matter that might concern Françoise.

FRANÇOISE: But, dear . . .

CLÉONICE: Keep your secrets to yourself; still, you can trust me. . . . Oh, I forgot one more thing: Mummy wants me to notify you that she is solemnly opening the doors of the Château de la Rive on the first of July, two months from now; that will be Inauguration Day for the embellishments she thinks she has added to it. The festivities will be mind-bogglingly luxurious and in the most appallingly bad taste, let me warn you now. As for you, sir, Mummy is expecting to send you an invitation, and I trust Françoise will allow you a dance with me.

FRANÇOISE: You really plan to leave after a fine speech like that?

CLÉONICE: Ah, but aren't you just terrified I might stay? [*Going out upstage.*] Good-bye! Good-bye!

Scene 9

[*Françoise, Henri.*]

FRANÇOISE: What's all this merriment? What have you two been talking about?

HENRI: Nothing in particular. . . . She's very entertaining. Will you go to that ball, Françoise?

FRANÇOISE: It seems to me that we have more serious questions to consider at the moment, now that we're on our own. My father sent me to you. . . . You're disturbed by the present and frightened of the future. . . .

HENRI: My future . . . I don't know if it's ruined. As for my present . . . all of a sudden it's become so full of problems, darling, that I'm ashamed how hasty I was a while back. I must ask you to forgive me, and forget it. . . .

FRANÇOISE: Why, that isn't the way you should be talking, Henri— not to me! I have some money of my own—not much, but it's solid and secure; and whatever ties or commitments we may have, it's our own property. . . .

HENRI: Oh, please, Françoise, please don't offer me any help! Considering how we stand at the moment, nothing could hurt me more than help of that kind.

FRANÇOISE: Well then, supposing . . . supposing your feelings for me were so serious that you still wanted to marry me, do you think your troubles could change the way I feel about you?

HENRI: The way you feel about me, Françoise darling, is the way a generous sister feels, I know that. But your soul is so tranquil, and your mind is so strong, that you can't appreciate what a humiliating life I'd lead if I owed everything to you.

FRANÇOISE: Maybe not; but you yourself could . . .

HENRI: Oh, I could keep myself gainfully employed—at least your father thinks so. I'm not so sure! What's more . . . Françoise, I have to think things over, I have to ask myself a few questions. Do I have enough strength of character, am I determined enough to deserve you, now that my situation is so different? [*He takes his hat.*]

FRANÇOISE [*frightened*]: Where are you going? What are you doing? What's going to happen to you?

HENRI: Oh, that's my business; promise me you won't worry too much, sister dear. First of all I'm going to Brittany, to check that my situation really is so bad . . . and then I'm going to sell what I have . . . possibly to Monsieur Dubuisson, at the highest possible price; that little girl is quite right! I'll see my lawyer today and set the thing in motion, so it will be well advanced by the time I return. . . . It might be a good idea . . . yes . . . if I paid a visit to this Dubuisson. He's just next door. I mustn't stay.

FRANÇOISE: Henri, you're not leaving me like this?

HENRI [*kissing her hand*]: Oh, I'll be back in a month—at the very latest. Do let me write to you—and treat me as a brother and a friend, the same as always. Things can't be any other way, can they? So then, good-bye, Françoise dear; see you soon! [*He leaves upstage.*]

Scene 10

[*Françoise; later, La Hyonnais, the Doctor.*]

FRANÇOISE [*crushed, sitting at the table*]: And that's the love of his life, his dream come true! . . .

LA HYONNAIS [*entering upstage*]: So he's going, is he?

DOCTOR [*entering from the left, followed by Marie-Jeanne*]: What? What's that?

FRANÇOISE: He's gone! . . . He's going to Brittany on a matter of business.

DOCTOR: Oh! He's thinking only of his own interests, is he? Hasn't he understood what we've been offering him?

FRANÇOISE: He doesn't want to accept anything from us.

DOCTOR: In other words, he doesn't really care for us!

LA HYONNAIS: Would you like me to go after him and bring him back?

DOCTOR: No indeed! He isn't worth our trouble.

FRANÇOISE: But he's going to be so unhappy! He left in such a state of agitation! . . . Oh my, now that I come to think about it— what if he's going to kill himself! . . . [*She goes to the fireplace and raises the blind from the plate glass window.*]

DOCTOR: What are you looking at?

FRANÇOISE: He's gone out of the garden, he's in the grounds of the château with Cléonice. . . . He's taking her arm . . . she's laughing. . . . Well, thank God; we can breathe easily!

MARIE-JEANNE [*taking her in her arms*]: Why, what's all this about, Miss? [*She sits her down.*]

FRANÇOISE: Nothing! I . . . I'm just . . . a bit faint. . . .

DOCTOR: She's fainted! Ah! I was sure of it: she was in love with him all along!

Act 3

At the Château de la Rive.—A very luxurious living room, decorated with flowers and lit up. Door at right, leading to the ballrooms. Door at left, leading to some rooms prepared for card games. Circular divan center stage; chairs and sofas.

Scene 1

[*Dubuisson, entering from the left; later, Madame Dubuisson, from the right.*]

DUBUISSON [*to some servants, who are just finishing the task of illuminating the room*]: Right, you've put enough lights here! No sense in burning all that oil and candlewax a whole hour early!

MADAME DUBUISSON: Why, Monsieur Dubuisson, aren't you any more dressed than that?

DUBUISSON: Well, what am I missing?

MADAME DUBUISSON: You've kept on your colored cravat! You look like a gardener! I wish you wouldn't keep acting like a peasant all the time—it's ridiculous.

DUBUISSON: Louison darling, there's nothing more ridiculous than trying to hide your roots. Me, I take pride in reminding all these fine gentlemen how I used to be shepherd, horse trader, pubkeeper at the "Buisson Fleuri." [*Madame Dubuisson shows signs of annoyance.*] Yes, and right under their noses, too! . . . I bled their cattle, traded their horses, sheared their sheep . . . with scissors that cut closer than their own. Are they laughing at me? . . . You bet—pretty sour sort of a laugh, though! . . . They've done more eating than sowing, the whole lot of 'em; while me, I've sowed and I've reaped, and just look at the result! . . .

MADAME DUBUISSON: Well, fair enough, you like taking them down a peg. That's all the more reason why you ought to marry your girl off to that little Count de Trégenec: you'll never do any better than that!

DUBUISSON: So long as his father gives him something . . . but what if he doesn't give him a cent? . . .

MADAME DUBUISSON: All the better in that case: the less he gives him now, the more he'll leave him afterwards. . . .

DUBUISSON: But in the meantime, the boy is going to be spending off us. And he does seem to be keen on spending—I know a thing or two about that.

MADAME DUBUISSON: You?

DUBUISSON: The Bargat and Pacaud firm knows something about it too. . . .

MADAME DUBUISSON: How come?

DUBUISSON: I know what I'm talking about! All I'm saying is, he likes spending money. . . .

MADAME DUBUISSON: Oh well, that's a habit he'll grow out of. . . .

DUBUISSON: You haven't exactly grown out of it yourself yet, Louison darling! . . . [*He sits on the divan.*]

MADAME DUBUISSON: I never do a thing without your consent. . . .

DUBUISSON: Consent isn't always approval.

MADAME DUBUISSON: Well, go ahead and complain! We still get on all right. You want the land at Luzy, you've got a bee in your belfry about that; I want a son-in-law with a title—I must have

one, if it's the death of me! And after all, Cléonice does have
to get married off. First she had that crush on her cousin Jules,
then we turned down the Duke de Belver, so from now on
we're going to have one enemy in high society.

DUBUISSON: Oh, fat lot I care about the Duke and the cousin! I've
sent Jules back to Paris.

MADAME DUBUISSON: Still, before he went, he got friendly with the
Duke—can't imagine how: the one's a gossip, and the other's
a creep. They've put both of their two grudges together, and
I'm worried about what they might get up to. The Duke can't
stand Monsieur Henri! . . . He came just so he could see him
here.

DUBUISSON: You invited him—the Duke?

MADAME DUBUISSON: I really had to!

DUBUISSON: All the same, Louison, you must admit it's a funny
thing, a duke and a count around our little girl!

MADAME DUBUISSON: And our dresses and laces, that you've been
grizzling about all week! Don't you reckon the fine ladies are
going to turn green when they see us all dolled up like that?

DUBUISSON: It's a lot of money . . . a lot of money! When I think
how the cost of what you and your daughter have got on your
bodies today would pay for thirty good pair of oxen at Poissy
market!

MADAME DUBUISSON: Well, is it doing us any harm? See how my
complexion glows when I'm in my diamonds! I don't rouge
myself up like all those young things with TB! . . . And your girl
too, you'll see she doesn't look bad at all in pink!

Scene 2

[*Cléonice, Madame Dubuisson, Dubuisson.*]

CLÉONICE: Well, I'm ready. How do I look, Mummy?

MADAME DUBUISSON: Not bad. Go and kiss your father, dear!

CLÉONICE [*going to her father*]: What's going on? Is he still angry
with us over the dressmakers' bills? [*She kisses him.*]

MADAME DUBUISSON: No, not him! Does he ever get angry?

CLÉONICE [*aside*]: Hullo, something's up; Mummy's sweet-talking
him.

MADAME DUBUISSON: Well now, dear, we've got something to tell you, there's a real good husband coming for you.

DUBUISSON [*aside to his wife*]: You're going to tell her already?

MADAME DUBUISSON: Sure—time is running out; he's going to be here soon.

CLÉONICE: Mummy, you're scaring me; I don't believe in "real good husbands," not after you tried to marry me off to the Duke! . . .

MADAME DUBUISSON: There's no question of that any more. What would you say to young Count de Trégenec?

CLÉONICE: You can't be serious, Mummy! He's in love with Françoise!

MADAME DUBUISSON: He's never given her a single thought.

CLÉONICE: How can you be so sure? Though I must say Françoise isn't making any moves in his direction either. But why should he want to marry me? He doesn't even know me: we only set eyes on each other twice . . . and that was a couple of months ago.

DUBUISSON: She's right; they don't know each other.

MADAME DUBUISSON: If people did know each other, nobody would ever get married.

CLÉONICE: That may be true, but it isn't very encouraging.

DUBUISSON: Don't you like him, this young fellow?

CLÉONICE: No, it isn't that, but . . . I mean, maybe he doesn't like me.

MADAME DUBUISSON: Well, who's forcing him to make the offer, then? . . . Don't be such an idiot!

CLÉONICE: Who's forcing him? His creditors, most likely.

DUBUISSON: She's not far wrong there!

MADAME DUBUIOSSON [*surreptitiously to her husband*]: Monsieur Dubuisson, do shut up. [*Aloud.*] She's still set on Jules, can't you see?

CLÉONICE: Oh goodness, must you bring up poor Jules all the time! If it wasn't for you, Mummy, I would have forgotten about him long ago.

DUBUISSON [*annoyed*]: Well, you just forget him right away, or else!

CLÉONICE [*aside*]: We're getting angry, are we? I'll stir them up good and proper! [*Aloud.*] Maybe I'm not able to forget him, father.

MADAME DUBUISSON: There you are, Monsieur Dubuisson, what did I tell you! Cléonice, do you want me to die from grief! . . .

CLÉONICE: Oh, surely not, Mummy! But anyhow, why don't you want me to . . . ?

MADAME DUBUISSON [*pathetically*]: Because I know what marrying for love is like, dear! It's torment! All this business of claiming to be in love with people! I myself nearly got swept away by my impulses when I was young; Monsieur Dubuisson there can bear me witness that I didn't want him at all! But in the end I listened to the dictations of reason and my parents. What really makes a girl happy? It's having nice clothes, carriages, going to dances and the theater. You see, darling, those are the only really serious things in life; everything else is just daydreams. Love passes away; aristocracy remains. Come along, dear, I can hear the carriages arriving, dry your tears, now! . . .

CLÉONICE [*aside*]: Tears? . . .

MADAME DUBUISSON [*in a fluster*]: Monsieur Dubuisson, do please go and change your cravat!

DUBUISSON: Oh rubbish—my cravat! . . .

MADAME DUBUISSON: Well, see to the food then.

DUBUISSON: Ah, that's different; we mustn't have any extravagances!
[*He goes upstage to talk to the servants, and leaves to the left.*]

MADAME DUBUISSON: Yes, dear, our impulses just lead us to our ruination. [*She tidies her daughter's hair.*] There's a pin coming loose from your headband. And believe me, I've had my troubles too—because we women lead a very public life, thank God we do! . . . [*In a brusque voice, to two servants who are looking out the windows upstage.*] What are you doing there? . . . Stay at the main entrance where people can see you! . . . My God, they're stupid creatures! . . . [*She goes towards them and gives them orders in an animated way.—Returning to her daughter.*] So, there's no two ways about it. . . .

CLÉONICE [*reflectively*]: Then you're insisting I have to marry the Count? . . .

MADAME DUBUISSON: Yes! . . .

CLÉONICE: And you're going to tell that to Jules?

MADAME DUBUISSON: You bet I'll go to that trouble!

CLÉONICE [*aside*]: If only he'd given me back that stupid letter! He claims he's burnt it. . . .

MADAME DUBUISSON: Now then, what are you brooding about? I tell you, I'll fix everything myself! . . . Look, there's Monsieur Henri. You must admit he's good-looking!

CLÉONICE: Oh, he isn't bad.

Scene 3

[*Cléonice, Madame Dubuisson, La Hyonnais, Henri.*

Henri enters by himself from the right.]

MADAME DUBUISSON: Ah, you're back again at long last, Count! Have you had a good trip? I thought you were never going to come back from your Brittany. [*Greeting La Hyonnais, who has just entered.*] Baron, you've been back from Paris for a week, I think? It's very kind of you to have accepted our invitation.... Well, well ... [*To Henri.*] Monsieur de Trégenec, let me make you a present of my... I mean, let me present to you my daughter Cléonice.... [*Aside.*] Curtsey, now! [*Aloud.*] The Count is to be your son-in-law... I mean fiancé. [*La Hyonnais has gone upstage; he goes downstage left.*]

HENRI: Really, Madame? ... Am I to understand—already? ... I didn't think...

MADAME DUBUIOSSON [*ingratiatingly*]: You didn't think your offer would be accepted? Who says it is? But it could be! ... [*To Henri, taking him aside.*] This isn't the time to go into all that! You have to talk it over with me first, you understand, I'm the one that runs the family. I'm going to wait for you in the big drawing room. [*Aloud, with a curtsey.*] Count! ... Cléonice, pay him your best regards now! [*She goes out to the right with Cléonice.*]

Scene 4

[*La Hyonnais, Henri.*]

LA HYONNAIS: Well then, it's true! You've taken this step? I didn't believe it.

HENRI: You've heard it already?

LA HYONNAIS: Yes, from the Doctor.

HENRI: Who told him?

LA HYONNAIS: Monsieur Dubuisson came yesterday to let him know. Also, your lawyer...

HENRI: My lawyer considered it advisable to act....

LA HYONNAIS: He wouldn't have taken such a step without your permission!

HENRI: He kept pushing me.... But tell me, what about Françoise? Does she know...?

LA HYONNAIS: That you've authorized this proposal? . . . Probably.

HENRI: And . . . is she coming to the ball?

LA HYONNAIS: Haven't you seen her yet?

HENRI: I've only just arrived. Two hours ago I was still in the coach.

LA HYONNAIS: There wasn't any urgent need to come here!

HENRI: The urgent need, actually, was to avoid seeing her. She won't be here this evening, will she? . . . If she knows . . .

LA HYONNAIS: Henri, if you're afraid to meet your best friends, you can't be at peace with yourself.

HENRI: Oh, sermons, my friend . . .

LA HYONNAIS: And you were dodging me too, just now! If I hadn't kept at your heels . . .

HENRI: Well, it's true! I don't want your advice, your ideas. . . . Why are you in this neighborhood again—and just when I've come back myself? . . . No answer? . . . You're looking for another excuse, and you're not able to tell me a lie! Look, Monsieur de La Hyonnais, I've just spent two months having stormy scenes with the Marquis de Trégenec. I plied him with questions, I pestered him, he lost his head; his dislike, his resentment, overcame his better judgment. . . . In a flash of anger, he told me the whole story.

LA HYONNAIS: He told you . . . ?

HENRI: I know the whole story! . . . And so do you. . . . But we mustn't speak about that—ever.

LA HYONNAIS: Henri! . . . I made a solemn vow to be silent; my behavior should have shown you that.

HENRI: Your behavior . . . yes, now I understand it. Jacques de La Hyonnais, did you really do it out of friendship for me?

LA HYONNAIS: Whether it's based on instinct or fancy, my concern for you is real and deep seated, Henri.

HENRI: Jacques . . . oh, look. . . . [*Holding out his hand.*] Let's be friends. I need a friend of some kind! . . . I've just been driven away from my father's property—I need someone I can open up to! . . . Otherwise, I'm all adrift—alone in the world! . . .

LA HYONNAIS: Don't have any doubts about me, Henri—I'll be on your side if that's what you want. . . . Think about your other friends, and give up this business of marrying for money! . . .

HENRI: If only I could . . . but my situation is hopeless. . . . Don't you see, you mustn't talk me out of this marriage; I'm not just marrying for practical reasons, I'm marrying for honor!

LA HYONNAIS: Well then, let me help you out; accept it from me, please. I'd be the one who was indebted—the one who would be perpetually grateful to you. Why, I'm a plain enough sort of fellow, don't you see?—I get my happiness from making people happy, and . . .

HENRI [*going up to him*]: No, no—you wouldn't be making me happy—you don't understand my kind of life. You're fond of abstraction and consistency; I want a bit of fun and sparkle in life. I need variety, unpredictability, horses, travels. You can immerse yourself in the study of dusty books; the only things I like to read are poems bound in gold and silk. I have a head full of dreams, curiosities, enthusiasms; and if my mind is eager for something, that's what my heart enjoys. Because I love—I'm tortured by a need to love—I have a kind of thirst for tenderness and devotion. . . . Who knows, maybe I have an artistic taste for love! . . . I need air, space, luxury, poetry, above all security, around my sanctuary. I couldn't be happy locked in a little room, nailed to a desk, bothered by yesterday's debts, scared of tomorrow's needs, counting up the cents in the drawer and the hours of work by the clock and the crumbs of bread on the table. My dream was to give Françoise a life worthy of her and me. . . . But poverty is killing my hopes—abject poverty is what I'm reduced to, and for life, as you must realize! I'm disowned, disinherited. . . . And so, since all I have left is a name and a title . . . since it's the only advantage that the Marquis de Trégenec can't snatch away from me . . . that name has to save me—it has to pay my ransom, by way of these ambitious commoners! [*He sits.*]

LA HYONNAIS: So you're turning your back on love—no regrets, no remorse?

HENRI: No regrets? Of course I have regrets! But Françoise is above feeling any selfish resentment. I talked to her frankly before I left; I'll always have the utmost respect for her.

LA HYONNAIS: And you don't think, then, that she could have been in love with you for the past ten years without telling you?

HENRI: Oh, you mustn't say things like that! Poor Françoise. . . . Yes, we could have been happy together—but it's too late. . . .

LA HYONNAIS: No—it's never too late to do the right thing. . . . Come and see her!

HENRI [*frightened, rising*]: Is she at La Chanterie? . . .

LA HYONNAIS: Yes; it's only a matter of crossing the grounds.

HENRI [*worried*]: She isn't at the ball, is she?

LA HYONNAIS: She wouldn't be very likely to come.

HENRI [*hesitantly*]: All right . . . no . . . I know how weak I am, how I react. . . . If I saw her, I'd be lost.

LA HYONNAIS: Quite the contrary; you'd be saved. In heaven's name, Henri, come on! This isn't the place for you. This silly vulgar family . . .

HENRI: Stop it, La Hyonnais—it's too late, I tell you. . . . I'm so utterly crushed and terrified—and Françoise would despise me. . . . Here, I'm not weighed down by any feelings of inferiority; if these social climbers ever accuse me of having married for money, why, I can look down on their cash—it's the only thing they can give me! Don't you see, it's too late to run away. And here's Plutus⁵ coming to carry me off, in the ironic guise of this money-grubbing peasant!

Scene 5

[Dubuisson, Henri, La Hyonnais.]

DUBUISSON [*aside*]: Aha! . . . There he is! . . . Wouldn't mind getting a talk with him before my wife does. [*Aloud.*] Count de Trégenec, anything I can do to oblige you. Baron de La Hyonnais is from the same neck of the woods as you—I had a chat with him yesterday at the Doctor's place; he's your friend, I gather, and understands business, so he isn't out of place here either. Well, Count, I'll put my cards on the table—it won't take long. You might have to say a lot of words with ordinary peasants, but you only have to say one with people of your kind; I've been around long enough to know that. You're doing me the honor of wanting to marry my daughter. She's descended from a lot of nobodies, which you know . . . I don't have no delusions on that score. We come from a haystack and a barrowful of dirt, her mother and me. Whereas you, you've got a long geology of ancestors. . . .

HENRI: Sir, I might make the same apologies for my status that you're making so skillfully for yours. I couldn't endure to be attacked because of the follies of my youth; nor could I ever join a family that thought I was too indebted to its wealth.

DUBUISSON [*aside*]: Oho! He's proud. . . . All right; suits me all the better. [*Aloud.*] I knew you were susceptive . . . so I've given some thought how to arrange things so that you won't be put out. We don't have any sacrifices to make for you. We'll buy back your property . . . from your creditors, I mean we'll pay off all your mortgages and I'll keep Luzy for your future children. That way, if I'm accepting . . . with pleasure . . . [*he bows*] a son-in-law that isn't bringing me a cent, I'm not paying for his title either; that's too important a thing . . . you can't put a price on that. And that way, you're not obligated to me for anything; which is what you want, isn't it?

HENRI [*smiling*]: I can see, sir, that Luzy has a very special charm in your eyes. I'm glad! This arrangement [*to La Hyonnais*] rescues me from my troubles without making me anyone's slave.

LA HYONNAIS: Then you're agreeing . . . so quickly?

DUBUISSON: Let him answer the way he wants, Baron!

LA HYONNAIS: Don't weaken! At least, before you commit yourself, see what the Doctor has to say.

DUBUISSON: 'Course! . . . If you want to ask his opinion . . . Still, since Mademoiselle Françoise is sick . . .

HENRI: Sick?

DUBUISSON: The Doctor isn't seeing anybody today.

HENRI [*to La Hyonnais*]: Jacques, let's go and see her, quick!

LA HYONNAIS: No; your lucky star seems to shine on: here they are.

DUBUISSON [*aside*]: Heck! . . . Luckily, my wife is with 'em. [*He goes upstage.*]

Scene 6

[*As above; Madame Dubuisson, Françoise, the Doctor, coming from the ballrooms.*]

MADAME DUBUISSON: Come and rest yourself here, love! . . . I'm sure you can't be feeling well.

HENRI: My Lord! Is this true, Françoise?

DOCTOR: She's never felt better!

MADAME DUBUISSON: All the same, she's pale as a corpse.

HENRI [*to Françoise—the Doctor has persuaded her to sit on the divan*]: So you've been unwell, then?

FRANÇOISE [*pale and trembling, but controlling herself*]: Oh, it's nothing serious, or I wouldn't be here. . . .

HENRI [*quietly—he has sat next to her*]: I can't tell you how deeply it moves me, to see you again like this! Will you forgive me for not having written to you? [*Monsieur and Madame Dubuisson withdraw upstage and talk quietly together.*]

FRANÇOISE [*aloud*]: It's up to my father to forgive you—for forgetting and being silent.

DOCTOR [*severely*]: Which I shan't forgive!

DUBUISSON: But of course he was caught up with plans, Doctor. I told you yesterday what it was all about.

DOCTOR: I do think I should have learned about those plans from him, rather than from you! [*La Hyonnais brings a chair to Madame Dubuisson; she and the Doctor sit.*]

FRANÇOISE: So it's true, Henri . . . ?

MADAME DUBUISSON: Yes, lovey darling, there's plans of a marriage between Monsieur de Trégenec . . .

HENRI: Excuse me, Madame; Monsieur Dubuisson and I are still at the stage of tentative discussions . . . nothing more!

FRANÇOISE: Oh! Really?

HENRI: I intend to think things over.

DUBUISSON [*sitting*]: Good Lord, you're the boss on that score, Count; don't worry about that! We can all discuss the business together.

MADAME DUBUISSON: I brought the Doctor and his daughter here for that very reason. Maybe Françoise doesn't know the Count's situation?

FRANÇOISE: Excuse me, Madame, but I do know it.

DUBUISSON: Things could be better. . . .

DOCTOR: All right, but what has that got to do with a marriage?

MADAME DUBUISSON: Unless he gets married, Monsieur is done for. His lawyer . . .

DOCTOR: His lawyer surely should have begun by selling property, so as to free up his client.

DUBUISSON [*sardonically*]: Free up, yes . . . unless the Count owes more than his land is worth.

HENRI: How would you know, sir?

DUBUISSON [*as before*]: Am I wrong?

DOCTOR: Whatever difficulties you may have, you know I have a certain amount of money at your disposal. . . . [*He rises, and goes upstage with Françoise.*]

DUBUISSON [*rising*]: Oh, if the Doctor's lending to you. . . . That's a different story! We won't mention the subject any more . . . we won't say another word . . . that settles everything.

MADAME DUBUISSON: What do you mean, that settles everything? We've had the insult of an offer to marry our daughter Cléonice, and just because the Doctor is lending his spare cash, that's all there's going to be?

DUBUISSON: Don't get yourself stewed up about it, darling. What the Doctor is doing is very handsome . . . very generous! A hundred thousand francs! A country doctor doesn't find that on his doorstep every morning! The Count is a very lucky man!

HENRI: That's quite enough, sir! You must know that I won't accept any such sacrifice; I don't deserve it.

LA HYONNAIS [*behind the divan*]: You could deserve it.

MADAME DUBUISSON: Yes, of course he could! He could do like you, and study medicine four, five year; after that, the Doctor could pass on a few of his customers. Not that there's much money in peasants, but it's so nice to help the poor and everything— with a good little horse, say fifteen or twenty leagues a day . . . or night—summer and winter. . . .

DOCTOR [*returning*]: As you can plainly see, that sort of thing never killed anyone; here I am to prove it.

MADAME DUBUISSON: And then, after twenty years, you finally earn enough to keep body and soul together.

DOCTOR: Even enough to help a friend, if need be.

MADAME DUBUISSON: On condition that he gives up his nobility and does the same as you.

DOCTOR: Gives up his nobility because he goes to work? Really, Madame Dubuisson, you have some ideas that the upper classes themselves have abandoned! And you yourself, having got rich by working . . .

MADAME DUBUIOSSON [*rising*]: Me? . . . Let me tell you this, Doctor, I never worked in my life! [*She goes up to Henri, who has remained slumped on the divan.*]

DOCTOR: I did believe the contrary, and I thought that was how you gained your wealth, not having any ancestors.

DUBUISSON [*mockingly*]: The Doctor's right there! You may have white hands today, Louison darling . . . but once upon a time . . . !

MADAME DUBUIOSSON [*in a rage*]: That's quite enough! No point in bickering. Seeing Monsieur Henri hasn't made up his mind

any more than he has, all we can do is wait for his good pleasure, unless a better prospect comes along for our daughter—
which may not be beyond the bounds of palpability.

DUBUISSON: There, there! You're just getting hot under the collar!

MADAME DUBUIOSSON [*aside*]: We're being fooled with and insulted. . . .

DUBUISSON: Not at all—you'll see. [*Aloud.*] Very sorry to trouble
you, Count, but could I have a couple of words please, on a
little matter of some urgency.

HENRI: With me, sir?

DUBUISSON: Yes. . . . Stay where you are, Mademoiselle Françoise;
stay where you are, gentlemen; it'll only take a couple of minutes.
[*He leads Henri downstage.*] You think the Doctor's going to lend
to you? . . . Suits me: I'm sure of getting my money, then.

HENRI: I don't owe you anything, sir.

DUBUISSON: 'Scuse me, but didn't you sign some bills of exchange
for the firm Pacaud and Bargat?

HENRI [*nervously*]: They're in your possession?

DUBUISSON: That's right; spiced with a little bit of legal protests,
judicial decisions . . .

HENRI: Eh?

DUBUISSON: . . . imprisonment for debt . . .

HENRI: I see . . . very well, sir. . . .

DOCTOR [*coming downstage right*]: What's the matter?

HENRI: Nothing, nothing, Doctor; Monsieur Dubuisson was just
saying to me . . .

LA HYONNAIS [*coming downstage left*]: What's up?

HENRI: Later . . . you'll find out. . . . [*Aside to Dubuisson.*] Keep it
quiet, sir; the Doctor wouldn't be able to find that sort of
money overnight. . . . I'll see to it. . . . I'll . . .

DOCTOR: But I want to know . . .

HENRI: It's nothing, I tell you, nothing at all. . . . [*Aside.*] I'm
doomed! [*He goes out to the left.*]

Scene 7

[*As above, except for Henri.*]

DUBUISSON [*watching Henri go*]: Aha! We're a bit crestfallen now!
[*To his wife.*] Leave me to it, darling; I'm not finished with him
just yet . . . I've still got something to say to him.

FRANÇOISE: What's going on between the two of you?

DUBUISSON: Something a bit cleverer than all the fine words of philosophy!

LA HYONNAIS: So then, sir, he's in your power, I see. . . . You're going to determine his fate, perhaps!

MADAME DUBUISSON: Sure looks like it.

DOCTOR [*forcibly*]: But this is senseless! You could ruin both his life and your daughter's!

DUBUISSON: Nah, you haven't got a clue about things, Doctor Laurent. You're a scholar, but you don't know what's what. . . . You ought to realize that nothing can go wrong when there's money—and when you can feel a bit of something right here. . . . [*He slaps his chest pocket.*]

DOCTOR [*astonished*]: In your heart?

DUBUISSON: No, no, in your pocket. Look here, Doctor, you poor fellow, you can work till you drop, but you still might not get your daughter married to the man she wants; wheresoas, you see, there's barons, marquis, dukes, counts after mine . . . and all she has to do is bend over and pick one up. [*He goes out to the left, and his wife to the right.*]

Scene 8

[*La Hyonnais, the Doctor, Françoise.*]

DOCTOR: Poor Françoise! Well, so much the better if you don't have to bend over and collect a husband.

FRANÇOISE: But what about him, father? Are you going to let these rich brutes simply walk over him? I'm sure he's in serious trouble at the moment—I can tell!

DOCTOR: He hasn't much resistance to trouble! What can we do for him? . . .

FRANÇOISE: We can find out, at least, why he went away looking so worried. You mustn't give up on him!

DOCTOR: If that's what you want . . . Wait for me here. [*He goes out.*]

Scene 9

[*La Hyonnais, Françoise.*]

LA HYONNAIS: You're in such distress! Do please try to calm down and get a bit of rest.

FRANÇOISE [*bursting into tears*]: Yes, it's true, I am upset! . . . I haven't been really alive for two months . . . and since yesterday, I do believe I must be dead! [*She sits on the divan.*]

LA HYONNAIS: Yes—since you found out about this scheme. But don't give up hope; you can still turn him back from it.

FRANÇOISE: Can I? . . . No, I can't do anything for him, because he doesn't love me!

LA HYONNAIS: He loves you in spite of himself—in spite of everything. He loves you with the utmost love he's capable of.

FRANÇOISE: Yes, of course, that's the point: it's terrible to say it, but he isn't capable of loving any more than that! . . . It isn't his fault; it's a problem that can't be cured!

LA HYONNAIS [*touched*]: Sometimes, when everything looks black, there may be a strange kind of joy in loving without any hope. Don't you ever feel that?

FRANÇOISE [*rising*]: I used to . . . yes . . . I used to feel that. . . . That was what kept me alive for ten years, Monsieur La Hyonnais— ever since I was a child, that was my comfort. I had the strength to tell myself that my secret would die with me! But two months ago I was utterly shattered! When it seemed to me that he might indeed possibly love me, I became weak—cowardly. I'd been so proud of having conquered and hidden my love—and yet I let it out. And don't you see—ever since that day, it's as if I've fallen out with myself. . . . I hate myself; I despise myself; I feel so humiliated! . . . The past itself has turned bitter on me. . . . Its memories were so true, and its patience was so quiet! . . . I imagined I'd never have anything to regret but a wonderful dream—whereas now, why . . . I'm ashamed of my own tears!

LA HYONNAIS [*very touched*]: No, never—you mustn't be ashamed of having suffered so bravely and loved so faithfully! Ashamed— you! Why, you'd have every right to be angry, and yet you're blaming only yourself and wanting forgiveness for your own unhappiness! Really, everything you're going through, every- thing you're saying, makes you all the more deserving of re- spect and . . . and friendship.

FRANÇOISE [*taking his hand*]: You're in tears too! . . . You're so good! . . . You're very kind . . . I can see that . . . I can feel it. . . .

LA HYONNAIS: What are you looking for?

FRANÇOISE [*hunting in her handkerchief and her bouquet*]: I don't know . . . somebody gave it to me . . . I've lost it. . . .

LA HYONNAIS: What was it?

FRANÇOISE: Just as I was on my way in to the ball, somebody, the Duke de Belver, I think—I was so preoccupied!—slipped a note into my hand. He can't abide Henri: it must be something against him. . . . Oh, here it is. . . . [*She finds the note on the sofa.*]

LA HYONNAIS: It might account for Monsieur Dubuisson's general air of triumph. . . . The Duke may be one of Henri's creditors. . . . Read it. . . .

FRANÇOISE [*wiping her eyes*]: I can't . . . can't see. . . . Can you read it?

LA HYONNAIS [*reading*]: "You could keep hold of this lover who . . ." Oh, the wretched fellow is insulting you!

FRANÇOISE: What does it matter? Keep reading. . . .

LA HYONNAIS: No!

FRANÇOISE: I want you to! Read it! . . .

LA HYONNAIS [*reading*]: "You could keep hold of this lover who is deserting you for a certain heiress. I have a most interesting letter from that young lady—a love letter to a young cousin— which you could use to break off the proposed marriage. Just say the word, and I'll give you the means of getting your revenge."

FRANÇOISE [*scornfully*]: That's a very flattering proposition!

LA HYONNAIS: The fellow is an utter disgrace!

FRANÇOISE: Doesn't matter; we must get back Cléonice's letter.

LA HYONNAIS: What for?

FRANÇOISE: To burn it. Otherwise, he'll be the ruin of the girl, and it'll look as though I've been his accomplice.

LA HYONNAIS: And yet if the girl is guilty of something . . . my own duty, personally, could be to warn Henri. . . .

FRANÇOISE: No, Cléonice hasn't done anything wrong—she's just a child. Go and see the Duke right away, Monsieur La Hyonnais. Ask him for the proof . . . on my behalf . . . but don't tell him anything about my intentions.

LA HYONNAIS: And miss the chance to tell him we both despise him?

FRANÇOISE: Oh—you're angry with him, are you? It doesn't bother me. . . . [*She starts to leave.*]

LA HYONNAIS: No, no, I'll be calm. . . . You mustn't have anything to do with a man like that.

FRANÇOISE: You promise you'll . . . ?

LA HYONNAIS: Ah, well—I don't really have the right to punish him, Françoise—I'm not your brother! [*He goes out to the left.*]

Scene 10

FRANÇOISE [*alone, reflectively*]: He's a wonderful friend—he really is a brother at heart! Ah now, if my poor Henri . . . He wouldn't be deterred by the girl's flightiness. . . . She's a bit of a flirt, she'd be able to get round him. . . . He'd do his best to square his feelings with his conscience! . . . I must talk to her . . . try to help her to be more true, more serious. After all . . . if she does have to marry him . . . at least she needn't cheapen him! . . . Yes: I'll act the sister to the end . . . do my duty as a friend . . . and then . . . My father is so kindhearted—if I didn't have him . . . ! My sadness is just killing him! . . . Why do we all have to be so weak spirited—so fond of the people who don't deserve it, and so unkind to the people who are fond of us! . . .

Scene 11

[*La Hyonnais, rather flustered; Françoise.*]

FRANÇOISE: Well? You look . . .

LA HYONNAIS: No, it's just that I've been in a hurry . . . I didn't like to leave you alone. . . . The Duke and I will have a meeting tomorrow. . . .

FRANÇOISE: Tomorrow?

LA HYONNAIS: Yes—about the letter. But here's Henri following me.

FRANÇOISE: Oh! . . . All right, find out what he's decided to do— quickly. I can't let him see me . . . these silly eyes of mine . . . I'm going to talk to Cléonice, and then I'll be back; see if you can keep him here. [*She goes out to the right.*]

Scene 12

[*Henri, La Hyonnais.*]

LA HYONNAIS [*watching her go*]: She does seem calmer . . . or stronger. [*To Henri.*] Look, tell me . . .

HENRI: No—you tell me—why did you just hit the Duke de Belver?
LA HYONNAIS: Oh—you saw it?
HENRI: Very distinctly; and you've arranged a duel for tomorrow morning.
LA HYONNAIS: The fellow was calling doctors quacks and charlatans. I happened to be going past . . . I heard it. . . .
HENRI: Now, what I heard was the name of Françoise!
LA HYONNAIS: It has nothing to do with Françoise. . . .
HENRI: Don't try to lie; you're avenging an insult for her!
LA HYONNAIS: I'm not avenging anybody; I'm a knight errant on behalf of the faculty of medicine, that's all.
HENRI: But if Françoise is being slandered—insulted—that could only be because of me.
LA HYONNAIS: Well, if that were the case, what would you do?
HENRI: I'd ask you . . . I'd order you to let me take your place.
LA HYONNAIS: In the duel with the Duke? You couldn't have any claim of the kind unless you'd decided to marry Françoise.
HENRI [alarmed]: Marry her?
LA HYONNAIS: Yes; otherwise, you'd compromise her all the more, and I wouldn't stand for it.
HENRI: You?
LA HYONNAIS: Tell me, have you given up Mademoiselle Dubuisson?
HENRI: Don't ask me any questions.
LA HYONNAIS: Oh but I must! Why did you refuse to give an account of yourself in front of us just a moment ago? And why are you so pale and worried now?
HENRI: Because I've just decided to do something desperate.
LA HYONNAIS: What is it? . . . Come on, speak up! . . .
HENRI: La Hyonnais, stop tormenting me! . . . These horrible debts . . .
LA HYONNAIS: Well?
HENRI: My liberty was under threat. . . . Monsieur Dubuisson has just given me the titles that he was holding against me; now, he has my promise! . . . But, please, don't talk about me any more; it's Françoise I'm concerned about.
LA HYONNAIS: Oh—Françoise! Since you're giving her up, you don't have any right to interrogate me about her.
HENRI [impetuously]: La Hyonnais—you're in love with Françoise!
LA HYONNAIS: Oh? You think so?
HENRI: I can see it! . . . You're pale, you're worried—you too! . . .

LA HYONNAIS: Well, what does it matter to you?

HENRI [*sadly*]: What indeed! . . . [*Rousing himself.*] And yet I do think you ought to treat her just as a sister, because . . .

LA HYONNAIS: Oh yes—if she were to be your wife, that's how it would be.

HENRI: Isn't that still how it is? Look, just where do you stand in relation to her and me? I don't understand it any more! . . .

LA HYONNAIS: Very well, you're going to understand it; it isn't in my power to keep it quiet any longer. Yes, I am in love with Françoise; yes—I've been in love with her ever since I met her. It isn't my fault! I'd given myself up to studies—I was fond of science and duty—I hardly realized my own feelings; I had no reason to mistrust myself. At the time, I thought you were seriously attached to Françoise; I didn't begrudge you your happiness, but I did feel it deeply. Yes—I valued it more highly than you did! . . . And that feeling would have been a pleasant one, your marriage would have been a great delight to me. . . . I shouldn't have thought of regretting the fact that I'd arrived a little late in the life of the woman you loved. . . . But you didn't love her!

HENRI: Didn't love her!! . . . As God is my witness . . .

LA HYONNAIS: No; you never *have* loved her. . . . And yet it was my duty to bring you back to her, and up till today, up till this very moment, in the midst of a thousand tortures and in spite of a thousand torments, I did everything to bind her to you. . . . Oh! On her side, I've been only too successful! . . . But since, on your side, it's been a waste of time sacrificing myself, since you can't find in yourself the will to deserve her . . . well then, I admit, Henri, I'm not in control of myself any more—I can't stifle my own feelings any longer. . . . The bravery and tenderness and intelligence and charm and moral beauty of that girl have utterly captivated me. It's a passion, an adoration, a fever, an ecstasy—in a word, it's love. Now, if you do come trotting loyally back to her, I'll simply have to say farewell to the two of you for ever. But if you don't, I swear I'll never leave her side— I'm going to protect her, I'm going to avenge her insults, I'm going to serve her, and I'm going to move heaven and earth to win her affection.

HENRI [*worried*]: Yes, you'd be a dangerous rival—you love her to distraction, I can see that.

LA HYONNAIS: Rival? Oh! . . . What kind of talk is that, Henri?

HENRI: Jacques—look—I don't know what I'm saying—I don't know what kind of muddle has taken hold of me. I don't know why I should be so troubled by what you've revealed to me. My God—what on earth is going on inside me? I'm being destroyed, torn apart. . . . I've turned my back on the finest and loveliest woman in the world. . . . I've been afraid to work, to be a slave, to live in obscurity. . . . I thought I was escaping from all my troubles, and now I have to face the worst of all! . . . [*He throws himself on the divan and hides his face in his hands.—Françoise enters and looks at him, without coming forward.*]

LA HYONNAIS: Here's Françoise, Henri. . . . [*Henri trembles.*] I'll leave you with her. . . . As regards what I've just been saying to you, you can't in all honor talk to her about that; but as regards the decision you need to make now, in all honor you really must tell her about it plainly. [*He leaves.*]

Scene 13

[*Henri, Françoise.*]

HENRI: Françoise, there's something I must say to you: it's good-bye forever! . . .

FRANÇOISE: Good-bye forever! . . . Where are you going, then?

HENRI: Nowhere at all, Françoise; I'm floundering in an abyss!

FRANÇOISE: Perhaps you've thrown yourself into it.

HENRI: No, no—Fate has pushed me in. Françoise, there's an unhappy secret in my life—one that you don't know about . . . an unjust father—maybe an insulted one. . . .

FRANÇOISE: I'd guessed as much. . . . And so I've stuck by you, the way we do stick by misfortunes . . . and so I keep sticking by you, now that your life is so desolate. . . . You must listen to one last piece of advice, Henri—as a friend, I have to give it to you. I know what you're like, you can't do without money. [*Henri reacts.*] I know that; well then, go and look for it in a family of some distinction . . . or else, at any rate, where you could really love the woman who was making you rich—love purifies and ennobles everything, doesn't it?

HENRI: You want me to be in love, I want it too. Everyone says this girl is charming. . . . Well, maybe she is; I can't tell. I did think so. I did think I could take a fancy to her seventeen years of

age, her chatter, her jewelry. . . . But I can't even look at her—
I don't see her, I don't hear her. . . . [*He rises.*] She flits past me
like a ghost—a cipher! Oh, Françoise, you can't tell me to love
somebody else unless you make me forget you first!

FRANÇOISE: Let's not talk about me any more, Henri.

HENRI: Oh but we must talk about you. You're my sister—I've been
so guilty toward you—I've done you so much harm.

FRANÇOISE: I'm not interested in that; I don't care about my own
private concerns. . . . You must do me the justice to see that I'm
not acting out of personal motives in this delicate matter. My
feminine vanity hasn't, I trust, received any real wound from
what happened between us.

HENRI: Vanity? You're an angel of modesty and tenderness! . . . Oh,
believe me, I know what gives you pain: it isn't resentment, it's
kindheartedness. . . . Anyhow, I haven't deceived you, have I,
Françoise?

FRANÇOISE: No. [*Aside.*] I've deceived myself!

HENRI: When I offered you my name, I did think I had an inheritance, I did think I was able to borrow. . . .

FRANÇOISE: That's true.

HENRI: And if, today, I seem to take back rather suddenly
what I had said, it's just that an utter disaster, an upsetting
revelation . . .

FRANÇOISE: Good heavens, am I blaming you at all? . . . [*Aside.*] How
can he hurt me so! [*She sits on the divan.*]

HENRI: So you do forgive me? . . .

FRANÇOISE: Yes, yes . . . for everything that has to do with me.

HENRI: And you will stay friends with me—you promise?

FRANÇOISE: Yes—you do want to deserve my friendship, don't you?

HENRI: Deserve it! Will I cease to deserve it if I get married? . . .

FRANÇOISE: That all depends on the circumstances. Can't you get
married without selling yourself?

HENRI [*alarmed*]: Selling myself?

FRANÇOISE: Why, yes . . . if you don't love the woman you marry,
you're sold to her. . . .

HENRI: Look here, Françoise, you have such rigid views about
things. . . . If I did hurt them unintentionally, would you just
turn your back on me—without any pity or regret?

FRANÇOISE: Turn my back on you? You? I'd never do that. I'd be
deeply upset for you—but as long as you were honest, I'd never
have any hard or bitter words.

HENRI [*swept away; on the edge of his seat, almost on his knees*]: Oh, Françoise, you're the angel of mercy; I don't think I could ever take my hand away from yours. [*He kisses her hands passionately.*] No, I can't do it, you see—when two hearts are united like ours, they can't be stifled or separated. . . .

FRANÇOISE: What are you talking about, Henri? . . . Just think . . .

HENRI: I'm saying . . . I'm saying that everything around us is just a bad dream! There's nothing true or real except our own feelings! I don't understand anything any more; I can't remember anything about myself any more—except that I love you and I don't want to lose you. I couldn't do it—never, you see! I wanted to forget about you, I wanted to leave you; a moment ago I was so miserable I wanted to tell you to love somebody else. It was crazy—and you couldn't have done it anyway—you feel as I do: that we'll always have one thought, one feeling, one being—never anything else!

FRANÇOISE [*distraught*]: Oh—what you're saying is so good and true. . . .

Scene 14

[*As above; the Doctor, La Hyonnais—they have heard Françoise's reply.*]

DOCTOR [*coming in from the right*]: What's he saying to you, Françoise?

FRANÇOISE: Father, you must know the truth—he does love me— and I never did accept that he'd deserted me—no, Henri, not for a day, not for an hour! [*To her father.*] What do I care about his failings and frailties and faults? That's just the way he is. It's all understandable, because it's the way he is! Isn't that how he's always been? . . . Haven't I always accepted him, whatever he did? . . . Yes—it's my problem, it's my pain—it's my deepest concern! And even if he broke my heart a thousand times, well, I'm used to suffering for him—maybe I need it. I think if ever I couldn't put a little happiness into his life any more, I wouldn't know what to do with my own!

DOCTOR: For goodness' sake—why are you telling him that, girl? Is he giving up . . . ? [*To Henri.*] Well, go on, tell us!

HENRI [*apparently bewildered*]: Tell you what?

DOCTOR: I want to know what went on between you and Monsieur Dubuisson that he won't tell me about!

HENRI [*as if coming out of a dream*]: What went on! . . . What? What went on?

DOCTOR: You're wavering? . . . So it's true then, what they're saying in the ballroom!

FRANÇOISE: What's that?

DOCTOR: That they've come to an agreement that he can't go back on—that the marriage is settled! [*Enter Monsieur and Madame Dubuisson.*]

FRANÇOISE: Settled?

Scene 15

[*As above; Madame Dubuisson, Dubuisson.*]

DUBUISSON: Sure. We're all in agreement; he's got the warrant in his pocket.

HENRI: No, sir; I'm giving you back these warrants—take them; they feel like a stain on me. . . . They're branding me—they're burning me! . . .

DUBUISSON: Oho! That's the way it is, is it? That'll teach me to put any trust in you!

DOCTOR: Trust in him! [*To Henri.*] You wretched thing—this is a punishment for your miserable weakness!

FRANÇOISE: Father! . . . [*Quietly.*] Please don't humiliate him in front of them.

HENRI: Françoise!

DOCTOR: Be quiet! You don't have the right to ask for either affection or pity from my daughter—after an insult of that kind! Yes, the very next minute—to be there and say to her . . .

FRANÇOISE: He didn't say anything to me, father—nothing at all!

HENRI: No—forget it! . . . I was out of my senses. . . . I haven't got any strength—my feelings are strong, but my actions aren't. . . . You expect me to live such a good life—but all these people ask from me is a name! . . . I'm not a hero . . . but I'm not a coward either. . . . [*To Dubuisson.*] All I've got left is my life, sir; you can have it if you want. I'm going—but I'm not running away! You can do what you like with me! . . . [*To the Doctor.*] Good-bye! . . . [*To Françoise.*] Good-bye, Françoise—good-bye forever! [*He leaves.*]

Act 4

At La Chanterie.—Scenery as for act 2.

Scene 1

[*Madame Dubuisson, Cléonice, Françoise, sitting together, doing embroidery and talking; Dubuisson, the Doctor, at the table.*]

DOCTOR: So, you can take possession tomorrow, if you want.

DUBUISSON [*turning in his chair and looking at Françoise*]: Sure! If it won't put Mademoiselle Laurent out too much, I'll have the workmen in tomorrow morning.

FRANÇOISE [*calmly*]: It doesn't affect me any more, Monsieur Dubuisson, from the time you're the owner. . . .

DUBUISSON: Oh, good Lord—it's all settled now. . . . All that was left was this little piece of paper [*he produces a piece of paper*] that your father just gave me. I paid cash down last week, so, as things stand, I can tear the place down in five minutes, any time I like! . . . [*He rises and looks at the windows etc.*]

FRANÇOISE [*smiling*]: You could at least wait until the ladies and I have gone out into the garden! . . .

CLÉONICE: What's Daddy saying? . . . He wants to tear down the house here? . . .

DUBUISSON: You bet! This building, it'd do nothing except get in my way, being right inside my property. . . .

MADAME DUBUISSON: Fact is, it's too small for us. . . . There wouldn't even be room to put one of our caretakers here!

CLÉONICE: Daddy, I want you to give it to me!

MADAME DUBUISSON: What for? . . . [*Quietly.*] Is this for some more rendezvous?

CLÉONICE: Mummy, never whisper to me—you never manage to lower your voice. . . . If you want to scold me, do it when we're alone. [*Aloud.*] This is the house where Françoise grew up—I want to keep it out of friendship for her. . . .

DUBUISSON: Grew up, yes—with . . .

MADAME DUBUIOSSON [*rising and going to the rear*]: With Monsieur Henri! . . . [*Aside to Françoise*]. You see, lovey, my daughter has got his interests at heart, whereas you, you don't think about him any more, now that . . .

FRANÇOISE: Now that . . . ?

MADAME DUBUIOSSON [*aloud*]: Look, Françoise, let's have a good open talk about it once and for all. . . . Are you or aren't you going to marry that Monsieur de La Hyonnais? . . . [*She sits at the table.*]

DOCTOR: Well now, how does that affect you, Madame Dubuisson?

MADAME DUBUISSON: Good Lord, you know perfectly well I still have the same notions about Monsieur de Trégenec, I'm not making any secret about that. Tell me, Françoise, do you ever hear any news from Monsieur Henri? . . .

FRANÇOISE: For the last three months—ever since he went to Paris on business—no, ever since the day of the ball—I've never exchanged a single word or a single line with him.

CLÉONICE: Oh—he doesn't write to you? . . .

FRANÇOISE: Never!

MADAME DUBUISSON: But Monsieur La Hyonnais has been writing to you while he's been in Brittany this last month; I know that.

DOCTOR: Oh? You've been making inquiries at the post office?

MADAME DUBUISSON: The postmistress is a close personal relative of ours. . . . Tell us then, is he going to be back soon, dear Monsieur Jacques?

DOCTOR: You can't wait to see him again?

MADAME DUBUISSON: Naturally! He's such a very proper young man— he's had a duel over Françoise! And along of that, he's from excellent birth, he's got some money, he's become a doctor, and all of that would suit your daughter much better than Monsieur Henri, who hasn't got anything anymore and was never brought up to fret and go without.

FRANÇOISE [*smiling*]: What do you think of Henri, Cléonice?

CLÉONICE: Oh goodness—I've told you hundreds of times: I think very highly of him, seeing he's so hesitant to propose marriage to me. . . . We saw him again in Paris the last time we were there, for the Exposition. I'm sure he was less proud than he used to be . . . and less ruined too.

FRANÇOISE: You're sure . . . that he'd be willing to marry you?

CLÉONICE: Sure? No—but to tell the truth . . . I don't think he's exactly averse to me . . . .

FRANÇOISE: Nor you to him, I suppose?

CLÉONICE: Far from it! I'd be in love with him, if . . . [*Lowering her voice, to Françoise.*] Well, I am in love with him, in spite of everything.

FRANÇOISE: Oh—seriously? [*Cléonice nods.*]

DUBUISSON [*watching them*]: What are you talking about? Don't go and get that boy into your head. Mustn't think about him anymore. . . .

MADAME DUBUISSON: Why not?

DUBUISSON [*going downstage left*]: Because we haven't got any hold on him anymore. His bills have been discharged.

CLÉONICE: Good heavens! Really? When was that?

DUBUISSON: Two days ago—the day before the three months I gave him was due to expire.

FRANÇOISE [*smiling*]: Really? So he found the money? [*To Cléonice.*] Well, dear, if Henri does ask to marry you, there wouldn't be any barrier to love on either side, now that he's bought his honor back. [*They get up.*]

MADAME DUBUISSON: Who's lent it to him?

DUBUISSON: His lawyer wouldn't tell me.

MADAME DUBUISSON: Do you know, Doctor? [*She waits in vain for the Doctor to reply; he rises and takes his hat.—To Dubuisson.*] He's pretending he didn't hear me. [*Aloud.*] Françoise, did you know that Monsieur Henri had his debts paid? [*To Dubuisson.*] She isn't answering either. Aha, I see: the Doctor's paid it—that's why they're selling you La Chanterie.

DUBUISSON: You think so? . . . Let's try to find out!

MADAME DUBUISSON: Oh yes, I'll keep pestering them till they tell me! [*Aloud.*] You're going into the garden, ladies? [*Françoise is talking upstage to Cléonice, and taking her hat to go out to the garden.*]

CLÉONICE: Yes, Mummy, I want to have a talk with Françoise. . . .

MADAME DUBUIOSSON [*to her husband*]: In that case, I'll latch onto the Doctor. . . . [*Aloud.*] Doctor Laurent, do give me your arm; I want to consult you about a little matter of my health, while I've got hold of you! . . .

DOCTOR [*letting her take his arm*]: Rubbish! I know your ailment—it's inquisitiveness. [*They go out upstage. Dubuisson finishes arranging his papers.*]

Scene 2

[*Dubuisson; later, Henri.*]

DUBUISSON: My wife isn't going to budge an inch, and the girl's in favor of him. Old Trégenec is rich. . . . Let's see, is there any other hold I can get on him? He's borrowed money, he'll have all the more need of it if he's going to live like a gentleman. . . . I'll have to organize a loan for him. . . . [*Seeing Henri, who is hesitating to come in.*] Why, here he is! . . . Heck, what's he doing here? . . . [*Aloud.*] Well, well, Count! Here you are in our neck of the woods, and I didn't know anything about it!

HENRI: I've just arrived; I called to see you, and when I didn't find you at home . . .

DUBUISSON: They told you where I was! And to what do I owe the pleasure of your visit?

HENRI: First of all, sir, I must thank you for the delay in payment you arranged for me.

DUBUISSON: Nah! Forget it; I would have given you six months . . . a year. . . . But you wanted to pay on the dot: right on the day and the hour. . . .

HENRI: Ah, sir, quite the reverse: I've come to tell you that I haven't been able to get the money together, that I'm not at all in a position . . . and, if you want to take extreme measures, here I am at your disposal.

DUBUISSON: What kind of nonsense is this? I just told you, I've been paid!

HENRI: Paid? Who did that?

DUBUISSON: It wasn't you, then?

HENRI: No, sir; there must be some mistake. . . .

DUBUISSON: Oh no—there's never any mistakes when you deal with me. Somebody has paid your bills of exchange. Who? It's none of my business; it's for you to guess. . . . But I've been reimbursed good and proper.

HENRI: Monsieur Dubuisson, you must think I'm very naïve; this is a clever ploy on your part to keep me tied to you. . . . But I must tell you . . .

DUBUISSON: Monsieur, I give you my positive word of honor, I'd be incapable of doing any such thing. . . . I'm an honest above-board man myself, I don't do those kinds of tricks at all. . . . The people that have been playing around with you don't really appreciate you the right way; they're not as much your friends as I would have been if you'd let me. . . .

HENRI: Friends? What friends? Who would do a thing like that for me, without my knowledge?

DUBUISSON: I'm not casting any suspicions on anyone, but suppose for instance it was the Doctor, you know? . . . [*Aside.*] I'll just

slip that one over him. [*Aloud.*] You've heard, of course, his
young lady is getting married?

HENRI: Really?

DUBUISSON: And considering how small his financial resources are,
you'd be wise to discharge the debt soon as you possibly can. . . .

HENRI: Oh, yes, of course! . . . This generosity is causing me the
very torment I wanted to avoid.

DUBUISSON: You see how it is, then. It's like I told you: I know what
you're like, you're proud. They've driven you away from a
marriage that was good and proper for you, and where did that
get you? . . . Now you're forced to look for another one that
maybe won't suit you so nicely. . . . Are you meant to stay a
bachelor—someone like you? Nah; and you can't earn a living—you've been too well brought up. . . . So then . . .

HENRI: Well, sir?

DUBUISSON: Well, heck—think about things, that's all I'm saying.
There's heiresses that are ugly, deformed; but there's some
pretty ones too . . . and some of them haven't been too
badly brought up either. Sooner or later, you'll give it some
thought. . . . Not that I'm throwing mine at your head; I'm not
in any big hurry to part with her, thank God. . . . Still . . . I'm
not saying she likes you . . . but I do think she doesn't dislike
you. You don't owe me anything anymore, nobody's going to
say that I'm buying you. . . . Look, are peasants that become
lords any worse than lords that become peasants all over again?
Do you want to start plowing the land while I'm buying it up?
That wouldn't be natural. You were born to do nothing, like I
was born to work. And right now, I'm comfortably off, and you
don't have so much as a pebble left to your name, and I'm
offering you an easy seat. Why look sour about it? Just sit on it!
It's your position in life, it's yours by right, and I, Christophe
Dubuisson, former plowhand, I'm giving it back to you.

HENRI: Sir . . . thank you, Monsieur Dubuisson! You're a fine man,
I know that, I do see that. Certainly your daughter is very likable and very pretty. I'd consider myself a happy man if she
cared for me; and as we're currently placed, I wouldn't be
ashamed to . . . But I can't possibly give you an answer at the
moment; I'm stunned by this peculiar turn of events . . . this
mysterious service that someone has just rendered me. I wish
I knew whom to thank or blame. Let me clear up the situation

and gather my thoughts. I don't want to come to you without knowing what I should refuse or accept to gain my freedom!

DUBUISSON: Suit yourself, take your time. You want to see the Doctor? . . .

HENRI: Yes, of course, I have to; I'm afraid he might be the one! . . .

DUBUISSON: Stay there. He's with my wife; I'll go and get him.

HENRI: You think he'll agree . . . ?

DUBUISSON: Yes, yes; why not? . . . I won't say any proper good-bye then, just Oh Rev Wah. [*He holds out his hand to him.*]

HENRI: *Au revoir?* . . . you think?

DUBUISSON: Yes, yes! I guarantee it. You just think about it. [*He leaves.*]

Scene 3

HENRI [*alone*]: So the Doctor is coming to my rescue, and Françoise is forgetting about me! . . . If only I'd kept my money; I would have been happy with her, a devoted wife like that. She would have pampered me, spoiled me; I would have been proud of such a wife—her delicate concern, her discriminating intelligence. . . . But when you're poor everything becomes unbearable and impossible; I know that now: three months of expedients, uncertainties, and abject poverty have taught me that much. I've had quite enough of that! [*Stopping in front of the window.*] Lovely weather—soft autumn sunlight. . . . The Bois de Boulogne would be delightful today, in a nice light carriage, or on a good horse. . . . Oh, here's the Doctor—and Françoise with him! . . .

Scene 4

[*Françoise, the Doctor, Henri.*]

DOCTOR: Well, so here you are, then? . . .

HENRI: Doctor—Françoise—I never hoped to see you again! . . . You do forgive me, both of you? . . .

DOCTOR: Yes; we're quite in the habit of that.

FRANÇOISE: Aren't you still our spoiled child, Henri? And you've come just at the right moment—we need you here! . . .

HENRI [*going to her*]: Me? . . .

DOCTOR: Yes, it's most important, and it concerns you particularly. . . . Monsieur de La Hyonnais will be here today, and we know from his letters that he has something to tell you—it'll save him the trouble of writing to you about things that we ourselves don't yet know. . . . Well, what's wrong with you?

HENRI [*troubled*]: Doctor, I understand: La Hyonnais is the one who paid my debts. . . . It could only have been you or he.

DOCTOR: And yet it wasn't either one of us. . . .

HENRI: Why hasn't anyone asked me for some guarantee? I wasn't even asked to give my word!

DOCTOR: It's a sign of how much they trust you.

HENRI: Or despise me! . . . Don't you see, the way things are working out between us is very hurtful to me. . . . Supposing it's true that La Hyonnais is coming back to . . .

DOCTOR: Go on!

HENRI: To marry Françoise. . . .

FRANÇOISE: Well?

HENRI: Well . . . well, if that's the way it is, then I want an assurance that he wasn't the one who paid my debts! Help like that—if it's to be done with any respect for me—ought to be done in broad daylight. But the way it's being presented to me, it's being forced on me like charity! Good God, have I come to that point! Do I have to bear the burden of a good deed that— in such a context—amounts to an insult!

FRANÇOISE: An insult! Oh, if that's the way you're taking it, I'm not going to keep quiet any longer. . . .

HENRI [*going up to her*]: Don't try to excuse him, Françoise. . . . A man might oust an ordinary rival, but not a friend; and he'd never put a friend through the humiliation of having to be grateful to him! So then, Monsieur La Hyonnais mustn't count on my gratitude; I can't wait to tell him to his face. . . .

DOCTOR [*having gone upstage*]: Go and complain to him then, if you dare; here he is!

Scene 5

[*As above; La Hyonnais.*]

HENRI: So!

LA HYONNAIS [*to Françoise and the Doctor, very excitedly*]: Yes, here I am—and I'm very pleased to be able to tell you . . .

DOCTOR [*shaking his hand*]: That you've been successful?

LA HYONNAIS: Yes—not without some difficulty.

FRANÇOISE: Completely successful?

LA HYONNAIS: More than I could possibly have hoped!

FRANÇOISE [*delighted*]: Oh, Henri, don't misunderstand him, go and shake hands with him—he's your best friend!

LA HYONNAIS: Misunderstand me?

DOCTOR: Yes, he was raving on and on; but that will pass.

HENRI [*haughtily*]: No, La Hyonnais, I wasn't raving at all! I can see things perfectly well, and I don't accept your help—let's have that clearly understood!

LA HYONNAIS: What kind of a welcome is that? Towards me!

DOCTOR: He imagines you've just been paying . . .

LA HYONNAIS: His debts? . . . Doesn't he know then? . . . [*Looking at Françoise and going up to her.*] Hasn't he guessed . . . ?

HENRI [*collapsing on a chair*]: Oh—Françoise! . . . Good heavens! She . . .

DOCTOR: Well, yes; she wanted to. She persuaded me . . . and I agreed. She's disposed of the little inheritance that her mother left her. This piece of property, the orchard, the cottage itself . . . [*He goes downstage left.*]

HENRI: Françoise—all that you had! You were so fond of this place! . . .

FRANÇOISE: Yes. [*Looking at La Hyonnais.*] All my memories! . . .

HENRI: But you don't have anything left!

FRANÇOISE [*indicating the Doctor*]: Oh yes I do! My father has worked for me; and for that matter, I can work too, if necessary. . . .

HENRI: Stop it, Françoise! It's tearing me apart! How can I make up for . . . ? Oh, Françoise, you're too noble-minded—it's crushing me, I can't thank you—except with tears of shame and despair! . . . But in that case . . . how has Monsieur La Hyonnais helped me?

DOCTOR: How has he helped you? Oh, he's helped you a lot—only he himself knows the full extent of it. . . . Speak up, Jacques; tell us what you've done.

FRANÇOISE [*to La Hyonnais*]: Go on!

LA HYONNAIS [*to Henri*]: A woman . . . a woman was struggling to sacrifice herself for you. . . . I didn't want to leave her to carry the burden of her self-denial all alone. I had to find some means of reestablishing you, seeing that she loved you. . . . And I looked for a way. Your father had rejected and abandoned you. I had to persuade him to be, if not fair, at least merciful; and that's what I resolved to do. Your mother had been accused, your legitimacy had been questioned. . . . I had to discover the truth, find the proof . . . and I did! Then I had to produce the proof, show it to be correct, produce reliable witnesses. I had to bring this heart-rending case before a tribunal consisting of one man—a prejudiced judge—an injured husband. Well, I argued the case and I won it. I'm bringing you a father's affection: he's asking for you and he's waiting for you. . . . I'm giving you back a family, an inheritance, a future. . . . Above all, I'm giving you back your right to marry the [*with a slight catch in his voice*] noblest and most admirable woman there is! . . . That's what I've done for you, Henri . . . and, believe me, nothing more could possibly be done . . . within the limits of human. . . . Anyway, that's what I've done. . . .

HENRI: Oh—it's a dream. . . . My mother cleared . . . my father . . . my honor . . . Françoise's love . . . friendship . . . self-sacrifice . . . forgiveness. . . . Everything at once! . . . . [*Going to La Hyonnais.*] And I was so unkind to you, Jacques. . . . There's no reason why you should take any interest in me. . . . You've . . . I can see it all now. . . . Do forgive me as a friend—I'd forgotten everything! You must forgive me for being swept away by my own happiness!

LA HYONNAIS: I've done my duty to my father—I promised him I wouldn't abandon you—and I've done my duty to myself too, because I'm here to say good-bye to Françoise and you, just as I said I would, Henri. Good-bye. . . .

FRANÇOISE: Don't go, Jacques! . . .

LA HYONNAIS: No, I have to.

DOCTOR: Don't go—listen to her.

FRANÇOISE: Monsieur de La Hyonnais, give me your hand, please. . . . Why, it's frozen! No, leave it in mine.

LA HYONNAIS: Françoise—you'll be the death of me! . . . Good-bye!

FRANÇOISE: No, don't take your hand away. This hand has been so loyal and true, it's supported me in my troubles and it's stood between me and despair. . . . Don't be ashamed of crying. You've seen me cry, and you comforted me with words from the heart; you've seen me weak, crushed, and you never criticized my weakness—or the weakness of the man I was crying for. You helped him, you put him back on his feet, you showered kindness on him. Bless you for it—and I want you to have my father's blessing too!

LA HYONNAIS: Lord—what are you saying?

HENRI [*coming downstage*]: Françoise!

DOCTOR: Go on, girl, speak out.

FRANÇOISE: Henri, I have loved you—with the kind of love a mother has—a passion, a thirst to sacrifice myself; you had so many troubles! When the time came and I was able to help you with a bit of money . . . oh, that was a very small thing really; I bought your peace and quiet—and mine—easily enough. Yes, Henri; I've been able to say, "I've given him everything, I've got nothing left," and I've also been able to say, at the same time, "I'm calm, I'm cured; my need for self-sacrifice is satisfied, my passion is assuaged; I feel well, I feel alive, at last I'm going to breathe freely and think about myself."

HENRI: By which you mean Jacques . . . ?

FRANÇOISE: It was Jacques I was thinking about!

LA HYONNAIS [*dropping into a chair, bewildered*]: Me?

HENRI: Françoise—a person like you can never tire of forgiving someone!

FRANÇOISE: I *am* tired of suffering pointlessly. What have you got to complain about, Henri? And how can I keep thinking about you, now that I know what love really is! You poor blind boy, I do thank you very much—you've opened my eyes to the brilliance of the real sun! And what I'm feeling inside me now— this sense of wonder, this sacred flame, this faith and zeal, this clear-headed delirium—yes, Jacques, this is love, the divine fire, the child of heaven! [*Holding out her hand to La Hyonnais.*] And this is what God is sending me, to reward me for having suffered so much and forgiven so much!

LA HYONNAIS: Oh, Françoise! [*Henri turns away.*]

Scene 6

[*As above; Madame Dubuisson, Cléonice, Dubuisson.*]

MADAME DUBUIOSSON [*entering left*]: Well now, has he made his final decision?

FRANÇOISE [*aloud*]: Not yet, but here's mine: I'm marrying Monsieur de la Hyonnais.

CLÉONICE [*kissing Françoise*]: Oh, you're so kind!

MADAME DUBUISSON: Yes, yes, real nice personage!

DUBUISSON [*upstage*]: Well then, maybe we can hold the two weddings together! [*He comes downstage right.*]

DOCTOR [*going to Henri*]: You're crying?

HENRI: Oh, if only I'd stayed poor!

DOCTOR: You'd never have known how to be poor!

HENRI: If she'd loved me, I would have loved working.

DOCTOR: No; that kind of love starts as a favor, and ends as a reward; and if you reject the one, you can't receive the other.

DUBUISSON: 'Course, that's right! The Count is going to make a very fine marriage, because he's marrying for money!

LA HYONNAIS [*to Françoise*]: And what about us? We're marrying for sound practical reasons too, aren't we?

FRANÇOISE: Yes, Jacques, in our own way—since we're marrying for love!

The End

The Paving Stone

(Le Pavé)

A Story in Dialogue

Characters

MONSIEUR DURAND
LOUISE, *his maid*
JEAN COQUERET, *his valet*
A COUNTRY NEIGHBOR

Scene: a house in the country. The interior of a study. Shelves laden with minerals, jars, books, and various instruments for the use of an amateur naturalist. A cluttered writing desk, a leather armchair; door at rear, opening onto a garden at the same level; door at right leading to a bedroom; window at left. A hunting rifle and a game bag on the wall.

Scene 1

NEIGHBOR [*offstage at rear*]: All right, Rosalie. I'll just wait for a little while and take a rest; if he doesn't come back, I'll be off. [*He enters.*] What an extraordinary fellow he is! I can't wait to find out if he's taken the plunge. My sister wrote me that she hadn't seen him, but the letter was dated the twenty-fifth, and it's the thirtieth now . . . and since he said he'd be back at the end of a week . . . The week is up. He must have introduced himself to his prospective bride by this time. After that, there will be some business for him to settle at home, his house will have to be set in order. . . . So long as his scientific fancies and lunacies don't keep him away from it too long! . . . But I'll shake some sense into him. Ah! Here he is.

Scene 2

[*Durand, the Neighbor.*]

NEIGHBOR: What on earth have you got there? An old paving stone? Oh yes—geology, mineralogy. . . . Well, hello, Durand my friend!
DURAND [*placing his paving stone on the table. He is in walking clothes*]: Hello, neighbor, I'm glad to see you. Oof! Boof! What a weight! How are things with you? . . . And what about my people here? The only one I've seen so far has been the cook . . . and I don't know . . .
NEIGHBOR: That makes two of us. She's the only one I've seen, too. But I know your other servants are doing well.
DURAND [*aside*]: Then why isn't Louise here when I come home?
NEIGHBOR: You seem very preoccupied with something—what are you looking for?
DURAND: Nothing. Yes I am . . . my traveling cloak. I had it just a moment ago.
NEIGHBOR: You've got it on your shoulders—which is very odd, considering how warm it is.
DURAND: Well, look at that! Isn't that peculiar!
NEIGHBOR: Absentminded as ever, are you? Really! That's become such a cliché nowadays. Now, if I were a scholar, I'd want to make myself noted for my excellent get-up and continual

presence of mind, to show people that I had a strong enough
head to hold my learning.

DURAND: That's what Louise says to me. Thanks to her reprimands
I keep everything in pretty good shape, as you can see; but I
can't help losing or mislaying my possessions. Anyhow, this time
I'm positive I haven't lost anything on the way; everything's in
my bag. Let me take it off. There are some new straps on it,
and they keep cutting into my shoulders; two or three times I
simply had to take it off and carry it by hand. [*He tries to take
off a bag he doesn't have.*]

NEIGHBOR [*laughing*]: Then what do you think you've got on your
back?

DURAND [*feeling himself*]: Nothing—quite right! I could have sworn
I could feel the straps. They must have bruised my arms.

NEIGHBOR: Well, where is the bag, then?

DURAND: I suppose I took it off just now in the hall. Yes, that's
right, I remember: I must have put it on the coat stand. [*He
starts to go out, and stops in front of a shelf.*] Why, what's this?
Schistose graywacke among the igneous rocks![1] . . . What an
imbecile that Coqueret is! He can never manage to put a speci-
men back in the right place when his stupid feather duster has
knocked it off! What a mania he has for dusting! But that's the
way Louise wants it, so one simply has to put up with it. As long
as everything hasn't been turned upside down! [*He starts examining and tidying things.*]

NEIGHBOR: Now then, look here, Durand my friend, try to think a
little bit less about your rocks and do me the kindness of listening
to me. I've come to talk to you about something different.

DURAND: Talk away, talk away, my friend, I'm all ears. . . . Only—
wait a minute—my hammer! Yes, I left it in my bag, but I'm
sure I'll find one here. . . . [*He opens a drawer and takes out a
hammer.*] Aha! Mister Jean Coqueret has been at it in my absence. Just look at this blunt tool—useless! . . . The brute! [*He
takes another.*]

NEIGHBOR: It's your own fault; you want to turn your servants into
geologists. . . .

DURAND: Well, I could have sworn, my friend, that he has a remarkable aptitude for it. He has what we commonly call a "sharp
eye," in other words he has admirably developed ocular senses;
but the moment you want to put an exact name or a rational
idea into his head, he's an idiot!

NEIGHBOR: Well, that should give you a bit of a laugh.

DURAND: It gives me a laugh when I'm in the mood to laugh. Would you believe it, he calls mica "midas" and crinoids "crinolines"?

NEIGHBOR: And what about Louise—does she take to your barbaric names?

DURAND [*fervently*]: Ah now, Louise—she's a phoenix of intelligence, my friend. Oh, if only I'd tried to teach her earlier! I never thought of it; I never saw any need for a housekeeper to know more; but just lately a thought occurred to me, and I said to her, "Why don't you learn a little geology? You could put some order into my specimens—I don't always have the patience to keep them tidy, and the way that little lackey keeps setting them up, they look like a representation of the primeval chaos." Well, my friend, believe it or not, in three months, Louise—and the very utmost of what that little peasant girl knows is how to read and write satisfactorily—she's set herself to study my *Index Methodicus*—you know, the introductory book I published last year—and lo and behold, now she knows the principal classes of rocks, and a fair proportion of the subcategories, just as well as you and I do.

NEIGHBOR: Just as well as I do! Thank you very much! I don't know the first thing about 'em—and I don't want to know. Poor girl! It must be terribly boring for her.

DURAND: Boring? For her? . . . You don't know what Louise is like! That girl's a treasure of devotion and self-sacrifice! As long as she can be of use, she's happy; she has no other thought or instinct than the wish to serve and please the people she cares about.

NEIGHBOR: You're talking about her with some feeling.

DURAND: Well, and why not? You're not reading any mischief into it, are you?

NEIGHBOR: No. I know you're the strictest man alive when it comes to principles and moral standards; but I was just wondering if, being as fond of her as you are, you might be thinking of marrying her.

DURAND [*laughing*]: Marrying her? Me? What an idea! Trust you to come up with an idea like that.

NEIGHBOR: Well, it's my turn to ask: And why not? You don't have any prejudices.

DURAND: I don't know what you mean by prejudices, but I know that I feel too pure and paternal an affection for that child ever

to think of imposing my forty-five years on her fresh youth. No,
no! Good heavens! Me with a young wife? Think of the mockery, and the future, and the catarrh, and the clamor, and the
corruption that inevitably infests ill-assorted marriages! Can any
daughter of Eve, in such a situation, stay faithful to an old man
without utter misery? No, I tell you! Leave Thérèse to Jean-
Jacques Rousseau.[2] Escapades of that kind may be all very well
for men of genius—and even in those cases they don't always
turn out very well.

NEIGHBOR: Since you're so level headed about things, I see I can
talk sensibly to you. A woman of thirty-two is what you need.
Did you see my niece in town?

DURAND [*examining his paving stone*]: *Gryphaea arcuata—Trigonia
gibbosa*[3] . . .

NEIGHBOR: Who? My niece? A griffin? A gibbon? Just what do you
mean by that, may I ask? There are no griffins or gibbons in my
family!

DURAND: Oh, I'm not talking about your niece, my dear fellow! I'm
looking at the contents of this magnificent block of oölite.[4] It's
a real find—I collected it on the highway, at the very moment
when the road mender was going to make use of it. The scoun-
drels, they're smashing up discarded paving stones to metal the
road—they're destroying all sorts of rare and precious specimens! And why, I ask you? If everyone had the sense to travel on
foot, as I do—whatever the place, and whatever the season. . . .

NEIGHBOR: You went to town on foot, and you came back the same
way?

DURAND [*examining his paving stone*]: Well, I'll be!—Seventeen species of fossils in a single stone! And when I say "fossils," many
of the specimens are in a perfect state of preservation! *Terebratula
spinosa, Nerinea hieroglyphica, Cidaris coronata, Pholadomya
fidicula*[5]—they're all here. . . .

NEIGHBOR: Fidicula fiddlesticks! . . . You're becoming quite intolerable, my friend, and since there's no way to extract one word
of commonsense from you . . . I'll wish you good day! [*He takes
his hat.*]

DURAND: No, no! Come now, you must forgive me! Do be patient
for a moment. . . . There's something here that fascinates me. . . .
Is it a maxillary tooth of a fish, or else . . . ?

NEIGHBOR: Hmm, maybe you're not quite as absentminded as you
make out! You're acting deaf so that you won't have to answer

me; but I'm here to tell you it's time you made a decision. You've been letting matters slip by. My sister tells me that you went to town to see her daughter and clean forgot to visit them.

DURAND: Why, I didn't forget anything at all. I admit I couldn't get up the determination to make that embarrassing visit, but I did see your niece out walking. I was most impressed with her; and as marriage is a serious matter and requires careful thought, I've come back home to think carefully for a little while.

NEIGHBOR: What on earth is there to think carefully about? You know everything about her—young widow, good family, no children, suitable age; she's respectable, educated, pretty, good natured. There can't be any question about her. She's at least as well off as you are. . . .

DURAND: That's all true, my friend. Why get yourself worked up about it? Am I disagreeing with you? I've seen her, I tell you. She's tall, blonde, slim, elegant; a bit on the thin side, though. . . .

NEIGHBOR: What on earth are you talking about?

DURAND: Oh yes, she is a bit on the thin side. . . . It's a pity! . . . And very blonde, too. . . . I would have preferred her to be a brunette.

NEIGHBOR: Well now, my friend—you and your ocular senses! You haven't any ocular senses at all—I can tell you that. Élise is small, dark, and "deliciously plump," as we used to say in my day. You've been looking at somebody else—why, you've mistaken her friend Madame de Saintos for her!

DURAND: Oh! . . . So your niece was the little brunette beside her? Yes, yes, I did notice her too. . . . Well, I declare! She *is* pretty! . . . A bit too dark and a bit too small. . . . Still, I'll think about it, she's worth thinking about. . . . I'll start thinking about it! Just give me time to get used to the idea of a little brunette—for the past three days I've done nothing but ponder the physiological peculiarities of a tall blonde.

NEIGHBOR: Durand, do you know what I think? You don't care about blondes or brunettes one way or the other. You haven't the slightest desire to get married, and you've hurried home so you won't have to think about it any more.

DURAND: No; I'm a straightforward man, and I haven't gone hunting for any excuse to avoid making up my mind. I came home . . . well, because my legs took me home. What do you expect? Habit, the need to work, the impossibility of being idle,

of dining in town and courting . . . I don't know anything at all
about such matters—good Lord, no! I'm not used to paying
court to a woman. I'd just be a donkey trying to be a lapdog,
I'm afraid; they'd find me utterly ridiculous—that's what I felt,
and I said to myself. . . . No, I didn't say anything to myself. I
took my traveling bag, I set off on a walk, and here I am back
home without quite knowing why or wherefore.

NEIGHBOR: Well, you may not know, but I for one can tell you. You
can't stand the idea of marriage; you'd rather stay an old bachelor. I might have expected it from an eccentric of your type.
You simply made me put my foot in it, when you asked me to
write to my sister. . . .

DURAND: Oh but excuse me; I didn't ask you at all; you were the
one who offered to do it—you talked me into agreeing.

NEIGHBOR: You didn't say no!

DURAND: I didn't say yes!

NEIGHBOR: So now you're not saying either yes or no? Well then,
I'll have you know that my niece wasn't created to sit around
waiting for your good pleasure! . . . She isn't lacking for suitors,
she doesn't know you, and she wouldn't have given you any
preference except to please me.

DURAND: Oh, in that case, my friend, it's all for the best! I don't
feel so bad about hesitating.

NEIGHBOR: Well, you can stop hesitating as of now; my niece isn't
for you. I'll write to her straight away and tell her to choose
somebody else, and I'll apologize to her for the stupid blunder
that my friendship for you led me into.

DURAND: My, if you're getting angry . . .

NEIGHBOR: You bet I'm angry! Lord knows, I've every right to be.

DURAND: No.

NEIGHBOR: Oh yes I have; and as I take my leave, may I have the
great pleasure of telling you that you're messing up your life
just splendidly with all this tomfoolery! Here's a very happy
man and a very useful citizen, whose only pleasure in life is
filling up his house with discarded cobblestones and smashed-
up seashells! Let me warn you that you're going to end up an
utter idiot—you'll become a silly pedant with an empty heart
and a scatterbrained head—an oddball—an old fuddle-headed
Polonius![6] . . .

DURAND [*laughing*]: Good heavens! That's a lot of ailments to have
all at once!

NEIGHBOR: Oh yes—and bit by bit you'll go mad, because people are made for domesticity, for company, and anyone who doesn't want to live like other people—anyone who doesn't have a taste for sensible things . . . That's all I'm saying, Monsieur Durand, that's all I'm saying; and please take good note of my words! [*He leaves.*]

Scene 3

DURAND [*alone*]: Now there's a litany for you! Just as well I'm a patient man! Still, you have to be tolerant of white-haired men, when you're a dozen years younger and don't have any white hairs yourself. Anyone would think I was going to turn doddery tomorrow morning—that I ought to hurry up and buy myself a walking stick. Humph! Go for a hike, you and your sermonizing! Anyhow, before I come to any decision, I really ought to consult the people who are close to me: my relatives, my friends, even Louise. Especially Louise: I wouldn't have any rest or well-being in life without her. Think how she'd feel if some cantankerous lady of the house started bullying her! Louise is utterly devoted to me—everywhere, in every respect, even to the point of taking up science so as to be of use to me. What other woman would have so much good sense and generosity? [*Looking at his collection.*] When I think how some ignorant tease could throw the whole lot out the window, force me to take an interest in her wardrobe, drag me off to dances! . . . But where is Louise, anyway? Maybe she's sick! . . . And that funny Jean Coqueret—why isn't he here? [*Calling.*] Coqueret! . . . Coq . . .

Scene 4

[*Durand, Coqueret.*]

COQUERET [*carrying Monsieur Durand's bag on his back*]: Here I am, sir! Hello, sir! Have you come back, sir?
DURAND: So it would seem. . . . Hello, my boy. Where's Louise?
COQUERET: Very well, sir. And yourself?
DURAND: I'm talking about Louise!
COQUERET: Thank you kindly, sir; and the same to you.
DURAND: When you're quite finished with your salaaming, perhaps you would be so kind as to answer me. I'm asking you where Louise is.

COQUERET [*worried*]: It's very kind of you, sir. Louise is . . . I don't know where she is, but I can promise Monsieur, she and I, we're just like brother and sister—no more and no less!

DURAND: Well, I should certainly hope so! [*Aside.*] Is he meaning some mischief by this, I wonder? No, he's too simple. [*Aloud.*] Oh, by the way, find my bag for me; it must be somewhere around here.

COQUERET [*who has put the bag on the table*]: There it is, sir; I found it!

DURAND: I must have lost it, then?

COQUERET: Oh no, Monsieur didn't lose it; he just left it beside the road on a heap of stones. I was coming back from the meadow, where I'd been to take the cow with Louise.

DURAND: So Louise stayed in the meadow? Why did you tell me you didn't know where she was?

COQUERET: Did I say that?

DURAND: You did.

COQUERET: That's odd, sir, that is. I thought I said, "She's with her cow."

DURAND: And why is she still bothering about cows? I relieved her of that job.

COQUERET: Oh, sir, she can't act the young lady—she's so fond of animals!

DURAND: Well, anyway, why did you tell me, "I don't know"?

COQUERET: I thought Monsieur was asking about the cook.

DURAND: Get along with you—still as silly and absentminded as ever! A real featherbrain!

COQUERET: Oh, no, sir! Since you went away for a week, I haven't been nearly as stupid, not by half!

DURAND: In other words, I'm the one who makes you stupid?

COQUERET: Oh, no, sir, it's my fault entirely! But since Louise started educating me . . .

DURAND: Oh! Louise has started . . . ?

COQUERET: Yes, sir. She said to me, like, "Look, Jean, you keep annoying the master, with your lack of sense and everything; you must make an effort to use your head and learn, so as to please him. Now, me, I've learned just so as I can teach you, and I'm going to teach you fast, while Monsieur isn't here."

DURAND: So . . . you say she's taken the trouble of learning entirely for you?

COQUERET: Yes, sir, it's like I'm telling you.

DURAND [*ironically*]: She's very good indeed, isn't she!

COQUERET: Oh yes, sir, she's awful good, and that's the truth!

DURAND [*aside, taking his hammer and working grumpily at his stone*]: And here I was thinking this fine enthusiasm was because she was so devoted to me! . . . But she just said those things to encourage him. . . . After all, she was only trying to make him less of a nuisance to me, so it was still done on my behalf. Excellent girl! [*Aloud.*] Let's see, what has she taught you, Mademoiselle Louise?

COQUERET: Louise? She started off at the start, with the . . .

DURAND: With the granites?

COQUERET: Yes, sir.

DURAND: All right, what is granite?

COQUERET: What is it? What is it? It's what you put at the beginning of the books and at number one on the shelves. It's the mountains up by Saint-Pierre.

DURAND: Good! And what else? It's made up of . . . ?

COQUERET: It's made up of . . . it's made up of . . . three things, which are . . . three things which are this . . . and this . . . and this.[7] [*He takes various specimens and shows them to Durand.*]

DURAND: I see! You don't know the names, you'll never learn them; but the eye and the memory for facts are there, all the same. At the very least you need to have some idea of the history of the planet. . . . Where did granite come from, in the beginning?

COQUERET: Oh, I know that, sir! It came from water—or fire—or air—whichever you like.[8]

DURAND: What! Whichever I like?

COQUERET: Louise told me, "Monsieur isn't sure, but he prefers to think it came from fire—it'll be whatever Monsieur decides."

DURAND [*aside*]: You'd think the two of them were setting out to make fun of me! Truth is, though, I don't have anything on that score but hypotheses. [*Thoughtfully, looking at the granite that Coqueret has brought him.*] Who can solve the very first problem for certain? Who presided over the spectacle, when these astonishing things were formed?[9] Ah, granite—the commonest and most mysterious of all rocks—the key that opens everything, except the starting point itself! Behind it, there's nothing established—only our flights of fancy and theories! It's the legendary poem [*Louise enters*] of our dreams, the impenetrable witness to days that are gone forever, the . . .

Scene 5

[*As above; Louise.*]

LOUISE [*having, on entry, shot a questioning glance at Coqueret, to which
he signals that their master is off in space—this gesture has nothing
ironic on Coqueret's part; on the contrary, it is respectful and admiring*]: Hello, sir.

DURAND [*jumping, and leaving his stone*]: Oh! Hello, Louise, my
good girl! [*He kisses her on the forehead, almost respectfully.*] Are
you at all happy to see me?

LOUISE: Oh yes, sir, very happy.

COQUERET [*quietly to Louise*]: Why don't you kiss him back? Go and
kiss him!

LOUISE [*quietly*]: No!

DURAND [*to Coqueret*]: Why are you whispering to her? [*To Louise.*]
What was he saying to you?

LOUISE: Nothing, sir, just silly things!

COQUERET: Oh no, sir, it wasn't silly things! I was telling her to kiss
Monsieur, just to please Monsieur! Honest!

DURAND [*rather touched*]: No; she's right to be more reserved, more
serious in her manners, now that she's grown up.

COQUERET: Is that why she doesn't want me to kiss her any more
myself? But with Monsieur it isn't the same thing; he's old.

DURAND: Old . . . old! . . .

LOUISE: Look here, sir, you just put yourself at ease. [*To Coqueret.*]
Go and find his coat and slippers for him. [*Coqueret hurries out
the door at right, which leads to Monsieur Durand's room.*]

Scene 6

[*Durand, Louise.*]

LOUISE: If you've come from town on foot, you must be tired!

DURAND: Tired? Me? Oh, has your pupil Monsieur Coqueret persuaded you that I'm very old, then?

LOUISE: You're not old, but you're not very young any more, either. And that nasty cold of yours, that you don't want to look
after! You've coughed three times already in the past three
minutes.

DURAND: Bah! So what? A slight touch of some lingering malady
makes you live fifty years longer! Tell me, what have you been

up to in my absence? You've been making yourself Coqueret's teacher, from what I hear, eh?

LOUISE: Oh! He told you . . . ?

DURAND: That you started him off on granite. But you're wasting your time: you'll never make him into anything other than a fool.

LOUISE: Excuse me, sir, but I'll make him into a good servant for you, because he's kind, decent, willing, and he's fond of you, too. That's certainly something!

DURAND: Yes, that's true; his instincts are good enough, but he'll never get beyond the instinctive.

LOUISE: Well, do you need a scholar to serve you? Aren't I here to sort out his little bits of clumsiness?

DURAND: Oh now, you, Louise, you're something else again! You have a fine memory, you're admirably teachable. It's a real pleasure to instruct you in anything. You mean a great deal to me, Louise dear. So much care and attention! To be served like a prince, coddled like a child, understood by someone who takes an interest in your work and helps you with your little hobbies . . . Why, what's the matter with you? You're sad? . . . What are you thinking about?

LOUISE: Nothing, sir; I was looking at this paving stone—it's a fine piece.

DURAND [*excitedly*]: Yes, isn't it? Just think, there's a fossil tooth there. . . . I imagine there could be an entire jaw, possibly it's . . . But you're not listening to me; something's bothering you!

LOUISE: No, sir.

DURAND [*looking at the paving stone*]: If it's what I think . . . it would be a real rarity. . . . But you're unhappy; that takes all the pleasure out of things for me. You're working too hard, I expect!

LOUISE: Me? Just the reverse, if you ask me; I don't do enough to repay you for all your kindness. After what you've done for me—brought me up, taught me, always been so good to me, gave my poor mother a home and looked after her right up to her last day. . . . See, she was a poor woman that nobody would have anything to do with, and you taught me to love and respect her in spite of everyone. . . . After that, if I didn't want to serve you and look after you when you're old and sick like she was . . .

DURAND: Me? I'll never be sick. With an active and sensible life, like the one I'm leading . . .

LOUISE: All the better then! But I would like you to have some need for me. You'd see then whether I remember it or not!

DURAND: Louise, you're an angel. I haven't done for you nearly as much as I should have. I've positively neglected you up till now. I didn't see how intelligent you were. I treated you like an ordinary peasant. I kept you at a distance, behind the door so to speak; I told myself it was enough to provide for your material needs, I never grasped that your mind needed cultivating too—that I'd be able to talk with you one day as a friend. Oh yes, I'm wide open to criticism. I've been absorbed in my books, and it's only in the last two or three months that I've begun to appreciate you and listen to you and look at you!

LOUISE [aside]: Oh, I would have been so much better off staying behind the door!

DURAND: Why are you daydreaming while I'm talking to you? Can't you see, I've set my heart on making up for my neglect. Don't I owe it to you? Haven't you done so much good for me? You've opened up my heart to friendship—and an even more tender feeling than that, one that I would never have known if it hadn't been for you: paternal feeling! That's the truth. I would have been just an old dried-up petrified pickaxer like my pebbles, wouldn't I? I would have become a gloomy unbearable hypochondriac! It was already starting to happen. I was getting moody at times—even with you. You say I've always been kind! You're forgetting that very often I've called you a fool and a scatterbrain. But that won't happen any more, no indeed; I can promise you that!

LOUISE [aside]: Oh dear! All the worse, in that case.

DURAND: No, no! . . . I won't be foolish any more. . . . I wouldn't dream of making you cry any more, you poor child! My eyes have been opened. I've realized . . . Yes, I was thinking about it just a little while ago, when I was on my way back here.

LOUISE: You were thinking too much. You left your traveling bag right in the middle of the road!

DURAND: You mischievous girl—you're scolding me. Well, of course I did! I was thinking about you. I was saying to myself, "A nice kind intelligent woman is a real treasure in a household—a ray of sunlight in a poor hermit's life! . . . Why do I have to go looking for a wife in town, when right beside me . . . ?"

LOUISE: Oh! You were thinking of getting married? Your neighbor did mention it to me. But you've given up the idea?

DURAND: Oh yes, you can rest assured! Nobody but you is going to give orders here!

LOUISE: But on the contrary, sir, I . . .

DURAND: Don't worry, I tell you! But I do believe I'm hungry, Louise; I don't know if I've had any lunch today. My whole chest feels on fire . . .

LOUISE: I bet you didn't even think of it! Well, your meal's waiting for you. Hurry up, sir.

DURAND: But . . . you're coming with me, aren't you? I won't have you passing me my plate any more; that's Monsieur Coqueret's job. You can talk to me and tell me about your chickens and your goat. Is he doing all right, your little goat?

LOUISE: Yes, of course, sir; to be sure he is!

DURAND: Ah, it feels good to be back home, and see my house again and my garden, and especially you! See you in a moment, little Louise! [*He leaves at rear.*]

Scene 7

LOUISE [*alone*]: Is there a better man on earth, or a kinder master than he is? No, there isn't. And the more he spoils me, the more frightened and worried I get! The good Lord knows it isn't my fault, what's happening! I never would have thought . . .

Scene 8

[*Louise, Coqueret.*]

LOUISE: And about time!

COQUERET [*carrying the coat and slippers*]: Don't be cross at me, Louise! It isn't my fault. I couldn't find the slippers, I could only find one of them. The rats had been and dragged the other one under the bed. I mean, it's Monsieur's fault! It's because he won't have any cats in the house, not after that big tomcat made your arm bleed all over and Monsieur was in such a state about it too and . . .

LOUISE: Run along and serve him, you chatterbox! He's in the middle of lunch! You understand? Who do you think I'm talking to?

COQUERET: Well, what do you think I'm doing? I'm getting there quick as I can! But listen a minute, Louise. In the meadow you wouldn't listen to what I was trying to tell you. You sent me back very crossly, you got to listen to me here!

LOUISE: No! We don't have the time.

COQUERET: It's the best time of all: Monsieur has just come back, he's in a good mood, I'm going to tell him straight out.

LOUISE: What? What are you going to tell him?

COQUERET: I'm going to tell him I love you, and I'm mad keen on you, and it's driving me crazy! . . .

LOUISE: Oh yes—you just try and tell him that, if you want him to send you packing!

COQUERET: Don't care; it'll have been said, and if you wouldn't mind saying the same . . .

LOUISE: That's enough. I've told you, it can't be done, I'm not about to get married just yet; you mustn't think about it, and that's all. I don't want to hear another word on the subject; I won't have it! [*Coqueret, who has put the coat and slippers on a chair, sits on top of them in despair and bursts into tears, with his head in his hands. Louise looks at him for a moment, then turns away and hides her face, crying too. Louise wipes her eyes.*] Monsieur is ringing; off you go!

COQUERET: No, I don't want to do any serving any more; I want to do away with myself!

LOUISE: Come on! Are you crazy? You want to keep Monsieur waiting?

COQUERET: Ten years I've been waiting on him every day; he can wait for me for once!

LOUISE: Are you trying to upset me?

COQUERET: Even if I did, I'd never do it to you as much as you done it to me!

LOUISE [*sternly*]: So, don't you care anything about me any more? It's all over, is it?

COQUERET: Why should I care anything about someone that just hates me?

LOUISE: You don't mean what you're saying. We've been brought up together, you know I'm very fond of you; but I can't possibly marry you. It isn't up to me. . . . Don't be silly! . . .

COQUERET: That's not true! You haven't got any mother any more, or relatives, or anything! The only thing it's up to is Monsieur, and he does everything you want, and if . . . [*The bell rings.*]

LOUISE: So, you won't obey? All right, I'm going myself! [*She goes out.*]

Scene 9

COQUERET [*alone*]: It's like that, is it? She doesn't love me at all? So then, maybe she loves somebody else better? What somebody else? She hardly knows anybody else except me; she never goes out anywhere, I'm never away from her, I'm jolly sure nobody else is chatting her up! So then, it's just that she doesn't like me, I'm too stupid for her! Oh, if it was only up to me.... [*He picks up Monsieur Durand's hammer.*] I'd break ... [*threatening the collections*] every last thing here! Oh yes I would! No—it'd upset Monsieur too much! And if I blew my own brains out, that'd worry him too—he's a decent fellow! Now that's what I call a man! He's a good fellow! He'd be worried sick about me—if he understood how I'm suffering, he'd order Louise to love me! Well ... why, that's it! I'm going to tell him exactly how things stand. Good—here he is! I'm going to tell him ... right this moment, too.... Ah, well, yes, only thing is ... I haven't got the guts!

Scene 10

[*Durand, Coqueret.*]

DURAND [*to the wings*]: No, girl, I don't want to eat any more; it isn't lunchtime. . . . Send me the cocoa here. [*Aloud, to Coqueret.*] Ah, you're here, are you? Why didn't you come when I rang, instead of sending Louise in your place? She's the one who goes to all the trouble!

COQUERET: Oh goodness! Louise and me, that's all the same thing, sir; her trouble is my trouble, and ...

DURAND: Eh? What are you trying to say?

COQUERET: I'm trying to say ... I'm trying to say that Monsieur must forgive me; I wasn't feeling well.

DURAND [*taking off his gaiters and putting on his slippers*]: Oh? We weren't feeling well? Louise didn't tell me that.

COQUERET: That was because she didn't want to cause Monsieur any worry.

DURAND [*smiling*]: You think I'm very fond of you, then?

COQUERET: I know Monsieur is very fond of me, because he knows I'm even more than very fond of him, and seeing Monsieur is so kindhearted ...

DURAND [*having put on his coat*]: Come now! If that's how you feel, you're not wrong to count on it. You really are intolerable— and yet you're a fine lad! What's the trouble, then? Headache?

COQUERET: No, sir.

DURAND: A cramp? A chill?

COQUERET: No, sir.

DURAND: Well, what is it, then?

COQUERET: I don't know, sir.

DURAND [*irritated*]: Where is it, then?

COQUERET [*cowed*]: Nowhere, sir. It's getting better; it's going away.

DURAND: Well then, what was the trouble a moment ago? Won't you talk? Are you making fun of me?

COQUERET: Oh no, Monsieur—the idea!

DURAND: Hmm—you know what it is? Your brains are addled— that's your trouble.

COQUERET: Yes, Monsieur, exactly; that's it.

DURAND: Try to get better, or you'll never be good for anything anymore. Off you go, go and find some cocoa for me . . . and my paper; hurry up!

COQUERET [*aside*]: I'll never have the guts! . . . I need to come up with an idea! [*He leaves.*]

Scene 11

DURAND [*alone*]: One goes to a lot of trouble to find happiness, and one always looks for it where it isn't. Ah! The philosophers described our vain desires very well when they called them the love of false goods! Such commonplace words—yet most profound! Certainly, there's something false and deceitful about the kind of satisfactions that money and ambition and pride can bring. Does a wise and healthy man have any need of the nerve-racking luxury of cities and frivolous shows and heartless love affairs? The simplest wildflower . . .

Scene 12

[*Durand, Coqueret.*]

COQUERET: Sir, here is your cocoa, with a letter for you. [*Aside, while Durand is opening the letter.*] I've hit on my idea, and this

one's brilliant! If it doesn't work—why, I must really be in for
some bad luck! [*He steps aside a little.*]

DURAND [*aside, opening the letter*]: Ah! It's from my neighbor. Is the
fearsome old fellow challenging me to a duel? [*Reading.*] "I
shouldn't have anything more to do with you, but at the moment, my hand is forced. Some people who want to meet you,
and who have just arrived here, absolutely insist that I should
invite you to dinner. As this will be your only chance to make
up for the harm you've done, I'm counting on you not to
refuse. I shall expect you at six." Curse these people! What can
I do? Still, I can't quarrel with my neighbor—he's a decent
fellow. . . .

COQUERET: Sir, they're waiting for the answer.

DURAND [*vexed*]: Say that I'll go.

COQUERET [*calling out through the window*]: Monsieur will go! [*Aside,
returning.*] I'll have to hurry up and speak to him soon, because
he's going to go out. [*Aloud.*] Sir . . . [*Aside.*] He isn't listening
to me, he's reading his paper. [*Aloud.*] Sir, you're a good
master . . . an intelligent man . . . a great scholar. . . . [*Aside.*] He
isn't listening to me at all! I'm going to whinge a bit. [*He
produces some deep sighs.*]

DURAND: Well, what is it? Toothache?

COQUERET: No, sir, it's in the heart.

DURAND: Nonsense! It's growing pains.

COQUERET: No, sir. Monsieur still thinks I'm a baby—but I'm over
twenty-two and a half.

DURAND: Fancy that! It's quite possible. All right, what's wrong with
your heart? Palpitations?

COQUERET: Yes, Monsieur, they're hurting me and burning me and
stabbing me!

DURAND: You've had them for some time?

COQUERET: Yes, sir, quite a while now.

DURAND: They happen when you're tired?

COQUERET: No, sir, they happen when I think about Louise.

DURAND [*starting*]: Oho! You've taken the liberty of falling in love
with Louise, have you, you rascal?

COQUERET: Good—he guessed it right away. That's good!

DURAND [*trembling with rage*]: Answer me, you wretch! You . . .

COQUERET [*frightened*]: It isn't me, sir, it's her.

DURAND: What do you mean, it's her? What do you have the hide
to mean by that?

COQUERET [*holding his head in his hands*]: Yes, sir, she was the one that had the idea of marrying me. I wasn't quite thinking as far as that just yet, myself. I kept telling her, "We're too young," but she said, like, "We're old enough, I'm seventeen, you're twenty-three; that's just right." But I kept telling her all the time, "It's too soon, Louise, it's too soon!" And then, Monsieur, she got so miserable that, all the time you were away, she did nothing else but moan and cry; and it was so bad that I got to feeling sorry, and the pity made me sad and sick, and I agreed to speak to you about it, sir, just to please the poor girl; because she'd never dare to tell you herself how much she loves me, same as even if you asked her, she'd just say I had a bee in my bonnet about it; but you've got to believe what I'm telling you and not what she's going to tell you, and, seeing as how I can see plain enough it's killing her, I've got it into my head to get married to her, and I've come to talk to you about it, because you're the best friend I've got, only so that you can order her to get married, and, seeing as how she's that obedient to you, as soon as you've said, "You have to!" she'll make up her mind, and you'll make her happy. That's what it is, Monsieur; and I do ask your pardon if I've said anything silly.

DURAND [*after a moment's silence, in an altered voice*]: Get out! [*Coqueret, dumbfounded, hesitates. Durand, beside himself, repeats:*] Go on, get out! [*Coqueret leaves, very crestfallen.*]

Scene 13

DURAND [*alone*]: It's impossible! Louise! . . . Oh! Louise! . . . In love with that boy? No, he's insane! I'll send him away; I'll send Louise away too, if it's true. . . . I'll kill her! [*A pause.*] What on earth can be the matter with me? Why should I care? . . . I care . . . I care because she's, in a sense, my adopted daughter, and the daughter of my heart and my intelligence can't possibly mismatch herself like that! What! Come down from the heights where my affection and admiration have placed her, and fall into the arms of a country bumpkin! . . . Ah! Women! Wasn't I told that they're the lowest creatures in creation? And here I was turning her into an angel—a saint! You can see how a scholar knows nothing, absolutely nothing, about real

life. . . . But—no, it isn't true, it can't be true—a thousand times
no! I must talk to her now, right away, and question her—to the
very depths of her soul; and I'll trample her underfoot if she
admits . . . Hold on—what *is* the matter with me? I've never in
my life felt in such a fury as this! And with good cause, yes, very
good cause, very sensibly. Sensibly? . . . No, anger isn't ever
sensible. I need to calm down, I need to get some fresh air, go
for a walk, breathe; yes, I need to go out hunting for a while,
and settle myself down again. [*He takes his rifle.*] After
which . . . quite deliberately, with the utmost composure . . . Off
we go! I don't feel at all well! [*He thinks he is leaving; he walks
around the room and drops overcome in front of his desk, with his head
in his hands and his rifle beside him.*]

Scene 14

[*Louise, Durand.*]

LOUISE: Sir . . . since you're going out to dinner, I think it's time
for you to get dressed. [*Durand signals to her that he does not want
to be disturbed.*] Oh! He's at work—he's at work thinking. Poor
master! Maybe he's upset. . . . No, he doesn't realize . . . but I
can see the danger myself, and I don't know how I ought to
act. . . . If he's in love with me, he's made up his mind to marry
me. A dreadful thing that would be! I'd die of sorrow! . . .
Because I couldn't possibly say no to him, not after everything
he's done for me. I'd be ungrateful and a coward and wicked.
What if I ran away? . . . That'd be worse still; he'd be too unhappy; but if I stay . . . poor Jean! . . . Good Lord, good Lord! . . .
Why did Monsieur have to be so friendly to a poor girl that
could have been happy just serving him with . . . ? Oh! He's
waking up out of his thoughts. . . . Gosh, he's pale! Could he be
sick? . . . That'd be the last straw!
DURAND [*brusquely*]: What are you doing there?
LOUISE: I was waiting to tell you what time it is; but . . . isn't Mon-
sieur well?
DURAND [*as before*]: Me? . . . You're mad!
LOUISE: Still . . .
DURAND: Don't talk to me. I'm busy. . . . I'm working! . . . Off you go;
leave me alone! [*Louise starts to go out.*] Where are you going?

Louise: You told me to go away.

Durand: That's no reason why I shouldn't ask you where you're going.

Louise: I'll go wherever you like.

Durand: That's no answer. . . . Where were you going?

Louise: Well, really, I don't know! I didn't have any idea; I was just going away because you told me to, that's all.

Durand [*disarmed*]: Listen, Louise. [*He looks at her.*] No; nothing; some other time. . . . I don't feel up to . . . [*Aside.*] It's absurd, I can't believe how upset I am! [*He sits down again, overwhelmed.*]

Louise: If you've got some complaint about me . . . the sooner you make it, the better, sir; I'd stop doing it right away.

Durand [*irritated*]: Oh! You're joking! You're repeating Monsieur Jean Coqueret's words!

Louise: I'd like to make you laugh. When you laugh, it's good for you.

Durand: I don't have the slightest desire to laugh. Sit down and answer me. . . . Come on, answer me seriously.

Louise: Answer what, sir?

Durand: What! What! . . . Haven't you anything to tell me—any secret?

Louise: Why . . . no.

Durand: You're hesitating! You're not telling the truth!

Louise: You're frightening me today. I don't know what to tell you—because I don't know what you're asking.

Durand: Let's cut it short. Do you want to get married—yes or no?

Louise: Me? Have I ever talked about that?

Durand: I'm talking about it myself, and I want an answer.

Louise: Well . . . no! I don't want to get married.

Durand: Why not? Come on, answer!

Louise: I don't know. . . . Do you want me to marry someone?

Durand: It doesn't matter what I want.

Louise: Oh but it does, sir. It's entirely up to you. Anything you told me to do would be good, anything you told me not to do would be bad. . . . All I'm thinking about is you, I don't have any wishes myself.

Durand: Too submissive. She's tricking me! [*Aloud.*] Then . . . suppose I told you . . . that I was advising you to get married . . . without leaving the house, of course . . . because I know you're attached to me.

LOUISE: Well, you'd have to tell me, "I want you to, and I want it to be with so-and-so." Otherwise how could I give any answer?

DURAND [*with an effort*]: Well, suppose I told you, "I want you to marry . . . that servant boy of mine"?

LOUISE: Why! . . . He's a very honest boy, very kind. . . .

DURAND [*bursting out*]: Aha! We're out in the open at last! She's in love with him!

LOUISE [*aside*]: It was to marry me himself. [*Aloud.*] Sir, I didn't say I was in love with him.

DURAND: You did say it.

LOUISE: No, sir.

DURAND: You told him so himself.

LOUISE: I didn't, and that's the truth!

DURAND: He told me you did.

LOUISE: He was telling a lie!

DURAND: Be careful! I'm going to make him repeat it in front of you!

LOUISE: If he did, it's because he lost his senses.

DURAND [*ringing the bell*]: I'll get to the bottom of this. Louise, there's still time. Just confess it to me—it'll be much better than an open scandal.

LOUISE: Oh good heavens! Why, what are you accusing me of? I haven't done anything wrong. I can't confess what doesn't exist!

DURAND: He's coming!

LOUISE: Let him come! [*Aside.*] Poor Jean! What's he gone and said to him, then?

Scene 15

[*Durand, Louise, Coqueret.*]

COQUERET: Monsieur!

DURAND: Come here and answer me, Mister Jean Coqueret: Do you want to marry Louise?

COQUERET [*eagerly*]: Yes, sir!

DURAND: And you think she'll agree?

COQUERET: Yes, sir, if you make her understand how things really are. Why wouldn't she want to marry me? She isn't anything more than I am. She isn't even as much. She's just a foundling,[10] and I've got my father and mother. She knows more than me, because you've taught her; but if she taught me too, I wouldn't ask for anything more. You pay her good, but you pay me more than I deserve too. And I've got enough to marry her, what's more. So we're pretty well suited for each other. I'm in love with her, and she can't hate me. I'm a decent man, she knows that well enough; and you know what I'm like too, sir. So, tell her you'd like it, and she'll be glad to obey you.

DURAND [*to Louise*]: You hear him! You're well suited to each other, you love each other, and all the two of you are waiting for is my permission to get married.

COQUERET: Yes, sir, that's how it is, you're talking very sensibly!

DURAND [*to Louise, angrily*]: Come on! Don't try any more of your lies!

COQUERET: Don't scold her, sir. If you scold her, she won't dare to admit it!

DURAND: I'm scolding her because she isn't being honest, and I don't know anything lower and more contemptible than telling lies.

COQUERET: Well, speak out, Louise, or tell me to go and jump in the lake, if I'm bothering you.

LOUISE: Jean, you've gone about it the wrong way! You might be in love with me, I'm not saying no to that, and I won't deny how I respect you; but I told you a while ago in the meadow, and again just now here, that I don't want to get married for a long time, and I told you not to talk about it any more. Did I say that to you, or didn't I?

DURAND [*to Coqueret*]: Is that what she said to you? Go on, answer! Speak up!

COQUERET: It's true she did say that.

DURAND: Then why did you lie to me and tell me she was crazy about you, and crying, and she'd been making advances to you, and she wouldn't dare to admit it to me?

LOUISE: You made it all up! That's an awful thing to do, telling lies like that!

COQUERET: I just wanted Monsieur to tell you to do what I said!

DURAND: Well, it's a disgrace; and so I'm turning you away!

COQUERET [*turning pale*]: Oh! . . . And what about you, Louise?

LOUISE [*distraught*]: Me . . . I . . .

DURAND: She won't have anything more to do with you either! Get out! Quick!

COQUERET [*very gloomily*]: All right, Monsieur, I'm going.

DURAND: Wait a minute—your wages! . . .

COQUERET: Thanks, I won't need any. [*He leaves.*]

Scene 16

[*Durand, Louise.*]

LOUISE [*running after him*]: Jean! Listen . . . just listen!

DURAND [*taking her forcefully by the arm and bringing her back*]: Let him go! Why should you interfere? When I've rid you of a gossip and a liar whose silly talk was dishonoring you! . . .

LOUISE: He didn't mean anything bad by it, sir. You can see he just lost his head! Poor boy! He was such a good servant for you, he was fond of you and everything. When he was simpleminded, it used to amuse you more often than it annoyed you, sir. . . . You'll be sorry about it, sir! Who knows, you might even blame yourself for . . .

DURAND: What would I have to blame myself for? Tell me! Because you're sorry about it? Are you as sorry as all that?

LOUISE: It's nothing to do with me, sir. I never talk to you about myself; I never asked you anything for myself! . . . But when it comes to you yourself, shouldn't I . . . ? Isn't it a bit cruel to send away a good fellow that served you honestly for ten years . . . since he was just a boy, because of one mistake, one little lie that didn't hurt you at all, and I was the only one that had the right to get angry about it?

DURAND: So you forgive him, do you? It's all right for someone be impertinent to you. . . .

LOUISE: He wasn't, never.

DURAND: Boasting about your affection! Isn't that an impertinence of the worst kind?

LOUISE: That all depends on the way he talked about it. He can't hardly explain himself. If he told you I was very fond of him, he wasn't lying. Weren't we brought up together under your very eyes, by good kind Rosalie? Shouldn't I think of him as my brother?

DURAND: No! Because I don't think of him as my son. He's too far beneath you in brains.

LOUISE: Oh! Brains! . . . Brains are a fine thing, I won't argue about that, but they're not everything: kindness is a lot more important, and I'll never forget, when all the other children my age used to turn their back on me and call me a foundling—poor kids that didn't even know what they were saying and thought they were doing something dreadful to me—there was one that always used to comfort me and stand up for me, and that was Jean—only Jean, and nobody else!

DURAND [*sadly*]: And me—what about me? Didn't I comfort you and stand up for you?

LOUISE: Oh, that wasn't surprising, coming from you, a man like you, that only has the idea of doing good, and is up above all the other people! . . . That's like the Lord God: it's not any credit to him to be like he is, he couldn't be anything else; but poor little Jean, that wasn't any better brought up than anyone else, before he came to you. . . .

DURAND [*aside*]: Oh—always him, always this Jean, the idiot, the clown, the fool! Women, women! It's enough to drive a man mad! [*Looking at Louise, who is gazing out the window.*] What's this? Are you talking to him—calling to him?

LOUISE: No, sir, I'm just looking at him, I'm just watching where he goes. You know, it bothers me, having seen him walk out and refuse his pay and look at me the way he did. . . . There he is walking alongside the water! . . .

DURAND [*touched*]: You think he might . . . ?

LOUISE: Throw himself in? Well, who knows? Twice today he did threaten to do it. He isn't very strong in the head. . . . Being driven out of here like that, you being so kind and fair, it's a big disgrace, and people in this part of the country could think he must have done something really bad! He's been disgraced for something he said without even realizing the consequence of it, poor Jean!

DURAND [*jealous*]: Louise, you're crying!

LOUISE: Well, yes, I am crying, sir. . . . He's been my good friend ever since we were children, we work together, he's just like I am!

DURAND [*automatically picking up his rifle*]: Oh! You wretched girl— you're in love with him—I don't know what holds me back from. . . . [*He takes a step towards the window.*]

LOUISE: If you want to kill him, kill me first!

DURAND [*dropping his rifle, aside*]: Lord God, save me and protect me! I did feel like killing her, too! [*Aloud.*] Look here, there's nothing to worry about, come away from the window. . . .

LOUISE: Come away from it? . . . Oh no, Monsieur! Look, there
he is running straight towards the river. . . . Monsieur—call
him back and forgive him! . . . [*Calling out.*] Jean! Come
back! . . . Monsieur is forgiving you, Jean! He isn't listening to
me! . . . Oh, I can't just let him do it! [*She runs out.*]

Scene 17

DURAND [*alone*]: The wretched girl—she's mad about him—mad
about that brainless noodle of a peasant! . . . No matter how
I've made fun of him and humiliated him and humbled him in
her eyes, he's young, he's a handsome lad, and that's all that
matters! She loves him because he's twenty years old, because
he's the first man that dared to talk love to her! She loves him
because it sickens me—yes—out of a spirit of contradiction—
to make me suffer and despair! . . . And yet, what if it was only
out of kindness and pity. . . . I've been too impulsive, too
violent. . . . Certainly I did frighten her. [*Looking out the window.*] Here they are coming back—he's following her like a
dog. . . . They're not talking. . . . She's bringing him back here!
What! Do I have to see him and talk to him? . . . No—I don't
want to—I can't stand the fellow! . . . They're stopping. . . .
They're talking together. . . . What are they saying to each other?
Maybe they're laughing at me. . . . Woe betide them if they're
planning some scheme because I'm so weak! . . . If only I could
catch them by surprise. . . . No, they're coming into the
house. . . . Still, in my room . . . I can listen! I might hear what
they're saying here, and if they dare to make fun of me . . . well,
I'll kill the pair of them! . . . Oh, what a dreadful thing! . . . No—
I . . . I don't know what I'll do. I ought to kill myself right now
before I go out of my mind. . . . [*He leaves by the door at right,
looking bewildered, taking his rifle with him. Louise and Coqueret enter
by the door at rear.*]

Scene 18

[*Louise, Coqueret.*]

LOUISE: Come on, come in, don't be scared, pull yourself together. . . . He isn't here. . . . Don't let him see you're upset, be

honest with him, and most of all, don't cry, because when I see
you crying, I just lose my head, I don't know what I'm saying
or doing any more! ... Let me handle the whole thing the best
that I can.

COQUERET: You can't handle anything, 'cause you hate me!

LOUISE: That isn't true; I do love you!

COQUERET: Yes—you love me like your pet dog and your chickens!
You cried that much when the white pigeon got eaten by the
weasel!

LOUISE: You're just talking stupid and idiotic things! I love you like
you deserve, but you can see plain enough, Monsieur...

COQUERET: What—Monsieur! Monsieur all the time! What is all
this to do with Monsieur? Does it affect him at all? Does he
think I'm someone bad? Doesn't he know what I'm like? Doesn't
he know that I'm just as fond of him as you are, and I'd chuck
myself in the fire for him just like I would for you, and if I was
in his place and he was in mine, I'd get him married to you just
like I want him to get us married to each other?

LOUISE: Don't talk so loud, Jean; Monsieur could be just over there
in his room! What you're saying, all that is exactly what you
mustn't say to him! That's what gets him angry! He doesn't
want ... he doesn't want married people serving him, you know
that plain enough; there are some masters that don't like that
sort of thing!

COQUERET: Oh yes—bad masters that's only thinking about themselves, but not masters like Monsieur Durand; he wants the
people that's with him to be happy. Don't you see, Louise, if
he's got angry, it's your fault! If you'd said the same as me ... but
you couldn't say the same as me; you don't want me at all.

LOUISE: That isn't true, Jean! Look, listen to me.... [*Taking him
over to the window, and talking to him in a low voice.*] I'd marry you
all right if he wanted it; and I ...

COQUERET [*joyfully*]: Really? ... Really and truly, Louise?

LOUISE: Yes, really! But it isn't as easy as you think! There are
things you can't imagine, and I'm scared to think about them
myself, and I'm even more scared to talk about them. Can't you
try hard and figure it out? Look, suppose Monsieur, seeing me
grow up, got to thinking in spite of himself...

COQUERET [*aloud, unintentionally*]: Louise! That isn't right at all,
what you're hinting at. What! You think ... you imagine ...?
No, that isn't right; that's all wrong! Monsieur is a sensible

man, and you're thinking he's just an idiot; he's a man that's got more sense than you and me, and you're thinking he's just a fool; I mean, Monsieur is about the most honest man there's ever been on this earth, and you think he'd have bad ideas about you? Now that gets me angry! . . . If anyone else said that to me, I'd have punched them in the nose by now!

LOUISE: Come on, you still don't understand, do you? I'm telling you, Monsieur is thinking of marrying me—I'm sure of it. Would he be jealous of me otherwise? 'Course not! I know him just as well as you do; the Lord in heaven never made anybody kinder hearted than he is, and he'd never stop me from loving anyone decent, not unless he made up his mind to marry me himself.

COQUERET: Well, that isn't true, Louise, it can't be! You just think! Monsieur, would he have brought you up like that, hand fed you and everything, just so as he could say to you one fine morning, "Here we are now, you're a young girl and I'm an old man, and you're going to pay me back for all the nice kind things I've done for you . . . when I was really doing them for myself; and you can't refuse me, because I was good to your mother; and I'll get hold of your heart by its weakest point, and even though you're in love with that little fellow Jean, you got to forget about him and not love anyone except me." No, no! Louise, that's selfishness! Lord above, Monsieur isn't like that. Go and get him, tell him you're in love with me, and you'll see. Yes—I'd put my hand in the fire for it, Monsieur will just say to you, "Louise, I only ever had the one intention when I took you in, and that was to make you happy, and if you thought anything different, you'd be doing me an insult and an injustice." That's what Monsieur would say to you, if only you had the courage to be open and honest about loving me; but you don't love me enough to have that kind of courage—maybe you've got high hopes that's pulling you forward by one arm when friendship is holding you back by the other.

LOUISE: Well, no, Jean, it isn't like that at all! I don't have any high hopes of that kind at all; I'm just in between two friendships and I don't know which one I should listen to. But still, what you just said to me has made me change my mind about one thing—I can see you're every bit as good as Monsieur is, seeing as how you won't go around suspecting him. Who knows, maybe Monsieur might even be not quite as good as you, just at the moment. . . . You've talked very sensibly, Jean; you're worth a lot more than I am, and that's why I've made up my mind. You go and wait for me in the garden, I want to talk to him right away—don't worry, I'm not afraid of hurting him any more. If he couldn't face being hurt, he wouldn't really be himself any more—he wouldn't deserve for us to respect him or admire him either—you've made me realize that. Off you go quick, and don't worry about anything! I do love you, Jean—I do love you with all my heart!

COQUERET: Oh, thank you, thank you, Louise. [*He leaves.*]

Scene 19

LOUISE [*alone, on the point of entering Durand's room*]: Wait on! Why has he taken the key away? He never takes it away. He knows perfectly well nobody would go in his room without knocking. Is he sick—is that why he's shut himself up like that? [*She knocks.*] Monsieur, it's me, Louise! He's not answering—he's not moving—maybe he's asleep. . . . Sleeping in the daytime, that's not in his habits. He doesn't like to. Must be terribly tired, then. That's a worry. Suppose he heard what we were saying. . . . No—you can't hear anything from that room, not unless you get right up against the door, and Monsieur isn't the type to go eavesdropping like that! And anyhow, Jean didn't say anything about him except good things . . . the things I want to say to his face. . . . Have I got the courage? He was so hurt just now! Oh, he was really hurt, because he was being unkind! The poor man—Lord God, I don't know what to do any more! . . . Is . . . ? Yes! He's taken his gun! What would he need his gun inside his room for? Nah! I'm just being silly! . . . I would have heard, for sure. . . . Still, I did go a bit far away when I went to get Jean. While I was running off, maybe he . . . [*Calling out.*] Monsieur! Monsieur! [*She knocks.*] No answer? Oh, I'm that scared, it's driving me crazy. Monsieur! . . .

Scene 20

[*Durand, Louise.*]

DURAND [*a book in his hand*]: Well now, what's the matter with you? Is the house on fire?

LOUISE [*confused*]: Oh goodness, Monsieur, excuse me, I was thinking . . . I thought you were asleep!

DURAND: Aren't I allowed to take a rest in my own house, and do you have to kick up such a racket if I do? What do you want? What are you after?

LOUISE: It's just that . . . seeing you're going to have dinner in town . . .

DURAND: Well?

LOUISE: You need to get dressed, Monsieur! You're not going out in your slippers and your morning coat?

DURAND: What does it matter? We're in the country!

LOUISE: And then, Monsieur . . . it's . . . it's just that Jean has come back.

DURAND [*pretending to be preoccupied*]: Which Jean? Monsieur Coqueret? Well?

LOUISE: Monsieur sent him away, and I . . .

DURAND: I sent him away, and you . . . I really don't follow any of this. [*He pretends to examine his paving stone.*]

LOUISE [*aside*]: Now he's back in his daydreaming again, thank the Lord! [*Aloud.*] So Monsieur isn't thinking any more at all about . . . ?

DURAND: Look here! You're upsetting and bothering me; we need to put an end to it. I sent Coqueret away for telling a lie. Has he cleared himself? Or is he sorry for what he's done?

LOUISE: Oh yes, sir, very much, and . . .

DURAND: And you've forgiven him? That's up to you, my girl, that's your business; if you think he deserves to be forgiven . . .

LOUISE: Very much so, and even . . .

DURAND: You'll appreciate, I can't attach any great importance to it myself! It's up to you to think it over, and if you think you ought . . .

LOUISE: Monsieur, you're still angry at him—or me!

DURAND [*dryly*]: Where do you get that idea, my dear?

LOUISE: Because you don't seem to care about it. I don't want to get married if it's going to upset Monsieur, but if Monsieur will just let me explain why Jean behaved the way he did . . .

DURAND [*acting his part more convincingly*]: My dear child, you can tell me about it some other day. You can see I don't have the head for it today. I'm busy with a thousand more serious matters: a job to complete, business matters to attend to, preparations . . .

because you know I have the prospect of an advantageous marriage.

LOUISE: Oh, really, sir? You've made up your mind, then? That's wonderful!

DURAND: That's wonderful! wonderful! . . . For me, quite possibly; but what about you? What if my wife didn't take a liking to you? . . .

LOUISE: Oh, that wouldn't happen, sir! I'd be so fond of her! I'd serve her so well! You'll see, she'll take a liking to me all right!

DURAND: Let us hope so. And yet . . . you're young . . . you're not . . . exactly pretty. . . . Are you pretty? Do people find you pretty? I must admit I wouldn't know much about that; I'm so used to your face that I'm not much of a judge of it.

LOUISE: Well, no, sir, I'm not pretty at all; but how would that affect Madame? . . .

DURAND: Oh, you know how some women are—jealous—silly things! What if mine got the idea that I paid you any particular attention, that I liked the look of you? That would be a very silly idea, certainly, a very big mistake; I never in my life thought . . .

LOUISE: Oh, sir, I know that plain enough, and Madame would see quick enough how she needn't worry about that—especially if I was married myself. . . .

DURAND: Ah, that's it! That's what we need to arrange; but you don't want to—or, at least, you're hesitant.

LOUISE: Oh, I've settled all that. The moment it could be useful, or even necessary for Monsieur to be happy and not have any worries, I'd be very glad to do what Monsieur would want.

DURAND [*ironically*]: You mustn't sacrifice yourself, though!

LOUISE: Oh no, sir, I'm not sacrificing myself; if you'll just let me follow my own feelings . . .

DURAND [*frowning*]: Your own feelings? . . . [*Controlling himself.*] Well, well, I'm very glad you want to own up at long last! I can see Jean wasn't lying to me, and everything is working out for the best after all! He's an excellent lad, good natured. . . . Tell him I'm sorry I misjudged him . . . and tell him, too, that it's more your fault than mine.

LOUISE: That's the truth! I shouldn't have gone and contradicted him.

DURAND: Go and find him, and leave me to my work. There's still half an hour before I have to go off and have dinner with my neighbor.

LOUISE: Your neighbor? Why, here he is, sir; he's come looking for you.

DURAND: Well then, leave us to ourselves. [*Louise curtseys to the Neighbor, who is entering. She leaves.*]

Scene 21

[*Durand, the Neighbor; later, Coqueret; later still, Louise.*]

NEIGHBOR: Aren't you any more ready than that? I dare say you were on the point of forgetting all about your promise!

DURAND: No, my friend; far from it. But do you need to have me in full dress?

NEIGHBOR: Yes, absolutely; the people that are wanting to meet you are some ladies.

DURAND: In that case, it's a different matter. [*He rings the bell.*] You didn't tell me that. . . . [*To Coqueret, who has entered.*] My black coat, and a white tie! [*Coqueret goes into the room at right.*]

NEIGHBOR: Are you feeling unwell? Your face does look a little more drawn than it did this morning.

DURAND: Maybe it does. I've been through a great shock.

NEIGHBOR: In what way? An accident?

DURAND: Yes—a paving stone . . .

NEIGHBOR [*pointing to the paving stone*]: Oh! You're still thinking about your griffins and gibbons?

DURAND: No! This is a different paving stone—one that, to put it metaphorically, fell on my head—a very heavy one, too—and it caught me daydreaming about selfish happiness! But you're right, my friend: dreams can lead us astray; sometimes one simply has to do the same as everyone else. [*Looking at Coqueret, who is presenting his coat to him.*] The most simpleminded people sometimes know more about decency and conscience than the proudest scholars in the world. [*Taking his coat.*] You'll allow me? [*To Coqueret.*] Thank you, my boy! And what about the cravat?

LOUISE [*having entered with the cravat*]: Here it is, sir!

NEIGHBOR [*while Durand is putting on his cravat*]: I'm glad to see you've come to your senses. With an intelligent man like you, there's always some way . . . I was so angry at you earlier! Oh yes, very angry! I said to my sister . . .

DURAND: Oh? Is your sister staying with you?

NEIGHBOR: She's the one who wants to see you. Without her—and without my niece, who took your side entirely...

DURAND [*putting on his shoes with Coqueret's help*]: Oh? Your niece is with you too? Good heavens!...

NEIGHBOR: What do you mean, "good heavens"?... Are you going to tell me again that she's too tall, too short, too dark, too blonde? The ladies wanted to come and kidnap you. They're outside in my carriage. Look! [*He takes him to the window.*]

DURAND: What! That's your niece, is it? Well, she certainly wasn't the one I saw before! I don't know her at all.

LOUISE [*near the window*]: Oh, sir, she's as beautiful as an angel, that lady is!

DURAND: Yes indeed—a serious and gentle angel!

LOUISE: See, you do have eyes after all!

NEIGHBOR: My dear fellow, you ought to thank your lucky stars. She's mad keen on science. Why, she's never set eyes on you, she's only heard all the good things that people keep saying about you, but she's been deep in books for the past week—her mother is scared she's going mad.

DURAND [*touched*]: Oh! You think she'd be interested...? [*To Coqueret.*] Help me with this shoelace.... [*To the Neighbor.*] And she's been so kind as to...?

LOUISE: Sir, your cravat is on all wrong. And you really oughtn't to look like a shaggy dog! [*She tidies his hair.*]

DURAND: Let's not keep her waiting! Come on, my friend, shall we be off?

COQUERET: What about our wedding, sir?

DURAND: Same time as mine, my boy! Very soon!

NEIGHBOR: Oh? You're arranging a marriage between them? Good for you! [*They leave.*]

Scene 22

[*Louise, Coqueret.*]

COQUERET: Well there you are, what was I telling you, Louise? As you can see...

LOUISE: Yes, Jean, you were right! Monsieur has saved his dignity, and you've saved our happiness!

The End

The Japanese Lily

(Le Lis du Japon)

A Prose Comedy in One Act

Characters

JULIEN THIERRY, *a painter*
MARCEL, *an attorney*
THE MARQUISE, *a young widow*
A SERVANT

Paris, in the time of Louis XVI.[1]

The interior of a flower painter's studio, small but attractive. Flowers everywhere—in flower stands, in flowerpots, in vases; canvases, easels, etc.; a large table, an armchair, other chairs; no luxury, very tidy. At rear, a large open door leading to a small peristyle where a staircase leading to the upper stories can be seen.—At right, in the studio, a window with a green curtain, half drawn; downstage left, a door.

Scene 1

[*Julien, Marcel.*

Julien is at the window; Marcel enters, holding a small earthenware pot wrapped in paper and containing a plant.[2]]

JULIEN [*to himself*]: Nobody in the garden! Isn't she coming out today?

MARCEL [*aside*]: He's very preoccupied! [*Aloud*]: Hi there! Hello, Julien!

JULIEN: Oh—Cousin Marcel! [*He shakes his hand.*]

MARCEL: So, you were lost in dreamland, you great artist?

JULIEN: Yes, you great attorney! I was looking at the spring blossoms. And what about your law business—is it blossoming too?

MARCEL: It's budding, my friend, it's budding. Oh, if only my chambers were paid for, things would be better—branches and fruits would shoot forth then. So, tell me—if you inherit, you'll help me, eh?

JULIEN: To pay? Oh, absolutely. But don't count on it, my poor friend—I shan't be inheriting.

MARCEL: Who knows?

JULIEN: Uncle Thierry has too low an opinion of artists in general and me in particular.

MARCEL: He'll come round, perhaps. That's up to you.

JULIEN: You want me to give up painting?

MARCEL: Not at all! Painting flowers and fruit and golden flies and butterflies and dewdrops—why, it's a very fashionable art form; your poor father excelled at it, and you yourself are already getting praised for it. I don't want you to give it up, I want...

JULIEN: Well, what?

MARCEL: I want you to give me some water.

JULIEN: You're thirsty?

MARCEL: No—it's for this flower. Have to keep its roots moist.

JULIEN: Very pretty—and lovely scent, too! I've never seen any like it. Is this a present for me?

MARCEL: Oho, I'd love to see you getting presents of that kind! This thing is worth, maybe, a thousand crowns.

JULIEN: Pity! Belongs to our uncle then, does it?

MARCEL: Well, who would you expect it to belong to? It's a lily, from Africa, or...

JULIEN: Or Asia maybe?

MARCEL: Or America, I can't remember; and it's called . . . hang on a minute! . . . Oh, Lord, I can't remember. Doesn't make any difference to me, you can well imagine; but I do know one thing: he entrusted it to me as if it were a baby being put out to nurse.

JULIEN: And where are you taking it?

MARCEL: I'm bringing it to you, and I'm entrusting it to you in turn. The portrait of this precious bit of vegetation is to be painted while it's in its full glory, and guess what our uncle is giving you for the privilege.

JULIEN: What?

MARCEL: Two hours.

JULIEN: He's going to lavish two hours of affection on *me*?

MARCEL: No, you're going to lavish two hours of hard work on the job. Never mind! Hurry up, Julien; get on with it.

JULIEN: Fine! So, he's starting to appreciate that a flower painter and a lover of rare plants can be of use to one another, is he? All the same, Marcel, he could have started a little sooner— being as rich as he is!

MARCEL: Well, he's starting now; he's referring his practice to you.

JULIEN: And to you too, I hope?

MARCEL: Partly. Clients of his kind keep more than one attorney occupied, but at least he is using me.

JULIEN: Well then, why shouldn't you inherit?

MARCEL: Me? Never; I've married into the middle classes.

JULIEN: Ah, that entrenched social climber pride of his—you think it's a serious case?

MARCEL: It's becoming a mania, an obsession. You realize of course that he fell out with you because you wouldn't marry a certain widow. . . .

JULIEN: The fat over-the-hill lady from the country?

MARCEL: She had a few little ermined ancestors up her sleeve, and that allured the rich man, but I admit she was a fraction past her prime. Now he has a different idea, and a less terrifying one.

JULIEN: Another scheme to marry me off?

MARCEL: Yes; twenty-five, also a widow, passably pretty, very pleasant, even a bit coquettish, so the report goes—Madame de Reuilly, the judge's widow.[3]

JULIEN: Very well! It's settled: I refuse.

MARCEL: Why? Are you out of your mind?

JULIEN: Yes. [*He stands, and goes to the window.*]

MARCEL: There's a straight answer for you; stops all arguments, too. Still, Julien . . . What are you looking at?

JULIEN: Nothing.

MARCEL: Oh yes you are! [*He looks.*] Why, it's Marquise d'Estrelle, another client of mine. Let me say hello to her.

JULIEN: No, no! She doesn't know I'm looking at her.

MARCEL: Oho—so you're looking at *her,* are you?

JULIEN: She doesn't have any idea. I've been very careful about it. As soon as she appears, I draw the curtain.

MARCEL: And, while she's walking in her little garden, you gaze at her through the chinks in the material? Are you so sure she's never noticed?

JULIEN: Oh my friend, she doesn't even know I exist.

MARCEL: Well, she's going to know.

JULIEN: How? Why?

MARCEL: Because, at the conclusion of a little lawsuit that I won for her only yesterday, this little building you're living in became her property.

JULIEN: Really?

MARCEL: Our uncle has some idea of buying it so that he can knock it down and extend his garden—it's separated on that side by some wall or other, and he's offering to purchase it.

JULIEN: Lord in heaven! Knock down this building!

MARCEL: It'll be decided today.

JULIEN: By whom?

MARCEL: By the architect, who ought to be here any minute to look it over. If it can be repaired cheaply enough, the Marquise will hold onto it and keep a tenant in it. If it would spell disaster, she sells it, and Uncle Thierry tears it down to raise tulips on top of it.

JULIEN: Impossible!

MARCEL: That depends on the tulips. If they feel like growing . . .

JULIEN: Oh, Marcel, don't make fun of me! This is desperate!

MARCEL: What—it's as serious as that? A woman you've seen . . . from a reasonable distance . . . and to whom you have never spoken . . .

JULIEN: She comes here, just close by, and sits on that bench. Sometimes she stays there for an hour or so, reading or thinking. Other times, she has one or two girlfriends with her, or an elderly man—some relative of hers; she talks with them. . . . Oh, she has such a soft voice and such a noble and touching way of

saying things! If I do eavesdrop on her, Marcel, I'm not being
indiscreet; I don't always do it on purpose, and anyhow I don't
take any interest in the things that are being discussed—unless
she is taking an interest in them. I listen only to her, and
everything she says makes me feel how good and true and
generous she is! . . . She's big hearted and pure hearted, you
see—quite incomparable. She has an upright mind—a rare
sensibility—and a magnanimous soul! In short, she's a heavenly
being, an angel on earth, and I simply adore her!

MARCEL: Ye gods! You're well and truly hooked, my poor
friend . . . and you haven't a hope. She's much too aristocratic.

JULIEN: And much too strict in her ideas and her notions of eti-
quette: she'd never take the slightest notice of me. Don't betray
me, then; I can love her in silence without doing her any harm—
you must see that.

MARCEL: I haven't the slightest wish to betray you. Still . . . who
knows? She's a widow, and not very well off. . . . If Uncle . . .
What are you thinking about?

JULIEN: Oh—sorry . . . you were talking to me?

MARCEL: Hello! Of course I was talking to you; are you deaf?

JULIEN: Tell me, Marcel—this architect who is coming—is he
Dubourg?

MARCEL: Well, yes—our old schoolmate. Where are you going?

JULIEN: I'll dash off and see him—he's just down the road.

MARCEL: But he's coming here!

JULIEN: Doesn't matter! I want to . . .

MARCEL: Well, what?

JULIEN: You'll see!

MARCEL: But what about the lily—the painting?

JULIEN: I know, I know, I'll be right back. [*He leaves.*]

Scene 2

MARCEL [*alone*]: Oh, this is insane! What's going on in that head of
his! There's an artist for you! I certainly did well to study petti-
fogging—otherwise I might easily have gone the same way myself! But let's see—I'll go and find the Marquise, I'll say to
her . . . Ah yes, I'm onto it now. . . . [*The Marquise appears.*] And,
at the same time, I'll be able to feel the temperature of the water.

Scene 3

[*Marcel, the Marquise.*]

MARQUISE: Oh—you're here, are you, Monsieur Marcel?

MARCEL: I'm quite at home here—quite at *your* home, I mean. Come in, Marquise!

MARQUISE: No, I'm just on my way up. I want to see the suspect story with my own eyes. Monsieur Dubourg would be up there, I suppose?

MARCEL: No, Madame, he hasn't arrived yet, and he's the one who has the keys. . . . Please wait here . . . at . . . It's a painter's studio, and there's nobody here.

MARQUISE [*entering*]: You sure? This is where the young painter lives?—One of your relatives, I believe?

MARCEL: Julien Thierry, my cousin. After all, it's your own property now, and as proprietor you have the right to visit and inspect. And you could have a look at his canvases while you're here. . . . It isn't a bad place.

MARQUISE [*looking*]: Very nice, in fact . . . charming . . . really! You did tell me he was talented and well behaved. But I'll still have to evict him.

MARCEL: Certainly, if the circumstances really are outside your control; otherwise . . . he does have a lease, so there would be an indemnity to discuss.

MARQUISE: Discuss? No; he can name the figure himself—he can be trusted. I don't understand business matters myself, as you well know! But I can't stay any longer—what if he came back? . . . He lives alone, doesn't he? He isn't married?

MARCEL: He's neither married, nor . . . To put it another way, he lives alone, responsibly and honorably.

MARQUISE: His studio is pleasant and teeming with flowers. He's comfortably off?

MARCEL: If he didn't pay his father's debts so religiously, he could live fairly well from his earnings; but . . .

MARQUISE: But he's conscientious and financially embarrassed? Don't take my side, Monsieur Marcel—I must insist on that.

MARCEL: Madame, if I may say so without offense, is financially embarrassed herself. She doesn't count the cost before she gives. If she listened to the advice of her humble attorney, she

would think—she's already given me permission to tell her so—
she would think seriously about remarrying.

MARQUISE: I'm deep in debt, then, am I, Monsieur Marcel?

MARCEL: So deep that you can't afford to rebuild this building—
and yet it does bring in a certain amount of rent. Madame
ought to put herself beyond these little annoyances! Really—a
person of her rank, with such a fine character . . .

MARQUISE: The same subject again, Monsieur Marcel? I can see
you're set on getting me to make a wealthy marriage.

MARCEL: It's entirely up to you, Madame; I know a young man . . .

MARQUISE: Oh—you know a young man! . . .

MARCEL: Handsome, a fine figure, attractive, sensitive . . .

MARQUISE: Ah now, that's the sort of person—that's charming!

MARCEL [aside]: It's working! Full steam ahead, now! [Aloud.] And
rich—very rich, in fact!

MARQUISE: That's an asset, if he wants to do good!

MARCEL: Yes, isn't it, Madame? The glory of good deeds may com-
pensate for the absence of titles; a misalliance isn't as serious
a thing nowadays as it used to be in the past, and . . .

MARQUISE: Oh, excuse me—would it be a misalliance? Let's drop
the subject. It would not be to my taste at all.

MARCEL [aside]: Ouch! [Aloud.] I do sincerely apologize to Madame for having hurt her . . . principles!

MARQUISE: You were going to say "prejudices"? Well, let me explain
myself to you—you're a gentleman. I don't have any prejudices, but I do think it's rather base to sell your name for
money, and it's equally absurd and undignified for a social
climber to want an alliance with an impoverished lady of
quality. Every sphere ought to keep its own pride, Monsieur
Marcel. . . . Let the *nouveaux riches* be proud of their riches—I
don't mind, if they've acquired them honestly; but let us be
equally proud of not owing anything to anyone. Let everyone
keep to their own place, without greed and without childish
ambitions!

MARCEL: Madame is absolutely right! [Aside.] Poor Julien! He'll
have to go!

Scene 4

[*As above, Julien; later, a servant.*]

JULIEN: Well, I've seen Dubourg, I . . . [*Seeing the Marquise, he utters a cry.*] Ah!

MARCEL: This, Madame, is my cousin the painter . . . your tenant . . . and, since you have some instructions to give him, here he is, ready to receive them.

MARQUISE: If you find me installed in your rooms in your absence, Monsieur, you have only Monsieur Marcel to blame. I gave myself the pleasure of looking at your work.

MARCEL [*sotto voce to Julien*]: In other words, she didn't look at it at all.

MARQUISE: And since we are here face to face, why shouldn't I mention to you that I wish to regain possession of this building?

JULIEN: But . . . Monsieur Dubourg and I agreed. . . . The repairs are urgently needed, that's true, but I don't wish to move house, so I'm undertaking them at my own expense. Naturally, any inconvenience involved in that would not affect Madame.

MARCEL [*surprised*]: Yes, but . . .

JULIEN: Excuse me, Marcel, this is my concern.

MARQUISE: So, Monsieur, you're refusing my request?

JULIEN: Your request, Madame? I thought . . . [*The servant enters, and gives a note to Marcel.*]

MARQUISE: You thought it was only a question of . . . ? What's that, Monsieur Marcel? The architect?

MARCEL: No, Madame, it's my uncle, Monsieur Thierry . . . who is asking for me on urgent business. . . . [*Sotto voce to Julien.*] Your reply to the marriage in question.

JULIEN: I've said no.

MARQUISE: Off you go, Monsieur Marcel, I shall handle this matter myself.

MARCEL: I'll be back, Madame; it isn't far away. [*Sotto voce to Julien.*] I'll stall for time. You'll think better of it. Don't hope for anything here; intractable pride, my dear fellow! [*He leaves.*]

Scene 5

[*Julien, the Marquise.*]

MARQUISE: Were you also being asked for, perhaps?

JULIEN: No, Madame.

MARQUISE: Very well, I shall speak to you frankly. Since this building can be repaired—and that would be my concern and nobody

else's—there is a lady, a friend of mine, whom I wish to lodge
here. So, I must ask you to specify a legal indemnity for your
departure at the earliest possible opportunity.

JULIEN: I'll leave today, Madame. My only wish is to obey you.

MARQUISE: And Monsieur Marcel will arrange . . .

JULIEN: No, Madame. One loses one's happiness; one doesn't sell it.

MARQUISE: One's happiness? Yours can't possibly be tied to this
modest apartment.

JULIEN: Excuse me, but it's so light here, so cheerful, so pleasant!
Flowers in front of my window, lawn at ground level, a chink of
sky up there, trees down there, the ripple of a little fountain,
the sparrows who have made friends with me . . . that amounts
to happiness, in the life of a poor artist in Paris.

MARQUISE: Well then, I should be sorry to hurt you. We might be
able to come to an agreement. I could lodge my friend on the
first floor, and you could keep the ground floor. You have a
view here, do you? [*She opens the curtain.*] Oh, but that's my
garden . . . and this window . . . I didn't think this room was
occupied!

JULIEN: I don't stay here . . . except to work; and the daylight would
be too strong, so I keep everything drawn.

MARQUISE: Well then, you don't enjoy the view about which you
were waxing so eloquent?

JULIEN: When you're not there, Madame. . . .

MARQUISE: And how do you know when I'm not there? Monsieur
Thierry, this window is something of an embarrassment to me.

JULIEN: Oh Madame, you don't think I'd allow myself . . . ?

MARQUISE: I don't think anything at all. I've never noticed anyone
in here, and I don't suspect you of being inquisitive. It would
be a sheer waste of time anyway—I don't have any secrets! But
that's beside the point. One likes to feel at home; why, you
yourself would feel embarrassed under a neighbor's gaze. If
you are so eager to stay here, I shall do my best not to disturb
you, but you'll appreciate that this aperture would need to be
walled up.

JULIEN: Walled up? Merciful heavens! You're plunging me into
darkness—a painter!

MARQUISE: Wait a minute! If I've got my bearings properly . . . the
grand and beautiful gardens of my neighbor Monsieur
Thierry . . . your relative . . . are over this way.

JULIEN: Yes, but . . .

MARQUISE: A window of whatever size you need could be opened here, and Monsieur Thierry certainly wouldn't have any objections. You'd stand entirely to gain by the exchange. Have a talk about it with your uncle . . . and as soon as possible, please do me the favor of having it done. [*Seeing Julien's dejection.*] You're very new here, I believe; only two or three months. . . .

JULIEN: Two months . . . two days, two hours can sometimes be the equivalent of a whole lifetime in terms of joys and sorrows. When I came here, the sorrow of having lost my father . . .

MARQUISE: A man of great talent, I know, and much admired by everybody!

JULIEN: Yes, Madame; the pain of the loss was still very immediate. I stopped going out, I stopped living. I needed solitude, and yet it was a torment to me. The tranquillity of this little retreat delighted me. My thoughts became calmer here . . . and more positive, too . . . a nobler ideal, endless dreams and aspirations . . . a whole world of hopeless desires. . . . Oh, your flowers are less mistrustful and less cruel than you are! They don't think themselves tarnished by the glance of a humble lover of nature, and God, who has made every good and perfect thing, won't blame me for worshiping him in his sacred works!

MARQUISE: A mind as lofty as yours would find unsullied delights and sacred models in any place. Aren't they all around you? The plants in this room are rarer than mine, and you mustn't neglect them for the sake of those that are outside. You must live for the wonderful art that your father taught you; his fame will guide you. And, since you like symbols, remember that lilies . . . such as that marvelously white one there! . . . owe their brilliance only to their purity; you must appreciate that it's natural for them to love darkness . . . and solitude. Good-bye.

JULIEN: Good-bye, Madame! . . . But . . . you noticed this lily . . . your image . . . allow me one single consolation, one single favor! [*He picks it.*]

MARQUISE: Oh—what are you doing?

JULIEN: Take it.

MARQUISE: But . . . no, Monsieur, I can't accept it!

JULIEN: Oh, what a wretch I am—you're refusing me even that! . . . But that's right, I was forgetting . . . I am poor and nameless—I don't have even the right to offer you a flower!

MARQUISE: It isn't that, Monsieur; but I don't accept flowers from anyone, and I should be afraid of the fragrance of this one.

Scene 6

[*As above; Marcel.*]

MARCEL: You're leaving, Madame?

MARQUISE: Dubourg isn't here; do please send him to me, Monsieur Marcel. [*She disappears.*]

MARCEL [*to Julien*]: Uncle is getting impatient and annoyed; haven't you done any work? . . . [*Seeing the picked lily.*] Good Lord! What have you done, you wretch? This is a criminal offense!

MARQUISE [*returning, alarmed*]: What is? What's going on? [*She rushes toward Julien.*]

MARCEL [*showing her the lily*]: A murder! A felony! Look, Madame!

MARQUISE [*dropping onto a chair*]: Oh! What a fright you gave me!

JULIEN: Fright? Oh, she's fainting! She's turning pale! [*He looks for a glass of water.*]

MARQUISE: No—nothing . . . thank you. . . . I don't understand . . . I thought . . . I don't know what I thought! Why the dreadful cries?

MARCEL: I'm deeply sorry to have alarmed you, Madame, but if you only knew! . . . Oh! It's a suicide, and that's the truth!

MARQUISE: What! A suicide! Who?

JULIEN: I don't understand any of it either. Marcel is crazy!

MARQUISE: Oh—he's the one, is he? [*Marcel bursts out laughing.*] You're laughing now?

MARCEL: Yes—I'm laughing, I'm crying, I'm fuming, I'd be swearing if I dared! We've all lost our wits. . . . Let's just calm down, let's come to grips with the situation, and you can be the judge, Madame. You'll know, either by sight or by reputation, our uncle, the ex-shipowner, the eccentric, the worthy and unpleasant and wealthy Monsieur Thierry?

JULIEN: Oh, what does it matter whether Madame . . .

MARCEL: Shut up, you wretch, you are beyond forgiveness! [*To the Marquise.*] You've heard tell of his passion for onions?

MARQUISE [*astonished*]: Oni . . . ?

MARCEL: Yes—bulbs, as he calls them, tulips, lilies. . . . This one, barely open in a warm greenhouse—thirty-two degrees Reaumur!—was entrusted to me for that accursed dauber to do a sketch of it.

MARQUISE: Yes, I understand. . . . I see. . . .

MARCEL: No, Madame, all you see is the deed. The consequence is beyond all anticipation. Our uncle had resolved . . . I've just been told in confidence . . . to leave all his property to Julien here present, on certain conditions. . . .

JULIEN: Be quiet! I . . .

MARCEL: Shut up! You . . . you have no sense at all. After this dismal accident, this inexcusable negligence or inexplicable malice, it's all up with you. I know what he's like, I can see him now, blind with anger—he's disowning you, he's disinheriting you. Here's a lily that has just cost you an income of thirty or forty thousand pounds!

MARQUISE [*aside*]: Poor boy! . . . And he did it for me! . . . [*Aloud.*] Hurry up, Monsieur Marcel, go and tell Monsieur Thierry that I was the one who perpetrated this evil deed.

MARCEL: You, Madame? He won't believe it.

MARQUISE: I was the one, all the same. I took a liking to the flower, and without knowing what I was doing . . . Off you go, Monsieur Marcel, quickly; I take full responsibility for it.

JULIEN: But I don't want to deceive . . .

MARCEL: Look here, I made myself answerable for you—I don't want to find myself accused . . . banished! Devil take it, no! It's my own skin I'm worried about. I must hurry, I must fly. . . . [*He stops; aside.*] She hasn't left; I'd be wise to find out the truth. [*He stays at the door, behind the curtain.*]

JULIEN: Marcel can appease Uncle's anger on his own account; I shall defy it and take the consequences. Oh, I would have been happy if . . .

MARQUISE: If . . . ?

JULIEN: If, instead of refusing so haughtily, you could have accepted this humble present!

MARQUISE: A present that may cost you very dear, it seems! Look here, Monsieur, what you did was quite senseless, and so, perhaps, is what I'm going to say to you. . . . But, far from treating you with scorn, as you seem to think, I find your mistake rather touching. . . . It seems to have a lack . . . a lack of thought, certainly . . . but also a lack of calculation . . . and, whether or not you're at fault, I can't help admiring a person who forgets his own interests so readily, and thinks only of giving other people pleasure.

JULIEN: If it would have been a pleasure to accept it . . . why were you so cruel as to refuse it?

MARQUISE: Cruel! I didn't imagine . . .

JULIEN: Cruel or not, why did you refuse it?

MARQUISE: Good heavens! There are questions of social custom. . . .

JULIEN: I've seen a little of society myself, Madame. My father's talents and intelligence brought more than one member of the nobility to him. I was there, and—as far as my youth allowed—I could observe what is socially acceptable and what isn't. If you had come to my father's studio, and he had offered you that flower, you wouldn't have refused him.

MARQUISE: Of course not; an old man has the right to be courteous; it would be ungracious to take any offense at that.

JULIEN: Then I was so unfortunate as to give you offense, was I?

MARQUISE: Good heavens, that isn't what I'm saying!

JULIEN: Oh yes it is—I've gone against social custom, I've been presumptuous, impertinent. . . .

MARQUISE: No . . . no.

JULIEN: Excuse me, but you are driving me out of your neighborhood.

MARQUISE: Well, Monsieur Thierry, that's necessary! You're not well suited here; isolation, daydreaming . . . with a lively imagination, one creates phantoms, one latches onto ideas . . . which one believes to be serious, even though they're nothing but artists' fantasies, impulses from a heart that doesn't understand its own workings. I myself . . . I don't know why I'm telling you about myself . . . it's because this refusal hurts you. . . . I'm in constant dread of myself. I don't like to torment people, I detest coquettishness; but I'm equally afraid that my frankness could be misunderstood—that the simplest and most natural response could be regarded as flirting. I don't accept compliments and bouquets from anyone. I shun observation—my position requires me to be cautious about that—and what I didn't accept from you, I certainly shouldn't have accepted from a duke or a peer. Please be assured of that, because it's the simple truth.

JULIEN [bowing]: In that case, good-bye, Madame, and may nothing trouble the serenity of your heart. Mine is breaking . . . and since I'm not to see you any more . . .

MARQUISE: Well?

JULIEN: No—nothing, Madame. Whatever else I lose, I don't want to lose the respect I owe you.

MARCEL [*aside*]: The idiot! If I don't meddle with things . . . [*Aloud.*] Well, here I am.

MARQUISE: Oh! Well?

MARCEL: Everything is lost! Uncle didn't believe me. He's out of his mind, he's cursing Julien, he's disowning him . . . unless . . .

MARQUISE: Unless what?

MARCEL: Unless he marries the judge's widow.

MARQUISE: What judge's widow? [*Julien gestures to Marcel to be silent.*]

MARCEL: No—I'll name her, so that Madame can judge for herself how stupid you're being: Madame de Reuilly!

MARQUISE: Oh! A very fashionable person, charming if not beautiful, maybe a little . . . a woman with numerous attractions. And why is he refusing so . . . so flattering a match?

MARCEL: Because Monsieur claims to be in love with somebody else—and let me explain how ridiculous it is—a woman who isn't in love with him, who doesn't like middle-class people, who finds herself too highly placed to consider him—in short, a woman . . .

MARQUISE: Whom you know, Monsieur Marcel?

MARCEL: Oh no, Madame, he never mentions any names.

JULIEN: Why, I could name her to the whole universe and it wouldn't compromise her! Who blames a good woman if a madman, an unlucky wretch, is pining away for her? [*Marcel reacts.*] Everything is over for me—the joys of youth, the hopes of the future, the triumphs of art, aspirations and illusions, everything! It's too late to fight against the disease; today it's become incurable. From now on, I can only nurture my wound, let myself be consumed by a dreadful passion, and succumb to it with dignity. I may be rejected and despised, I may be cursed and disowned, but I'll still keep—and I want to keep pure and sacred—the very fire that is devouring and killing me! [*He drops onto a chair, his head in his hands.*]

MARQUISE [*quietly, to Marcel*]: He's so frenzied, it worries me. . . . Poor unhappy soul! He seems so good—and so honest! You must comfort him, Monsieur Marcel—you must tell him. . . .

MARCEL: What can I tell him?

MARQUISE: Oh—really, I don't know! . . . Tell him that his sorrow deserves to be pitied. . . . [*Aloud.*] Goodness! What is he to be told? What advice could be given to the woman he loves so much? Wouldn't she have some constraints? Wouldn't she have

to take other people into consideration? And if she's as blame-
less as he says, shouldn't she wish to deserve the respect that
people have for her? What would people think of her, if she
encouraged the hopes of a man she doesn't know? And how
could she get to know him? Could she accept him as one of her
intimate friends, when she hasn't accepted anyone else? She
would feel sorry for him, no doubt . . . deeply sorry for him,
perhaps, since she must be kindhearted; he wouldn't love her
if she were vain or insolent or cold. . . . But I do believe she
must try to discourage him, even if she . . . [*Aside.*] Oh! This is
cruel! And my heart is so weak—I can't hide that any longer!
[*She runs out, hiding her face in her handkerchief.*]

Scene 7

[*Julien, Marcel.*]

MARCEL: Wake up, wipe your eyes; the game is won.

JULIEN: Oh, leave me alone! I'm a broken man, Marcel.

MARCEL: Why, don't you understand? Uncle knows nothing about
the accident to his lily; I didn't go to see him, I stayed out
there, I listened, I returned on cue, and I saved the whole show
by talking about Madame de Reuilly. Without my help, and
without the opportunity, you would never have dared to make
your declaration; I deserve the credit for that little dash of
eloquence that carried the day.

JULIEN: You're going soft in the head!

MARCEL: Not at all—you're the problem case, you're blind.
Uncle . . .

JULIEN: Oh! What are you talking about? It's beside the point. . . .

MARCEL: It's absolutely the point. The Marquise has to fall in love
with you, then you can inherit; you have to inherit, then you
can marry the Marquise!

JULIEN: The Marquise is above . . .

MARCEL: All pecuniary motives—I know that; but society, which
would condemn her if she married a poor painter, will absolve
her if she marries a respectable millionaire! And what about
you—would you dare to accept her hand, if all you had to offer
her was privation and poverty? No. Why, marrying for love is a
fine thing, I'm not disputing that: I love my wife, I work, she

saves, that keeps us busy and binds us together. But when you're
married to a Marquise, you should be able to dispense with
little economies—they'd be a torment and a disgrace to her.
You have to surround her with comfort and dignity, you have
to be rich—I admit it—and you *are* rich, I can answer for that.
Before three days are up, Uncle and I will have put in such
good work that the Marquise will be listening to the very proposals she rejected out of hand this morning.

JULIEN: What do you mean? Did you dare . . . ?

MARCEL: I mentioned someone, but she doesn't yet know it was
you. Today she loves you for being down and out . . . tomorrow,
she'll forgive you for not being so any longer!

JULIEN: You're talking nonsense! . . . She doesn't love me!

MARCEL: Wait a bit! She isn't far off. She's dreadfully worried; she
was crying just now.

JULIEN: She was crying?

MARCEL: She's looking this way . . . yes, yes, she's afraid you might
be desperate.

JULIEN: What are you going to do?

MARCEL: A simple test. [*Very loud, near the window.*] Devil take the
accursed flower! Devil take grand passions that drive people
crazy, and grand ladies that just laugh at them! Come on, let's
get out of here, I don't want you staying here another day, it'd
be the death of you! Come on, let's go, I do insist! [*He opens
and shuts the side door noisily, pushes Julien behind an easel, and
hides on the other side of the room.*]

JULIEN [*sotto voce*]: What—you expect—you think . . . ?

MARCEL: Just do what you're told, quick!

JULIEN: I'm scared.

MARCEL: Quiet!

Scene 8

[*As above, the Marquise.*]

MARQUISE: Gone! Maybe forever! I'll never see him again! . . . Oh—
why did I ever set eyes on him? [*She picks up the lily.*] Poor
flower! Poor Julien! Oh, what's wrong with me? I'm in such
torment! He was happy here—happy because he loved me—
and I'm driving him away—I'm killing him! . . . No! It's out of

the question! . . . But what can I do? I can't possibly go running
after him! . . . Oh, I'll write to him . . . write what? [*Writing.*]
"Dear Monsieur . . . " No! "Dear Julien!" Just "Dear Julien"?—
well, never mind! "I'm taking the lily, and I accept it!" [*She
kisses the lily.*]

JULIEN [*falling at her feet*]: Oh—thank you!

MARQUISE: Julien!

MARCEL [*aside*]: Well, well—a friend happy, a Marquise for a
cousin . . . and my chambers paid for!

The End

A Good Deed
Is Never Wasted

(Un Bienfait n'est jamais perdu)

A Proverb

Characters

ANNA DE LOUVILLE
LOUISE DE TRÉMONT
M. DE VALROGER
M. DE LOUVILLE [*Anna's husband*]
[A SERVANT]

The Château de Louville.—A drawing room.

Scene 1

[*Louise, Anna.*]

ANNA [*standing, agitated*]: Well, you can say what you like, but I refuse to see him.

LOUISE [*seated, doing embroidery; calmly*]: Why?

ANNA: When a man compromises so many women, he's every decent woman's born enemy.

LOUISE: Would you please tell me what the fine words "compromises women" mean?

ANNA: That's the question of a primitive savage. Are you asking it seriously?

LOUISE: Very seriously. I am a primitive savage.

ANNA: What a claim! Are there any primitive savages left in this present age? Nowadays there aren't even any at Carpentras.[1]

LOUISE: Ergo, there could be some in some other place. Can't you produce any answer? Is the question too difficult?

ANNA: It's very easy. A man who compromises women is Monsieur de Valroger.

LOUISE: That doesn't tell me anything; I don't know him.

ANNA: Haven't you ever seen him?

LOUISE: Where could I have seen him? He's a new star in Paris society, and I haven't been there since I lost my husband.

ANNA: Well, I've been living in this château for two months, and I don't know the gentleman either, but my husband knows him; he says he's an absolute Regency rake.[2]

LOUISE: Nonsense! That's an extinct species. Monsieur de Louville is teasing you.

ANNA: Who can tell? I'm sure he would be very displeased with me if I received the man in his absence.

LOUISE: Then you've done well to turn him away. Let's change the subject.

ANNA: Oh! Goodness, there's nothing to stop us talking about him.

LOUISE: We've nothing to say on the subject, since neither of us knows him.

ANNA: Especially since, if we did know him, we'd have nothing good to say.

LOUISE: Then let's be glad that we don't like spinach, because if we did . . .

ANNA [*going to a window and looking out*]: What tired old jokes you make!—Look at that! He's horrid!

LOUISE: Who?

ANNA: The fine seducer Monsieur de Valroger. He's extremely ugly.

LOUISE: What is he doing in your grounds, when he knows that you won't receive him?

ANNA: He must have wanted to see at least the grounds, and, as the gardener can never say no to twenty francs . . . I'll have him thrown out.

LOUISE: The gardener?

ANNA: Certainly. He must have accepted money to give the man a chance to see me.

LOUISE: What a waste of money that was!

ANNA: Oh? You think my figure isn't worth the expense?

LOUISE: Indeed it is—but he might have reflected that he could see it for nothing.

ANNA [*drawing the curtain abruptly*]: He hasn't seen me.

LOUISE: That's only because he didn't want to. Evidently he isn't as curious as you are.

ANNA: Aren't you yourself curious to see a man who has been talked about so much? He's right here, close by!

LOUISE: Oh, I suppose it won't cost anything to take a look. [*She goes to the window and looks out.*] Well, to be frank, I'm not of your opinion. He's very nice to look at.

ANNA: Nice! Like the public executioner!

LOUISE [*returning*]: Ah, how you hate him—this poor Monsieur de Valroger!

ANNA: And you defend him?

LOUISE: Against whom?

ANNA: I don't know, but you're desperately keen for me to receive him.

LOUISE: Perhaps it might be better than all this regret at missing out.

ANNA: Speak for yourself.

LOUISE: Myself? Oh, I know I shall see him at my own home. My mother told me he was going to call.

ANNA: And you expect to receive him?

LOUISE: Certainly.

ANNA: Ah!—Well, you're a widow, you have children. . . .

LOUISE: And I'm not nearly as young as you: say it, it doesn't bother me—quite the contrary, in fact. When you reach my age without self-recriminations, you can count the years with pleasure.

ANNA: Get along with you, you virtuous flirt!

LOUISE: My dear child, you'll have the same pleasure yourself, provided you don't let too much curiosity into your life.

ANNA: I beg your pardon? I've no idea what you're talking about.

LOUISE: Yes you do. You know perfectly well that curiosity is an affliction of the soul—a disease! Virtue leads to a calm and healthy life.

ANNA: Excellent! A sermon?

LOUISE: Naturally; I'm getting old!

Scene 2

[*Anna, Louise, a servant.*]

SERVANT: The Marquis de Valroger wishes to know if Madame is at home to him.

ANNA: Again? Didn't you tell him I've gone out?

SERVANT: I did, but he saw Madame at the window, and, thinking that she had come back . . .

ANNA: The impertinent creature! Tell him I'm not seeing him.

LOUISE [*to the servant*]: Just a moment. . . . [*To Anna, sotto voce.*] Do have him in!

ANNA [*likewise*]: Oho! You see—you're the one who's willing! [*To the servant.*] Let him in. [*The servant leaves.*]

LOUISE: Yes, I want you to see him. I want to show you that there's no such thing as a dangerous man in the presence of a decent woman.

ANNA: But my husband . . . Admittedly, he didn't forbid me to see him! . . .

LOUISE: Your husband respects you too much to worry about anything; and in any case, I'm here.

SERVANT [*announcing*]: The Marquis de Valroger.

Scene 3

[*Louise, Anna, Valroger.*]

VALROGER [*going to Anna*]: If I had the audacity to persevere, Madame . . .

LOUISE: It's because you saw me at the window? [*Sotto voce to Anna, who is astonished.*] Let me handle this.

VALROGER [*indicating Anna*]: Madame was the one I saw.

LOUISE: Madame is my friend, Madame de Trémont,[3] and you are in my house; I alone must beg your pardon for having kept you waiting.

VALROGER [*teasingly*]: It is very kind of you to apologize, Madame, but I was not aware that I did have to wait.

LOUISE: Still . . . you were told that I had gone out. I hadn't.

VALROGER: You are adorably frank, Madame! Then I must reflect that your first instinct had been to show me the door?

LOUISE: Precisely.

VALROGER: Once and for all, you mean?

LOUISE: I admit it, since I have thought better of it.

VALROGER: I'm very glad that you have; but to whom do I owe . . . ?

LOUISE: You owe it to Madame, who told me the most admirable things about you.

ANNA: Well! Of all the . . . ! [*Louise signals to her to be quiet.*]

VALROGER [*to Anna*]: Then I must thank you even more than your friend.

ANNA [*dryly*]: Don't thank me; I don't deserve the honor!

VALROGER [*teasingly*]: Oh! Madame, you say that in such a tone of voice. . . . I'm bewildered as to whether I should fear or hope!

ANNA [*loftily*]: Hope for what?

LOUISE: Hope to impress us. [*Offering Valroger her hand.*] Well, sir, it's done; we are most impressed.

VALROGER [*kissing her hand*]: Really! [*Aside.*] What a strange woman she is!

LOUISE: How could it possibly be otherwise? I myself never knew that you were such an excellent man, and so kind to all the needy in our neighborhood. My friend here has only just told me.

VALROGER [*astounded; to Anna*]: What! You knew . . . Indeed, I have been rehabilitated very cheaply! Is there the least merit . . . ?

LOUISE: Yes, there is always merit in providing thoughtful assistance with discretion. It may not be so meritorious for us women—we have nothing else to do with our time; but a man of the world, not swept away by his pleasures into a whirlpool of selfishness and forgetfulness! . . . Come now, I see that my praise is embarrassing you . . . it's over. I owed you the explanation, and we shall not mention it again.

VALROGER: Why, no, Madame; since you have raised the subject, I want to know all about it. Before Madame de Trémont went to the trouble of telling you I was an angel, it seems you thought I was a demon, since you so pitilessly kept me away from your sanctuary?

LOUISE: You shall know everything, because you're too well bred to ask me where I acquired the information. I was told that you were wicked.

VALROGER: Wicked! Now there's a dreadful word. Would you please explain it to me, Madame?

LOUISE: I can only give you my personal understanding of the word. A wicked man is a man with hatred in his heart, and you were accused of hating women.

VALROGER: How can anyone hate women?

LOUISE: To pursue them only for the pleasure of compromising them is to hate them. To compromise them is to rob them of the respect and trust that they deserve; it's to do them the greatest injustice and the greatest harm. That's what a wicked man is.

VALROGER: Very well. And what is a wicked woman?

LOUISE: The same thing. She's a heartless coquette.

VALROGER: Well, here's a bizarre occurrence, Madame de Louville! I myself had been told that you were a wicked woman, in the sense you give to the word.

ANNA [*letting it slip*]: Me?

VALROGER [*realizing the deception*]: You? [*Aside.*] Well, well! These ladies are having a little fun at my expense! [*Aloud, to Anna.*] Oh, you, Madame de Trémont, you are supposed—correctly, I trust—to be a sincere and considerate woman; but your friend Madame de Louville, who has just given such a fine definition of wickedness, has the reputation of being as wicked as Satan!

ANNA: Well, there's a nice reputation! But it's scandalous! . . . I . . . [*To Louise.*] Aren't you angry?

LOUISE: To be angry about it would be to admit that I deserve it.

ANNA: But Monsieur believed it—still believes it, presumably?

LOUISE: Indeed; who can tell? That's for him to say.

VALROGER: Ha, ha!

ANNA [*angrily*]: What do you mean, "Ha, ha"?

VALROGER: Ho, ho!

ANNA: Those aren't answers!

VALROGER: What can I say? It's true that Madame has virtue written in flaming letters all over her face, and the welcome she has just given me would turn the head of the merest novice, but angelic creatures of her kind are very often the most dangerous and treacherous ones. They contrive to put you at their feet, and as soon as you're there, they kick off their pink slippers and reveal their cloven hooves.

ANNA: Well then, if you don't believe either one of us to be sincere, and if you are so ill disposed toward . . . Madame in particular, why did you come to see her? Nobody invited or urged you to do so, as far as I know.

VALROGER: Oh but excuse me, I was imperiously summoned here to reply to a challenge.

ANNA: Well, I didn't know that.

VALROGER: No, you didn't know it; but possibly Madame de Louville does!

LOUISE: I have my suspicions. Without knowing you, and simply on the word of other people, I said many ill things about you. Your easy conquests of fast women made me angry. I hated you—as we do hate someone who confuses us with other people—and, while I did say that I would never see you in my life, I still wanted to see you so that I could defy you to your face. That was the challenge to which you replied by coming here.

VALROGER: Ah, now you're being sincere!

LOUISE: I often am; it's my way of being coquettish. The great diplomats do the same.

ANNA: I hate and despise coquettishness!

LOUISE: And I confess that we all have some of it. It's much better to acknowledge our own weaknesses than to hear ourselves perpetually reproached with them. Yes, I confess that, especially between twenty-five and thirty, we women are all a little perverse, because we are all a little mad. We are intoxicated with the pride of our beauty if we are beautiful, and with that of our virtue if we are virtuous. And if we are both—oh! then there's no limit to our vanity; any man who dares to doubt our power becomes our mortal enemy. He must be conquered at any price; and to be conquered, he must be driven to love us. What would his adoration be worth if he didn't suffer for us a little? Shouldn't he be made to pay the penalty for his irreverence? So you embark with him in the nutshell known as conflict on the dangerous flood known as love; you make game of the dangers, and you hold out till some unforeseen reef, an utterly trivial one, perhaps a slight touch of spite or childish jealousy, shipwrecks you and your delightful traveling-companion. That's the very common and very familiar result of such reciprocal challenges. At first you hate each other, then you adore each other, and after that you despise each other—or possibly yourself. And yet it would have been so easy to meet in a natural way, greet each other politely, and go your separate ways without harboring any bitterness over casual words or thoughtless blusterings!

ANNA: My dear, your remarks are priceless. But still—speaking as a decent woman without any particular troubles, as all the world knows—I don't see where your confession leads you, and I must admit that it goes beyond my own experience. I shall therefore leave you to ask Monsieur for forgiveness of your sins, and I shall withdraw. . . .

LOUISE: Without inviting him to visit you?

ANNA: Without inviting him. I have no reason to ask his pardon, since he is convinced I regard him as an angel!

VALROGER: Might I at least be allowed to go there and offer you my thanks?

ANNA: Yes, Monsieur, at the Château de Trémont, [*aside to Louise*] where I shall never set foot again! [*She leaves.*]

Scene 4

[*Louise, Valroger.*]

LOUISE: You do appreciate, don't you, that I am now on bad terms with Madame de Trémont?

VALROGER: I can see, Madame de Trémont,[4] that your relations with Madame de Louville have been slightly strained on my account.

LOUISE: Oho! You have guessed what I was about to reveal to you?

VALROGER: Yes. Madame; I saw that, being a good friend, you wanted to nip an evil in the bud.

LOUISE: An evil?

VALROGER: Yes. I came here, as you very well know, to avenge myself, never mind how, for the contempt and aversion that Madame de Louville claimed to feel towards me. Now that will no longer be possible; you have shown her the danger too clearly. In addition, you made me look ridiculous in her eyes, because I didn't at first see the trap you had prepared for me. So I must abandon my quest for revenge. But don't be too triumphant, I was only moderately intent on it.

LOUISE: Then I must thank you for being merciful to virtuous women in the person of my young friend, and take you up on your promise.

VALROGER: What promise?

LOUISE: Your promise to leave alone—permanently—this young woman who loves her husband, an excellent husband, a good man who is known to you . . .

VALROGER: He isn't a friend of mine.

LOUISE: He soon will be, now that you are settled in our neighborhood. You'll go hunting together, you'll meet each other everywhere, you'll respect him, you'll see that his private life is happy and decent. But any private life, however admirable, could possibly be disturbed by some slight word. You are a dangerous man, in the sense that you can't take a single step without some scheme or adventure being attributed to you; but you're a gentleman all the same, and you'll promise me to give up . . .

VALROGER: Excuse me! Before I commit myself, I'd like to know . . .

LOUISE: What?

VALROGER: I'd like to know how—why—you, who are said to be the pure and virtuous woman par excellence, seem to hold other women's virtue so cheap, even to the point of begging that they should be spared?

LOUISE: Oh! I'll go much further than that. I hold my own past virtue cheap too. I'm not at all sure that in my youth, if I had been pursued and plagued by a cunning seducer, I should have retained the tranquillity I now possess.

VALROGER: In your youth?

LOUISE: Yes; and as I have been extremely happy in my own private life and treated with great respect by everyone around me, I am very tolerant towards women who lose their way on intricate and confusing paths.

VALROGER: Do you know, Madame, I'm tempted to regard you as the true coquette I expected to find here.

LOUISE: Well, naturally!

VALROGER: Madame de Louville is a child. Beauty, youth, pride, temerity—all that is very familiar, very far from challenging and very unexciting. But a truly strong and ingeniously humble woman, who is generous toward her sisters, calls herself old, and yet is prettier than the youngest of them—why, say what you like, that's priceless, as you must see, and it would be an immense triumph . . .

LOUISE: To offer it up?

VALROGER: No, to conquer it.

LOUISE: Conquer! Why, there's a charming word! Are you propositioning me?

VALROGER: If you like.

LOUISE: And if I don't like?

VALROGER: It's too late. You provoked it, and you didn't protect yourself against it in time.

LOUISE: Indeed, that's true. Well, sir, you are very kind, and I thank you.

VALROGER: In other words, you regard what I have said as a cheap compliment?

LOUISE: Far from it; I feel too flattered for that.

VALROGER: What excruciating mockery, my dear! I'm beginning to think you're a coquette in good earnest.

LOUISE: It's part of my role.

VALROGER: The role of guardian angel to Madame de Louville?

LOUISE: Precisely! If I don't take possession of your heart today, a certain proverb won't come true.

VALROGER: Well, it won't; I detest you.

LOUISE: Oh no you don't.

VALROGER: You believe the opposite?

LOUISE: Not at all. I'm nothing to you either way.

VALROGER: And you're paying me back in the same coin, very lavishly!

LOUISE: No, not in the least.

VALROGER: Am I to understand that you detest me too?

LOUISE: Quite the reverse. Look me in the eyes.

VALROGER: With pleasure.

LOUISE: Well?

VALROGER: Well?

LOUISE: Do I look as though I'm making fun of you?

VALROGER: Definitely.

LOUISE: Oh! You're a cunning fellow! Well, you've been overrated; you're a well-behaved respectable young man, you've never understood the look in a woman's eyes.

VALROGER: In the eyes of a woman like you, quite possibly.

LOUISE: And just what is "a woman like me"?

VALROGER: A sphinx. I've never seen such assured disdain.

LOUISE: And I've never seen such obstinate mistrust. Come now, what kind of oath should I swear to prove I love you?

VALROGER [laughing]: You love me—you!

LOUISE: With all my heart!

VALROGER [aside]: She's mad! [Aloud.] Swear it on your honor if you want me to believe you.

LOUISE: The honor of a woman? You don't believe in that. In melodramas people swear by their eternal salvation—but you won't believe in that either.

VALROGER: Swear by your friendship for Madame de Louville!

LOUISE: Better still—by my daughter's innocence!

VALROGER: How old is she?

LOUISE: Six.

VALROGER: Then I do believe in it. So you do love me, then, just like that, very sweetly, with all your heart, like any man who might happen to come along?

LOUISE: I wouldn't love just any man who might happen to come along. Listen to me. You'll see that I'm not joking, and that my affection for you is very serious.

VALROGER: Oh! You'll have to explain that, please!

LOUISE: Do you remember a boy called Ferval?

VALROGER: Not in the least.

LOUISE: Augustin de Ferval.

VALROGER: Very vaguely...

LOUISE: Well, since all the i's need to be dotted, you may possibly recall a certain young lady called Aline, who was no Queen of Golconda?[5]

VALROGER: Well, Madame?

LOUISE: Well, Monsieur, that pretty creature, who was under your protection, was taken seriously by an unruly young lad just up from the provinces....

VALROGER: Ah! I follow, I do remember now! It must have been five or six years ago. Do you know our little friend Ferval?

LOUISE: He was my brother—a child who was rash enough to provoke you and on whom you chose not to take revenge, since
you gave him the satisfaction of taking a shot at you and then
replied with a pistol loaded with blanks. He never knew that;
but some of your friends secretly told his mother, who repeated
it to his sister. You'll appreciate, then, that the aforesaid sister
can't be joking when she says that she's very fond of you!

VALROGER: Then it's true, as people say, that a good deed is never
wasted, because your friendship must be a fine thing; and yet . . .

LOUISE: And yet?

VALROGER: You shouldn't offer it for such a trifle, Madame! It's a
dangerous stimulant.

LOUISE: Dangerous to whom?

VALROGER: To me.

LOUISE: Come now, why answer me like that? What's the point of
keeping up the conventional maneuverings and polite pleas-
antries, when I myself am simply calling everything by its proper
name?

VALROGER: You're forgetting your own words: I'm a wicked man,
and my heart is ice cold.

LOUISE: I've never believed that.

VALROGER: Well then, you've been wrong; you should have believed it.

LOUISE: Why aren't you telling the truth? I don't understand you
any more.

VALROGER: I am telling the truth. I'm in love with you.

LOUISE: If that were the truth, it would scarcely prove your heart
to be ice cold.

VALROGER: Ah, but wait! I'm in love with you after my customary
fashion—without loving you at all.

LOUISE: I understand; my trust humiliates you, my loyalty hurts
you, so you're taking revenge by telling me something you
think will offend me.

VALROGER: Yes, Madame, I do mean to offend you.

LOUISE: Why?

VALROGER: To make you hate me.

LOUISE: Because the friendship of a decent woman is an insult to you?

VALROGER: That's as may be. I don't want yours.

LOUISE: You're brutally sincere!

VALROGER: Yes. I'm a hardened seducer, just as you're a quintessen-
tial coquette.

LOUISE: And thus I'm outwitted and rebuffed! I'm a coquette in good earnest, and I tried to compete with a slyer and more vindictive creature than myself, who puts me in my place and means to make an example of me. Is that so?

VALROGER: Exactly.

LOUISE: And how am I to escape?

VALROGER: You won't.

LOUISE [*deliberately raising her voice*]: In other words, you're going to do to me what you intended to do to Madame de Louville?

VALROGER: Yes, Madame.

LOUISE: You'll come to see me?

VALROGER: Every day.

LOUISE: And if I won't let you in? . . .

VALROGER: I'll linger beneath the windows. I'll sleep in the garden, under a tree.

LOUISE: Then I'm saved! You'll catch a cold.

VALROGER: I'll cough so much that you won't be able to sleep. You'll send me herbal tea!

LOUISE: Which you'll refuse to drink?

VALROGER: On the contrary, I shall drink it.

LOUISE: And then?

VALROGER: And then you'll take pity on me and let me in.

LOUISE: And then?

VALROGER: I'll keep coming back.

LOUISE: I'll let myself be compromised?

VALROGER: No; you'll run away, but I'll follow you everywhere. Everywhere you go, you'll find me opening the carriage door and offering you my hand.

LOUISE: That's an old trick, that is.

VALROGER: Everything's an old trick. I haven't discovered anything new; you can't improve on what always works.

LOUISE: And that's what it means to compromise a woman?

VALROGER: Not at all! To compromise a woman is to exploit appearances which you have arranged, in order to slander her or to let her be slandered. Personally, I don't slander anyone. I'm a man of the world and a gentleman. I'll tell the whole world that I'm doing the maddest things for you and getting nowhere—which will be true till you start doing similar things for me.

LOUISE: And why should I?

VALROGER: Because madness is contagious.

LOUISE: And I'll become mad myself?

VALROGER: Don't rely on the past.

LOUISE: As you know, I don't take any pride in that. All the same, what is past has been attained.

VALROGER: No! Your virtue was helped along by an absence of danger—you said so yourself. And yet you must have aroused passions; but there would scarcely be one man in a thousand with the perseverance to devote month after month and year after year to the conquest of such a woman. . . . Now I know— I can see—that you've never met such a man.

LOUISE: And you fancy you are?

VALROGER: I am.

LOUISE: You enjoy that?

VALROGER: It's the only thing I do enjoy.

LOUISE: You were born hostile and vindictive, as people are born poets or shopkeepers?

VALROGER: A man's happiness lies in cultivating his special talents.

LOUISE: Even the bad ones?

VALROGER: Ah, so you do admit that I'm bad?

LOUISE: That's what you're after, is it? You have a need to frighten everyone; when you don't achieve that, you think your performance is wasted. If someone trusts you, it humiliates you. It's an obsession with you—I can see that clearly enough—but such an obsession would never be satisfied with me. I don't think you're really bad at all.

VALROGER: You're evading the question. If I am what I claim to be, you should hate me.

LOUISE: And you want to be hated?

VALROGER: Yes; it's absolutely essential to me, the very first step.

LOUISE: Well, since I don't allow you the first step and therefore will presumably escape the last one, I must say that, wicked or not wicked, I can't hate the benefactor of the needy in my neighborhood and the savior of my brother.

VALROGER: Useless to invoke the past—you'll hate me all the same!

LOUISE: How do you propose to achieve that?

VALROGER: First of all, I shall try to woo Madame de Louville.

LOUISE [*looking at an embroidered door curtain*]: What good would that do, if it didn't make me jealous?

VALROGER: You asked me to spare her. I have to be relentless, to show you conclusively that I'm worthless.

LOUISE [*showing him the door curtain, which is wavering*]: Court her
by all means; now that she's heard the whole conversation,
she'll be able to defend herself. Your plans are betrayed, and
perhaps . . . [*She goes to the window.*] That carriage on its way . . .
Yes, reinforcements are arriving.

VALROGER: Her husband?

LOUISE: Precisely.

VALROGER: Madame de Louville may be out of contention, but I
can do without that strategy.

LOUISE: That's all I wanted. Thank you, dear sir; she is saved, and
I don't have any fear of you myself.

VALROGER: Thank you, dear Madame; so you accept the challenge!

LOUISE: What challenge? You want me to fear you so that I may
come to love you? That's a superfluous prologue, since we've
reached the dénouement straight away. What you want isn't
love—you're glutted with that, you don't care for it any more;
what you want is to upset my virtue—in other words, my soli-
tary tranquillity. Well, hearts that are closed to the unhealthy
disturbances of wild passion can feel purer and kinder emotions—which you could be proud of inspiring and preserving
eternally fresh. It isn't a humiliation to be maternally loved by
a mature woman; and it wouldn't be at all glorious to make her
absurdly infatuated with you.

VALROGER: A mature woman! . . .

LOUISE: I am thirty-six, my fine sir!

VALROGER: That isn't true; your daughter is only six!

LOUISE: Ah, but my son is fifteen!

VALROGER: Oh, come now!

LOUISE: I don't have his birth certificate in my pocket; otherwise . . .
But you've calmed down, and you'll admit you're a little embarrassed to find yourself mistaken, for all your clairvoyance, about
a woman's age. You'll see my son for yourself, and that will cure
you instantly. Yes, you will come to see me—every day, if you
like—and without first being condemned to sleep under a tree.
You'll catch your colds for other women, and I shall always
keep a supply of herbal tea at home. You'll find that I'm sur-
rounded by a few people who never leave me—my son, my
daughter, and my nephew, son of the Augustin de Ferval whose
life you saved in spite of himself; plus my mother, who blesses
and prays for you every day, and my sister-in-law, the said
Augustin's wife, who is in on the secret, and who regards you

as a saint—however perverted you are supposed to be. See whether there's any way to creep into our midst like a wolf into a sheepfold! All the members of this pleasant little world are delighted that you have settled in our neighborhood. Our poor Augustin has passed away—he died last year, and the mourning I am wearing is for him—but thanks to you we kept him among us for six years and saw him happy, married and a father. His wife and child are treasures that he left among us. The whole grateful family, great and small, will throw their arms around your neck and your legs; and when you've been well and truly kissed on both cheeks like a long-awaited friend for whom no gift is too good, you'll come to feel that you're flesh and blood just like any other man—and not the ghost of Don Juan, a hero from some alien time and place. That will melt the layers of artificial ice around your heart—which is alive and human, since it is generous and compassionate. Your evil spirit will laugh at itself, and you'll deign to love and even protect ordinary decent people—which is much easier than setting traps for them, and much more pleasant than striving desperately to belittle them. You'll keep your craft and your cunning for women who provoke it and who can afford to play that particular game. Since you're a decent man yourself, you'll be forgiven your odd little quirk of wasting your time surveying and studying and testing the weakness of our sex while you arouse its perversity. Why, you'll be forgiven everything, even your incorrigibility. People will think that this business of punishing female wrongs is a wretched task, and that you must be a most unfortunate man. They'll try to tend you like an invalid, or amuse you like a convalescent. If at times you're tempted to make war on your own friends, they'll say, "It's only a test: he wants to see if we deserve the respect he has for us." Then they'll do their best to show you how much they prize it. And let me tell you now, they'll be most disappointed if they don't manage to bring some good wholesome affection into your life. Friendship may not be convulsive, but it isn't ice cold either. So, without the slightest trouble on your part, you'll gain a great victory among us: the victory of having genuinely touched, moved, delighted or grieved a few hearts that are not commonplace, and that don't open themselves to everyone.

VALROGER: Well, Madame de Trémont, I have such love for you, just as you are, that I should consider myself an idiot and a coward if I had planned to disturb that noble and touching serenity. You've understood perfectly well that I was above such an act, and in any case I would never presume to seriously threaten someone like you; but I hereby stop the frivolity and surrender my weapons to you. I was rightly informed that you were the sincerest and kindest and strongest of women; and I have long understood one thing: generosity is your sex's most powerful weapon. Virtue without modesty is always a provocation, just as resistance without conviction is always a pose. I am happy and proud to say that I understand and respect you. . . . And, since you do me the honor of accepting me as a brother, would you care to consecrate the bond?

LOUISE: In what way?

VALROGER: A moment ago you talked of kissing me on both cheeks. . . .

LOUISE: That was a metaphor!

VALROGER: Why shouldn't it be the formula that seals a pact of honor?

LOUISE: And haven't you another reason too?

VALROGER: Another reason?

LOUISE: You don't wish to utter it! No; in your eyes it isn't a reason at all. You're too generous to require an act of reparation, but may I tell you something? When you came in here, if I'd followed my first impulse, I should have flung my arms around you; and don't think such gratitude would have been overdone. I know the whole story, Monsieur de Valroger; I know that one of those cheeks has been struck by the glove of my poor silly brother, and since I don't know which one . . .

VALROGER: Both, Madame, both!

LOUISE: I shan't contradict you; but any act of reparation requires witnesses, and lo and behold, here are ours now. [*She kisses him on both cheeks in front of Monsieur de Louville and his wife, who have just entered. Anna cries out in surprise, Monsieur de Louville bursts out laughing. Valroger goes down on one knee and kisses Louise's hand.*]

VALROGER: Thank you, Madame, thank you!

LOUVILLE [*laughing*]: Bravo, my friend! That's what I call storming an impregnable citadel!

VALROGER: The fortress is me, I fancy; and I've surrendered unconditionally. [*Quietly, as Louise turns laughingly to Anna.*] Tell me, Louville, isn't there any chance of marrying that woman?

LOUVILLE: Get along with you! She could be forty!

VALROGER: Even if she were fifty!

LOUVILLE: Nonsense! She loved her husband, she worships her son. . . . No, it's impossible!

VALROGER: That's too bad; it would have been the only way to turn me into a responsible man!

The End

Introduction

1. George Sand, *Œuvres autobiographiques*, ed. Georges Lubin, 2 vols. (Paris: Gallimard, 1970–71), 1:998–1001.

2. S. B. John, "The Drama of Money and Class," in *French Literature and Its Background*, ed. John Cruickshank, 6 vols. (Oxford: Oxford University Press, 1969), 5:67.

3. George Sand, *La Mare au diable* (Paris: Calmann Lévy, 1865), 165–75.

4. "The Lord Chamberlain . . . has declined to license any play that is not in blank verse and three hundred years old," says a character in *Utopia Limited* (W. S. Gilbert, *The Savoy Operas* [London: Macmillan, 1926], 613).

5. The best-known cases are Charles Reade's bowdlerized adaptations of *Claudie: The Village Tale* (1852) and *Rachel the Reaper* (1874). The full extent of the practice remains unknown.

6. Jules Lemaître, *Impressions de théâtre*, 11 vols. (Paris: Société française d'imprimerie et de librairie, 1889–1920), 1:150–62.

7. Lemaître is quoting the last speech from act 2, scene 5 of Musset's play.

8. Émile Zola, "George Sand," in *Œuvres complètes*, ed. Henri Mitterand, 12 vols. (Paris: Cercle du livre précieuse, 1966–70), 11:771–4.

9. George Sand, *A Woman's Version of the Faust Legend: The Seven Strings of the Lyre*, tr. George A. Kennedy (Chapel Hill, N.C.: University of North Carolina Press, 1989).

10. Gay Manifold, *George Sand's Theatre Career* (Ann Arbor, Mich.: UMI Research Press, 1985), 150.

11. Théophile Gautier, *Histoire de l'art dramatique en France depuis vingt-cinq ans*, 6 vols. (Paris: Hetzel, 1858–9), 2:52–60.

12. T. S. Eliot, *The Family Reunion*, ed. Nevill Coghill (London: Faber and Faber, 1969), 51. Eliot's ideal performer of the part was Paul Scofield, whose Harry—recorded on T. S. Eliot, *The Family Reunion*, directed by Howard Sackler (New York: Caedmon Records, 1965)—might

make an excellent starting point for any actor attempting Sand's Marquis, in spite of the obvious differences in mood and genre.

13. William Archer, *The Old Drama and the New: An Essay in Re-Valuation* (London: William Heinemann, 1923).

14. Alexander Pope, *Selected Prose*, ed. Paul Hammond (Cambridge: Cambridge University Press, 1987), 160.

15. George Sand, *Correspondance*, ed. Georges Lubin, 25 vols. (Paris: Garnier, 1964–91), 2:589.

16. Martin Cooper, *Gluck* (London: Chatto and Windus, 1935), 249.

17. "Let us conceal nothing that might be seen as mitigation of the Duke's conduct," she says characteristically at one point in the novel; yet the very same passage contains a relentless cumulative list of his defects (George Sand, *Le Marquis de Villemer* [Paris: Michel Lévy, 1861], 51–2).

18. The classic English-language discussion of the difference is T. W. Robertson's *Birth*, a sort of latter-day *Il turco in Italia* in which the budding dramatist Jack Randall observes the action from the sidelines and intermittently meddles with it, trying to decide to which category it belongs (*The Principal Dramatic Works of Thomas William Robertson*, 2 vols. [London: Sampson Low, Marston, & Co., 1889], 1:1–47).

19. Wladimir Karénine, *George Sand: Sa vie et ses œuvres*, 4 vols. (Paris: Plon, 1899–1926), 4:394.

20. Sand, *Correspondance*, 18:288–9.

21. Manifold, 101.

22. Karénine, 4:297.

23. Sand, *Correspondance*, 20:74, 75.

24. George Sand, *Théâtre de Nohant* (Paris: Michel Lévy, 1865), 160.

25. In informal correspondence she referred to *Le Pavé* as "a kind of proverb" (*Correspondance*, 16:488), but that was not how she characterized it in print. Once again (as the phrase "kind of" indicates) we note that her works fit into categories less readily than those of her main dramatic contemporaries.

26. The recent reprints by Indigo et Côté-femmes éditions provide useful reading texts, but are not critical editions and contain too many typographical errors for scholarly use.

The Marquis de Villemer

The Marquis de Villemer was first performed at the Odéon on 29 February 1864, with Charles-Emmanuel Ribes (Urbain), Francis Berton (the Duke), Saint-Léon (Dunières), Georges Rey (Pierre), Eugène Clerh (Benoît), Edmée Ramelli (the Marquise), Marguerite Thuillier (Caroline),

Émilienne Leprévost (Diane), and Borelli-Delahaye (Léonie). When the play was being cast, Sand expressed particular concern over the choice of actor to play Urbain, pointing out that the role could easily be made to seem "lugubrious," and stressing that it should be assigned to a performer who can make it "likable and interesting" (*Correspondance*, 18:120).

1. The Faubourg Saint-Germain: a particularly aristocratic district of Paris.

2. The courts of Henri IV (reigned 1589–1610) and Louis XV (reigned 1715–74) were notorious for sexual exploitation of socially inferior women. Their names recall the corruption of the old French aristocracy to which the Marquise belongs and illustrate her tendency to judge offenses differently depending on the social position of the offender, as well as setting the scene for the particular accusation against Caroline in the last act.

3. In the French text, the tales are specifically the *Fables* of Claris de Florian (1755–94), which were very widely read in nineteenth-century France.

4. On 11 May 1745, during the War of the Austrian Succession, French forces led by Marshal Saxe (Sand's great-grandfather) defeated a combined British, Dutch, and Austrian army in a hotly contested battle at Fontenoy (now in Belgium). The victory was long remembered, both as a model of military tactics and for the heroism of the combatants.

5. Carl Maria von Weber (1786–1826), German composer. The choice suggests a certain amount of artistic discernment, yet does not pose any challenge to the Marquise's conservative tastes.

6. The Duke is in danger of being arrested for debt.

7. Fictitious. Note how deftly the very slight hint of political instability contributes to the impression of a society gradually crumbling at the foundations. Anything more explicit would be less effective.

8. At this point, Sand wrote to Francis Berton (who played the Duke in the original production), "the Duke ought to hesitate for a moment, as if he was already on the point of weakening. But his pride takes over, and he refuses. People are surprised at that—it's the author's fault—please help the author out" (*Correspondance*, 18:281).

9. After the Flood, Noah sent out a dove from the ark; her return bearing an olive leaf was the first sign that the waters were subsiding (Genesis 8:10–11).

10. The French term, *toquée*, was evidently still a new, not very familiar piece of slang in the early 1860s; it is one of Thénardier's words in Hugo's *Les Misérables* (1862).

11. "All the dialogue in this scene ought to be *very spontaneous* up to Urbain's big speech," Sand wrote during rehearsals for the original production (*Correspondance*, 18:283).

12. One of Caroline's major duties is to read to the Marquise; she is now preparing a new book for this purpose (in the nineteenth century, most books were issued with unopened leaves, which required cutting before the book could be read).

13. In the French text, *Frontin*, the archetypal pert, audacious valet of eighteenth-century French comedy; his literary descendant Figaro is more familiar to English-speaking audiences.

14. The Duke is quoting a slogan uttered by the somewhat fickle hero of Musset's popular one-act play *Il faut qu'une porte soit ouverte ou fermée* (1848).

15. The *Dictionnaire historique et critique* compiled by Pierre Bayle in 1697; long a standard reference work, but very antiquated by 1864.

16. The artist Denis-Auguste-Marie Raffet (1804–60) was noted mainly for his lithographs of scenes from recent French history.

17. Sand's rehearsal notes stress that she should not seem to be *extinguishing* the lamp (*Correspondance*, 18:283).

18. Marie de Rabutin-Chantal, Marquise de Sévigné (1626–96) was France's most famous letter writer. The Duke attempts to break his news as Madame de Sévigné, in her celebrated letter of 15 December 1670, broke the news of a proposed marriage between the Grande Mademoiselle (the King's first cousin) and a mere duke: "I'm going to tell you the most amazing thing, the most surprising, the most marvelous, the most miraculous, the most triumphant, the most stunning, the most unheard-of, the most singular, the most extraordinary, the most incredible, the most unforeseen . . ."—and so on. The allusion has ominous undertones relevant to the play's final scenes: the 1670 match was promptly broken off as a result of pressure from the royal family.

19. "In this speech," Sand wrote, "Caroline comes to a spontaneous decision, and her very first words frankly reveal an impossibility; she shouldn't be affected by grief except towards the end, when she has demonstrated her strength of character and can reveal some of her distress" (*Correspondance*, 18:284).

20. "This remark should be spoken without any pause. . . . A pause before 'I'm afraid' would suggest more vanity in Caroline's character than she has; instead, she should pass over the fear very lightly. If there is any pause to be made, it should be between 'Wait a minute!' and 'We do have one comfort left . . .'." (Sand, *Correspondance*, 18:284).

21. Don Rodrigo Díaz de Vivar, eleventh-century Spanish military leader and hero of numerous folk tales; familiar to French theatergoers from Corneille's play *Le Cid*.

22. "Don't delay the 'No!' when the Marquise is about to go down on her knees," Sand advised Marguerite Thuillier, who played Caroline in the original production (*Correspondance*, 18:284).

Françoise

Françoise was first performed at the Gymnase-Dramatique on 3 April 1856 with a cast of celebrities: Rose Chéri (Françoise), Francis Berton (Henri), Ferville (the Doctor), Adolphe Dupuis (La Hyonnais), François Lesueur (Dubuisson), Anna-Josephine Lesueur (Madame Dubuisson), Marie Delaporte (Cléonice), and Mélanie (Marie-Jeanne). Sand's preface discusses the original production, and incidentally provides some fascinating insights into her conception of the work and its characters. Dupuis is praised for his "delicate and elegant comedy" in the part of La Hyonnais, as well as his "heartfelt emotion"; this should dissuade us from taking the character too solemnly. The two senior Dubuissons are not stage villains but "basically kindhearted people who have been swept away by a form of vanity characteristic of countryfolk—a desire to emulate the nobility"; he displays, "underneath a pose of mockery and derision, the instinctive respect of serfs' sons for knights' sons," while she has " a more simple-minded showiness and a goodnatured, fun-loving ostentation." Henri, as befits a more complex character, receives a more detailed analysis. "Love of family and work, devotion, honor, and friendship—what could seem more natural, to any healthy mind? Yet the spirit and morality of the present day often impede these gentle impulses and unpretentious virtues. The struggles of a man torn between the lively temptations of our epoch and the peaceful charms of duty contain some truths worth telling, in my opinion. We have all witnessed such struggles, we have all known such a man. He wasn't villainous or detestable; often he was likable and kind; his conduct wasn't deliberately wicked; and therefore people pitied him, people went out of their way for him. He didn't consciously exploit such pity; indeed he rejected it, he was afraid of it. He didn't have enough courage either to accept it or to go without it; his intense thirst for happiness made him unhappy; he had spells of unproductive remorse and ineffective enthusiasm. What, then, was his error? A lack of faith and knowledge, a false idea of the true joys of life, a blind ignorance that threw away the substance to seize the shadow, an urge to avoid anything that would inconvenience himself, a notion that indolence is restful and inactivity enjoyable. These baneful dreams are the products of a materialistic civilization that hasn't yet accepted the true moral civilization, even though it feels some vague disturbing desire for greater balance and for a level of mental well-being that would match its physical well-being" (Sand, *Théâtre complet,* 4 vols. [Paris: Michel Lévy, 1866], 4:1–3).

1. Vichy: a town in central France, frequented since ancient times for the supposed therapeutic properties of its hot mineral springs.

2. Saint Cecilia: legendary martyr and patron saint of music, often depicted playing the organ.

3. As well as being grotesquely ornate and pretentious, the name is a singularly unfortunate choice, with resonances that are a little more apt than Madame Dubuisson can have wanted. The parents of the historical Cleonica or Kleonike (5th century B.C.E.) effectively prostituted her to the king of Sparta, who woke in the night and killed her, thinking her to be an intruder (Plutarch, *Cimon* 6:4–5; Pausanias 3:17:8).

4. The "Flowering Shrub," the name of the inn where Madame Dubuisson worked as barmaid and her husband (we later learn) as publican; no doubt the shrub was depicted on the sign outside the premises. The Dubuissons appear to have created their surname by adding an aristocratic-sounding *Du* to the name of their former workplace.

5. Plutus: the Classical god of wealth, not a very exalted deity; generally portrayed as fickle and blind.

The Paving Stone

The Paving Stone was first performed at Nohant on 7 September 1861, with Alexandre Manceau (Durand), Marie Caillaud (Louise), and Auguste Jallas (Coqueret); there was no Neighbor. This was a semi-improvised performance: "We asked the actors beforehand for the basic drift of the dialogue that they wanted to say, and on that basis (simplest things are always best, in our opinion) we drafted a detailed outline of the thoughts and conflicts, expectations and oversights, endeavors and impulses that their feelings and characterizations seemed to us to involve.... They were free to develop our suggestions as they pleased, and often we saw them shape their parts with remarkable intelligence; because of the freedom of their work, in the heat of the moment their performances were full of strikingly realistic and highly perceptive touches" (Sand, *Théâtre de Nohant*, 159–60). It should be noted that the two principals were both experienced performers: Manceau was one of the Nohant theater's driving forces, and Caillaud (a twenty-one-year-old peasant whom Sand had taught to read and write) had made a remarkable impression two years earlier in *L'Auberge rouge*. The first professional performance took place at the Gymnase-Dramatique on 18 March 1862 with Pierre-Chéri Lafont (Durand), Marie Delaporte (Louise), Pierre Berton (Coqueret), and Anna-Josephine Lesueur (the Neighbor, rewritten as a female role).

1. Throughout the play, Sand's use of geological terms is predictably sure-footed. Graywacke is a not an igneous rock (a *roche primitive*, in nineteenth-century French geological terminology) but a sedimentary one.

2. Thérèse Levasseur was the lower-class mistress of the French philosopher Jean-Jacques Rousseau (1712–78). She was not noted for her fidelity to him.

3. Two relatively common fossil bivalves.

4. Oölite, a granular fossiliferous limestone, is one of the characteristic rocks of the Upper Jurassic in France. All the fossils named by Sand could indeed be found in it—though as Durand says, it would be unusual to find so many of them in a single slab.

5. A fossil brachiopod, gastropod, sea urchin, and bivalve respectively.

6. In the French, the Neighbor refers to Cassandro, the stereotypic foolish old man in Italian *commedia dell'arte;* we have substituted a name more familiar to English-speaking playgoers.

7. The "three things" are the minerals quartz, feldspar, and mica.

8. During the eighteenth century, there was a prolonged (and acrimonious) geological debate between Plutonists (who proposed that the earth's rocks had solidified from molten lavalike substances) and Neptunists (who proposed that the rocks had been deposited by water).

9. Durand is recalling the Lord's questions to Job: "Where wast thou when I laid the foundations of the earth? declare, if thou hast understanding. Who hath laid the measures thereof, if thou knowest? . . ." (Job 38:4ff).

10. A foundling: *une champie,* local dialect for a child "found in the fields" (that is, an illegitimate child).

The Japanese Lily

The Japanese Lily was first performed at the Vaudeville on 14 August 1866 with Delacour (Julien), Charles Colson (Marcel), and an unidentified Mademoiselle Savary (the Marquise).

1. Louis XVI reigned from 1774 to 1792; the play is thus set shortly before the French Revolution.

2. In the novel, the lily is described as a previously unknown species, *Antonia thierrii,* with flowers at first "dark green, glossy, and tapering"; in full bloom, "the interior of the corolla glistened with incomparable sheen and whiteness, flecked [*tigrée*] with bright pink" (George Sand, *Antonia* [Paris: Michel Lévy, 1861], 58, 86). This symbolism would be well worth reproducing on stage, in theaters small enough for the flower's details to be visible.

3. More precisely, Madame de Reuilly is a *présidente,* that is, the wife (or, in this case, widow) of a *président,* but we have avoided the use of this term, which would convey a misleading idea of her social status to many English-speaking readers!

A Good Deed Is Never Wasted

A Good Deed Is Never Wasted was first staged at the Théâtre de Cluny on 7 November 1872 with Larochelle as Valroger and Cécile Germa as

Louise. In French drama, a proverb is a dramatic sketch or play (usually in one act) illustrating some familiar popular saying, which may or may not be stated during the work itself. The genre developed during the eighteenth century; the best-known examples were written by Alfred de Musset (1810–57).

1. The joke is that instead of the expected "Patagonia" or "darkest Africa," Anna cites a realm much closer to home. The inhabitants of Carpentras, twenty-four kilometres from Avignon in the south of France, were proverbial for their supposed ignorance and uncivilized outlook. Some local name with suitable associations could probably be substituted in a present-day English-language performance.

2. Sand is again evoking the moral corruption of the old pre-Revolutionary French aristocracy—in this case during the Regency (1715–23) after the death of Louis XIV, before Louis XV legally came of age.

3. Throughout scene 3 and the initial speech of scene 4, all allusions within the dialogue to "Madame de Trémont" refer to Anna de Louville, and all allusions to "Madame de Louville" refer to Louise de Trémont, since the two women are now posing as each other. The speech prefixes, of course, give their true identities. (Note, in passing, the dramatic effectiveness of setting up this deception on the spur of the moment and before the very eyes of the victim, rather than having it arranged by the two women in an expository scene beforehand.)

4. The deception has now been unmasked; from this point on, therefore, the names "Madame de Trémont" and "Madame de Louville" refer to their rightful owners.

5. Aline, Queen of Golconda (a legendary realm of fabulous wealth in the Indian subcontinent), was the ever-faithful heroine of Stanislas-Jean de Bouffers's *La Reine de Golconde* (1761). The story was frequently retold on the Parisian stage during the eighteenth and nineteenth centuries. As a result, "Aline" became a popular female name in nineteenth-century France (it was the name, for instance, of Renoir's wife). Donizetti's opera *Alina, regina di Golconda* (1828) is nowadays the most familiar version of the story.

Bibliography

Archer, William. *The Old Drama and the New: An Essay in Re-Valuation.* London: William Heinemann, 1923.

Bailbé, Joseph-Marc. "Le Théâtre et la vie dans *Le Château des désertes.*" *Revue d'histoire littéraire de la France* 79 (1979): 600–12.

Benoist, Antoine. *Essais de critique dramatique.* Paris: Hachette, 1898.

Cooper, Martin. *Gluck.* London: Chatto and Windus, 1935.

Didier, Béatrice. *George Sand écrivain.* Paris: Presses Universitaires de France, 1998.

Dimoff, Paul. *La Génèse de Lorenzaccio.* Paris: Droz, 1936.

Eliot, T. S. *The Family Reunion.* Directed by Howard Sackler. New York: Caedmon Records, 1965.

———. *The Family Reunion.* Ed. Nevill Coghill. London: Faber and Faber, 1969.

Faguet, Émile. *Propos de théâtre.* 5 vols. Paris: Société française d'imprimerie et de librairie, 1903–10.

Fahmy, Dorrya. *George Sand: Auteur dramatique.* Paris: Droz, 1935.

Gautier, Théophile. *Histoire de l'art dramatique en France depuis vingt-cinq ans.* 6 vols. Paris: Hetzel, 1858–9.

Gilbert, W. S. *The Savoy Operas.* London: Macmillan, 1926.

Hammond, William T. "Analysis of the Plot and Character Drawing in the Theatre of George Sand." *Birmingham-Southern College Bulletin* 22 (1929): 45–54.

John, S. B. "The Drama of Money and Class." In *French Literature and Its Background,* ed. John Cruickshank, 6 vols. Oxford: Oxford University Press, 1969. 5: 67–83.

Karénine, Wladimir. *George Sand: Sa vie et ses œuvres.* 4 vols. Paris: Plon, 1899–1926.

Lemaître, Jules. *Impressions de théâtre.* 11 vols. Paris: Société française d'imprimerie et de librairie, 1889–1920.

Manifold, Gay. *George Sand's Theatre Career.* Ann Arbor, Mich.: UMI Research Press, 1985.

Pope, Alexander. *Selected Prose.* Ed. Paul Hammond. Cambridge: Cambridge University Press, 1987.

Powell, David A. *George Sand.* Boston: G. K. Hall, 1990.

Razgonnikoff-Gerardy, Jacqueline. "George Sand et le théâtre romantique." *Les Amis de George Sand* 20 (1998): 51–5.

Robertson, T. W. *The Principal Dramatic Works of Thomas William Robertson.* 2 vols. London: Sampson Low, Marston, & Co., 1889.

Sand, George. *Antonia.* Paris: Michel Lévy, 1861.

———. *Correspondance.* Ed. Georges Lubin. 25 vols. Paris: Garnier, 1964–91.

———. *Francia, Un Bienfait n'est jamais perdu.* Paris: Michel Lévy, 1872.

———. *Le Lis du Japon.* Paris: Michel Lévy, 1866.

———. *La Mare au diable.* Paris: Calmann Lévy, 1865.

———. *Le Marquis de Villemer.* Paris: Michel Lévy, 1861.

———. *Œuvres autobiographiques.* Ed. Georges Lubin. 2 vols. Paris: Gallimard, 1970–71.

———. *Théâtre complet.* 4 vols. Paris: Michel Lévy, 1866.

———. *Théâtre de Nohant.* Paris: Michel Lévy, 1865.

———. *A Woman's Version of the Faust Legend: The Seven Strings of the Lyre.* Trans. George A. Kennedy. Chapel Hill, N.C.: University of North Carolina Press, 1989.

Sarcey, Francisque. *Quarante ans de théâtre.* 7 vols. Paris: Bibliothèque des Annales, 1901.

Smith, Albert. "Fantasy in the Plays of George Sand." In *George Sand: Collected Essays,* ed. Janis Glasgow. Troy, N.Y.: Whitston Publishing Company, 1988. 160–71.

Szogyi, Alex. "George Sand's Theatre: Her Personal Mythology." In *George Sand: Collected Essays,* ed. Janis Glasgow. Troy, N.Y.: Whitston Publishing Company, 1988. 194–202.

Wentz, Debra Linowitz. *Les Profils du théâtre de Nohant de George Sand.* Paris: Nizet, 1978.

Zola, Émile. *Œuvres complètes.* Ed. Henri Mitterand. 12 vols. Paris: Cercle du livre précieuse, 1966–70.